B IS FOR
BAD CINEMA

THE SUNY SERIES
HORIZONS OF CINEMA
MURRAY POMERANCE | EDITOR

Also in the series

William Rothman, editor, *Cavell on Film*

J. David Slocum, editor, *Rebel Without a Cause*

Joe McElhaney, *The Death of Classical Cinema*

Kirsten Moana Thompson, *Apocalyptic Dread*

Frances Gateward, editor, *Seoul Searching*

Michael Atkinson, editor, *Exile Cinema*

Paul S. Moore, *Now Playing*

Robin L. Murray and Joseph K. Heumann, *Ecology and Popular Film*

William Rothman, editor, *Three Documentary Filmmakers*

Sean Griffin, editor, *Hetero*

Jean-Michel Frodon, editor, *Cinema and the Shoah*

Carolyn Jess-Cooke and Constantine Verevis, editors, *Second Takes*

Matthew Solomon, editor, *Fantastic Voyages of the Cinematic Imagination*

R. Barton Palmer and David Boyd, editors, *Hitchcock at the Source*

William Rothman, *Hitchcock, Second Edition*

Joanna Hearne, *Native Recognition*

Marc Raymond, *Hollywood's New Yorker*

Steven Rybin and Will Scheibel, editors, *Lonely Places, Dangerous Ground*

B IS FOR BAD CINEMA

Aesthetics, Politics, and Cultural Value

Edited by
Claire Perkins
and
Constantine Verevis

Cover art: film still, Denis Lavant in *Holy Motors* (2012).
Courtesy Canal+/The Kobal Collection

Published by
STATE UNIVERSITY OF NEW YORK PRESS, ALBANY

© 2014 State University of New York

All rights reserved

Printed in the United States of America

No part of this book may be used or reproduced in any manner whatsoever without written permission. No part of this book may be stored in a retrieval system or transmitted in any form or by any means including electronic, electrostatic, magnetic tape, mechanical, photocopying, recording, or otherwise without the prior permission in writing of the publisher.

For information, contact
STATE UNIVERSITY OF NEW YORK PRESS, ALBANY, NY
www.sunypress.edu

Production, Laurie Searl
Marketing, Anne M. Valentine

Library of Congress Cataloging-in-Publication Data

B is for bad cinema : aesthetics, politics, and cultural value / edited by Claire Perkins and Constantine Verevis.
    pages cm — (SUNY series, horizons of cinema)
Includes bibliographical references and index.
ISBN 978-1-4384-4995-1 (hardcover : alk. paper)
ISBN 978-1-4384-4996-8 (pbk. : alk. paper)   1. Motion pictures—Aesthetics.   I. Perkins, Claire (Claire Elizabeth) editor of compilation. II. Verevis, Constantine editor of compilation.
  PN1995.B15 2014
  791.43'01—dc23   2013012454

10 9 8 7 6 5 4 3 2 1

For Dad
—CP

For Anna, Chrissie, and George
—CV

Contents

Illustrations ix

Acknowledgments xi

1. Introduction: B Is for Bad Cinema 1
    Claire Perkins and *Constantine Verevis*

Part I
AESTHETICS

2. Explosive Apathy 21
    Jeffrey Sconce

3. B-Grade Subtitles 43
    Tessa Dwyer

4. Being in Two Places at the Same Time: The Forgotten Geography of Rear-Projection 65
    Adrian Danks

5. Redeeming *Cruising*: Tendentiously Offensive, Coherently Incoherent, Strangely Pleasurable 85
    R. Barton Palmer

6. The Villain We Love: Notes on the Dramaturgy of Screen Evil 105
    Murray Pomerance

7. From Bad to Good and Back to Bad Again? Cult Cinema and Its Unstable Trajectory   129
   Jamie Sexton

PART II
AUTHORSHIP

8. Coffee in Paradise: *The Horn Blows at Midnight*   149
   Tom Conley

9. The Risible: On Jean-Claude Brisseau   165
   Adrian Martin

10. *The Evil Dead* DVD Commentaries: Amateurishness and Bad Film Discourse   181
    Kate Egan

11. Liking *The Magus*   197
    I. Q. Hunter

12. BADaptation: Is *Candy* Faithful?   215
    Constantine Verevis

Contributors   241

Index   245

Illustrations

Figure 1.1	Monsieur Merde (Denis Levant) and fashion model (Eva Mendes) in *Holy Motors* (2012). Courtesy Canal+ / The Kobal Collection.	3
Figure 1.2	Jack Smith's muse, Maria Montez, in *Cobra Woman* (1944). Courtesy Universal / The Kobal Collection / Ray Jones.	5
Figure 1.3	Joan Fontaine on the movie poster for *Born to Be Bad* (1950). Courtesy RKO / The Kobal Collection.	7
Figure 2.1	George Clooney walks away from an explosion in *Syriana* (2005) Courtesy Warner Bros. / The Kobal Collection.	23
Figure 2.2	Megan Fox and Shia LaBeouf make their escape in *Transformers: Revenge of the Fallen* (2009). Courtesy Paramount / The Kobal Collection.	27
Figure 3.1	Bad subtitles for *The Lord of the Rings: The Two Towers* (2002). Source http://www.angelfire.com/rings/ttt-subtitles/000-020/index.html.	44
Figure 4.1	Cary Grant and Grace Kelly in rear-projection shot from *To Catch a Thief* (1954) Courtesy Paramount / The Kobal Collection.	74

Figure 5.1	Undercover cop Steve Burns (Al Pacino) in *Cruising* (1980). Courtesy Lorimar / The Kobal Collection.	98
Figure 6.1	Anthony Hopkins as the villain Hannibal Lecter in *The Silence of the Lambs* (1991). Courtesy Orion / The Kobal Collection.	121
Figure 7.1	Cult favorites Rick (Humphrey Bogart) and Ilsa (Ingrid Bergman) in *Casablanca* (1942). Courtesy Warner Bros. / The Kobal Collection / Jack Woods.	137
Figure 8.1	Elizabeth (Alexis Smith), the orchestra's harpist in *The Horn Blows at Midnight* (1945). Courtesy Warner Bros. / The Kobal Collection.	154
Figure 9.1	François Négret and Vanessa Paradis in *Noce Blanche* (1989). Courtesy Films du Losange / The Kobal Collection.	170
Figure 10.1	Amateur horrors in *The Evil Dead* (1982). Courtesy Renaissance Pictures / The Kobal Collection.	183
Figure 11.1	Lily (Candice Bergen) in *The Magus* (1968). Courtesy 20th Century Fox / The Kobal Collection.	202
Figure 12.1	Ewa Aulin is a child of the universe in *Candy* (1968). Courtesy Selmur/Dear/Corona / The Kobal Collection.	231

Acknowledgments

The editors would like to thank the School of English, Communications and Performance Studies and the Faculty of Arts, Monash University, Melbourne, for the generous support provided for hosting "B for Bad Cinema," a conference co-convened by Alexia Kannas, Claire Perkins, Julia Vassilieva, and Constantine Verevis (Monash University, April 2009), from which this book project was developed. Thanks also to the School of English, Communications and Performance Studies for furnishing the book with images. The editors would also like to thank R. Barton Palmer and Murray Pomerance, not only for their direct contributions to the volume, but for their advice at various stages of its development. At SUNY Press, James Peltz and Murray Pomerance have acted as supportive and encouraging editors from the start, and are thanked for their feedback and sharp editorial vision at various stages of the project. Finally, a special word of thanks to our contributors: it has been a genuine pleasure to work with each one of you.

I

Introduction

B Is for Bad Cinema

CLAIRE PERKINS AND CONSTANTINE VEREVIS

A batsqueak of genius, dishevelment and derangement.
—Peter Bradshaw ("Cannes 2012: *Holy Motors*")

Taken from the *Guardian*, Peter Bradshaw's review comment for *Holy Motors* (Leos Carax, 2012) has become the most famous description of a film that was anticipated, received, and reviewed in a state of near-constant hyperbole. Rarely mentioned outside of the superlatives that guaranteed it the leading spot in *Film Comment*'s "Top Films of 2012" poll, descriptions of *Holy Motors* include, "the most astonishing film at Cannes" (Powers, *Vogue*) and "one of the most electrifying films you will ever see" (Ebiri, *New York Magazine*). At the same time, reviews of *Holy Motors*, Carax's long-awaited fifth feature and first film since the critical and commercial failure of *Pola X* (1999), have also emphasized the delirium of Carax's vision, describing the film as: "[an] ecstatic, idiotic, fizzy, frightening provocation" (Lodge, *Time Out*); "an exhilarating lunatic odyssey" (Collins, *The Telegraph*); "[a] baffling, bonkers and utterly brilliant [film]" (Mottram, *Total Film*); a "mad hatter's monsterpiece" (Hillis, *The Village Voice*), and "[a] balls-to-the-wall crazy, beautiful and unbelievably strange [work]" (Kohn, *Indiewire*).

For those who see Carax's film as a meditation on life, death, and artifice—and a profound reflection on the history and future of cinema itself—*Holy Motors* is a "visionary, game-changing masterpiece" (Romney, *Screen Daily*). More urgently, though, the superlative qualities of *Holy Motors* are perceived to lie in an energy that is framed as *craziness*; in what Bradshaw details as a "ferociously eccentric" drive to really use the fluidity of cinema in a way that "makes most other films look very buttoned-up" ("Cannes 2012: *Holy Motors*"). "Craziness" is a term that here stands for freedom, and in turn stands for goodness. At the same time, it readily—if not straightforwardly—opens onto *badness*.

In the tradition of polarizing "event" films—*The Tree of Life* (Terrence Malick, 2011), *Dancer in the Dark* (Lars von Trier, 2000), *Twin Peaks: Fire Walk with Me* (David Lynch, 1992)—the enthusiastic reactions to *Holy Motors* are naturally offset by those who see it more coolly. Many critics prefaced their own approval by noting that some audiences would find the film irritating, pretentious, and overdone. Writing in *Sight and Sound*, Ginette Vincendeau makes note of the film's "invention and energy," but also writes that the film's structure—a series of performative episodes around the character of Oscar (Denis Lavant)—and its investment in "images and feelings over storytelling" results in "uneven," indulgent filmmaking (89). An *Indiewire* blogger finds the film "sloppy" and "bitter," reading the perceived references to Carax's own uneven career as a statement that "those who can't get their movie made, sneer at those who can instead" (Jagernauth). In a more expansive comment, Jonathan Rosenbaum questions the French tradition that involves "a certain licence to behave like a depraved lunatic and receive approval, endorsement, and other cultural rewards in return for this boorishness." All of these receptions are cautioning against mistaking a *distinct* work for a *good* work. In this logic lie some fundamental aspects of the interest this collection takes in the concept of *bad cinema*.

What counts as "good" and "bad" in cinema? How should film discourse approach a film that is "bad" to some people and "good" to others? Can there be an "objective" component in determinations of "bad" and "good," or are such judgments entirely subjective and impressionistic? It is worth recalling that the reflections of many commentators on *Holy Motors* locate the wildness of the film in Denis Lavant's embodiment of "Monsieur Merde," the mute, strident, and sewer-dwelling gremlin created by Carax for the "Merde" episode of the triptych *Tokyo!* (Joonho Bong, Leos Carax, and Michel Gondry, 2008). If "good" or "bad" derives from "shit," how do "badness" and "goodness" collide, converge, supplement each other, complement each other, or perhaps annihilate each other in particular films or groups of films?

In what is perhaps his most telling review comment, Bradshaw describes *Holy Motors* as a "gorgeous furry teacup," foregrounding its "goodness" as surrealist provocation, or shock. This gesture connects with *Cinema 2: The Time-Image*, where Gilles Deleuze writes: from the very beginning, "it is as if cinema were telling us: with me . . . you can't escape the *shock* which arouses the thinker in you." But, Deleuze immediately adds, "this pretension of the cinema, at least among [its] greatest pioneers, only raises a smile today" (156–57). The reason for this is that while it was believed that the cinema—an industrial art that had achieved "self-movement"—was capable of imposing this shock, classical cinema simultaneously evolved from a belief in the ideality of representation and the stability of Truth. For Deleuze, "the shock would be confused, in *bad cinema*, with the figurative violence of the represented [i.e., imposed by commercial Hollywood cinema] instead of achieving that *other* violence of a movement-image developing its vibrations in a moving sequence which embeds itself within us" (157, emphasis added). Deleuze continues, stating that the "artistic essence of the image," its capacity to deliver a shock—akin to that of *Holy Motors*—is realized only in "a sublime conception of cinema," whereby "the imagination suffers

Figure 1.1. Monsieur Merde (Denis Levant) and fashion model (Eva Mendes) in *Holy Motors* (2012). Courtesy Canal+ / The Kobal Collection.

a shock which pushes it to the limit and forces thought to think the whole as intellectual totality which goes beyond the imagination" (157).

Deleuze locates this *sublime conception of cinema* in the film theory and practice of Abel Gance, F. W. Murnau, Fritz Lang, S. M. Eisenstein, and Antonin Artaud who, for "a brief minute, . . . 'believes' in cinema" (165). The latter opens up Deleuze's account of bad cinema—one in which "violence is no longer that of the image and its vibrations but that of the represented" (164)—to the Surrealists and the theorization of a sublime (epiphanic) moment: "[that] dangerous moment of representation which points to an elsewhere . . . [and allows one] to think or fantasize a 'beyond' of cinema, a world beyond representation which only shimmers through in certain moments of the film" (Willemen 240–41). Underground actor-filmmaker Jack Smith seemed to understand this when he wrote that the "allure of movies was a thing of light and shadows": "a bad film is one which doesn't flicker and shift and move" ("Perfect Filmic" 31). More particularly, Smith rallied (in his films and writings) against conventionally "good" movies—"the hypocrisy of good acting, good this, good that"—to argue that the performance of a "bad actor"—we could add, the affect of bad film—was potentially "rich, unique, idiosyncratic, revealing" ("Belated Appreciation" 5). In the case of his aesthetic muse—Universal Studios "Queen of Technicolor," Maria Montez (figure 1.2)—Smith wrote that those who saw "the World's Worst Actress" could appreciate only the most conventional pattern of acting ("GOOD PERFS"), and failed to see that "one of her [Montez's] atrocious acting sighs suffused a thousand tons of dead plaster [Hollywood studio sets] with imaginative life and a truth. . . . To admit of Maria Montez validities would be to turn on to moldiness, Glamorous Rapture, schizophrenic delight, hopeless naivete, and glittering technicolored trash!" ("Perfect Filmic" 28).

Smith's moldy aesthetic—his project for anti-aesthetically redeeming the debris of everyday life and film culture—resonates with more recent evaluations of (film) work that is characterized by its aesthetic impoverishment and affective excess. In film studies, this is most notable in Jeffrey Sconce's influential " 'Trashing' the Academy," an essay that draws upon Pierre Bourdieu's account of taste preference and class privilege to build a discussion of "paracinema" as a counter cultural valorization of all forms of trash cinema (372). In a different context, John Frow appeals to Bourdieu's work on the sociology of symbolic forms to investigate the circumstances of the construction of such (counter) cultural groups and to more broadly interrogate the "problem of value"

Figure 1.2. Jack Smith's muse, Maria Montez, in *Cobra Woman* (1944). Courtesy Universal / The Kobal Collection / Ray Jones.

that is foundational to the discipline of cultural studies (4). The chapters in this book spring from such discussions of taste and value to consider unworthy cinema—that is, aesthetically and/or morally disreputable film work—and mark out the broad contours of bad cinema. While some of the essays in this edition do share a kinship to discussions of "paracinema"—B movies and cult films—the observations herein do not describe the reality of a single aesthetic object, or represent a single methodology or critical agenda, but *variously* describe bad cinema in terms of its aesthetics, politics, and cultural value. Together the chapters in this volume suggest the protean nature of bad cinema, as well as the challenges such a concept poses to the ways many critics and audiences commonly think about films and film culture.

This collection takes up the idea of bad cinema and the organization of cultural value in a contemporary context where there is no longer a clear distinction or hierarchy between high and low culture, canonical and cult films, good and bad cinema. As the works of Sconce and Frow demonstrate in and through their indebtedness to Bourdieu's critique of taste, this situation is related to changes in audience structures and the role that critics and academics play in the circulation of cultural value. Some chapters in this book treat value as a problem of film aesthetics and (as in Deleuze's description) of the imbrications of film in an industrialized system of aesthetic production. Insofar as a connection is maintained to social structure and process these questions of value are also linked to issues of knowledge and power, and so raise broader social and political questions. Other chapters in this volume dwell not so much on the nature of the film object but rather deal (as in Smith's account) with its affect and the circumstances of its consumption. In these essays the championing of a particular type of cinema often has less to do with any objective aesthetic criteria of cinematic worth than with the social position and cultural status of the critic. In these ways, the chapters in this book seek to broadly understand what bad cinema might mean within contemporary conditions of film production and reception, and to examine on what basis and in which situations we continue to make judgments of taste and value within the field of film studies.

This volume continues and extends—but does not limit itself to—the trends in film scholarship that have made cult and exploitation films and other low genres increasingly acceptable objects for critical analysis. Individual chapters cover a range of issues, from the aesthetic and industrial mechanics of low-budget production through the terrain of audience responses and cinematic affect, and on to the broader moral and ethical implications of the material. As a result, this volume takes an interest in a wide range of film examples—overblown Hollywood blockbusters, faux pornographic works, and European art house films—to consider that material which lurks on the boundaries of acceptability in terms of taste, style, and politics. The book does not argue for any single value system (high or low, good or bad) but questions the insertion of the critic into the field of value and recognizes that this is a wider institutional problem, not an individual one. The very term "bad cinema" indicates how critically intertwined issues of taste, style, and politics are in all film practice and criticism. In this way, this collection of essays (like Frow's *Cultural Studies and Cultural Value*) seeks to make its most general contribution to an interrogation of some foundational categories for contemporary film studies: representation, culture, and audiences.

The twelve chapters in this volume pose a wide range of historical, political, and aesthetic questions around the idea of bad cinema, but despite their diversity they suggest points of reflection and convergence. As Dana Polan has pointed out, in the cinema (and beyond) the concept of badness (as well as goodness) covers at least two related ideas: on the one hand, the notion of *moral* (or political) badness, in which "cinema is interrogated for the ethics of its representations and their imputed effects." On the other hand, the idea of *aesthetic* badness, where "cinema is judged for artistic quality [with some films] found to be bereft of beauty or related values" (202). In Polan's essay these ideas of moral and aesthetic badness are mediated by a third term: namely, that of *auteurism*, and specifically the figure of Nicholas Ray. Polan puts forward Ray's 1950 film, *Born to Be Bad*, not only as a useful case study of badness, but also as evidence of how aesthetic and moral badness need to be understood as historically contingent terms (figure 1.3). More generally, as demon-

Figure 1.3. Joan Fontaine on the movie poster for *Born to Be Bad* (1950). Courtesy RKO / The Kobal Collection.

strated by Thomas Elsaesser, auteurism (in its French, post–World War II incarnation) brings a sophisticated appreciation of aesthetic problems to a body of films—Hollywood output from 1940 onwards—to occasion an interpretive shift. Specifically, the attribution of a high *aesthetic* value to industrial products previously considered crassly commercial, vulgar, and *morally* bad (Elsaesser 200). From these leads, this volume groups its chapters into two corresponding and connected conceptual areas: aesthetics (part I) and authorship (part II).

The diverse inquiries, across and within each of the two areas of this edition, recognize that it is impossible to approach the idea of bad cinema without considering an audience for whom it is bad. Sconce's work on paracinema—the movement that has grown up around sleazy, excessive, or poorly executed B movies to advocate them over and above A-list features—is the best known reception-based approach in cult and "badfilm" debates, and a source that has been widely drawn upon (see Mathijs and Mendik 100, as well as several authors in this collection). The most significant contribution that Sconce's work makes to these debates is to identify paracinema not as a body of texts, or *genre*, but rather as an interpretive filter that is fundamentally interested in ironic readings of diverse texts. In Sconce's words, "paracinema is . . . less a distinct group of films than a particular reading protocol, a counter-aesthetic turned subcultural sensibility devoted to all manner of cultural detritus" ("'Trashing' the Academy" 372). What is described here, and also in Sconce's later work (*Sleaze Artists*), which takes up Pauline Kael's "Trash, Art, and the Movies" to complicate orderly thought about bad cinema, is a phenomenon of taste: a way of reading that valorizes the inept, absurd, grotesque, and bizarre forms that have been rejected or ignored by legitimate film culture.

In part I, "Aesthetics," the practice of identifying films as good or bad objects is linked to broader and more transparent issues of social representation. In a 2009 issue of *Sight and Sound* that created a pantheon of bad directors in a broader celebration of "mad, bad and dangerous" films, Mark Cousins suggests that "each of these 'wild' directors has a psychic energy that is manic to a degree and might well be fuelled by sexual rage, or colonial exploitation, or a Marxist hatred of consumerism, or a fear of modernity or the body . . . or by historical events" (23). Here, various kinds of "explosive" social materials are evaluated not only in the discursive terms of artistic worth but according to the real effects to which they give rise.

In his contribution to this volume, R. Barton Palmer precisely describes how this pattern of evaluation is always anchored in some determining factor: "something is bad for something or seems good to someone in respect to some interest, and such contingent evaluations identify particular elements of a text and the context of its reception, in the process providing a kind of public 'reading.'" The chapters in part I demonstrate this point by engaging a broad range of aesthetic "interests" that work as a determining force in the evaluation of badness (and goodness). In these chapters, film objects, or parts of film objects, that are publicly bad—sensationalist, incompetent, pornographic, gratuitous—are assembled and reoriented in relation to a concern that exceeds this nomination at a political or historical level. In this way, the authors draw out the constructive and *affirmative* aspects of bad cinema.

While none of the chapters in part I deals explicitly with the type of (neo-)camp or exploitative material more commonly investigated in paracinematic readings, many demonstrate something of this reception-based protocol by attending to examples of formal and narrative devices often marginalized or ignored in film criticism: explosions, subtitles, rear-projection, and character villainy. Further, the chapters are linked by their common focus on cinematic affect, or what Joan Hawkins calls the "operative criterion . . . that characterizes paracinema as a low cinematic culture" (4). The authors frequently frame a central aesthetic technique as something that directly engages the spectator's body to induce or provoke affects that are overwhelming, dislocating, distracting, or thrilling. The aesthetic badness of Hollywood film—as both artistic failure and narrative design—is here linked to the "low" form of exploitation and "body genres" (Williams), and more broadly to an estimation of how specific genres figure in audience estimations of good and bad. The essays move beyond identifying these effects as evidence of the various texts' production and distribution contexts to consider how they open a space for the re-conceptualization of what makes a film good, or bad.

In the first chapter, "Explosive Apathy," Sconce addresses how the trend of his titular term can describe the "narcissistic" and "obnoxious" tendencies of much contemporary Hollywood blockbuster cinema. Citing examples from such films as *Robocop* (Paul Verhoeven, 1987), *The Matrix* (Andy and Larry [now Lana] Wachowski, 1999) and *Syriana* (Stephen Gaghan, 2005) where protagonists walk nonchalantly away from enormous explosions that they patently can not survive, Sconce characterizes explosive apathy as a technique that threatens to undermine a film's verisimilitude with its combination of excess and "stupid movie physics." Referring to a 1980s paracinematic sketch on NBC's *SCTV*, "The Farm Film Report"—where films were reviewed by actors pretending to be hicks according purely to the presence or absence of explosions—as a prescient comment on a now dominant cultural trend, Sconce identifies the obnoxiousness of explosive apathy. Its effect, he says, is a self-reflexive moment of narration, "self-conscious to the point of being exhibitionist, and exhibitionist to the point of demanding, rather rudely, attention and even respect." Connecting the tendency to theories of intensified continuity and impact aesthetics that seek to define the visceral effects of contemporary (action) cinema, Sconce argues that explosive apathy nonetheless goes beyond a functional imperative to integrate narrative and spectacle. It makes the "awesome" *obscene*, by engaging action technique in and of itself to overwhelm the audience with an attitude that is ultimately hostile and condescending: "the explosively apathetic announce in their very silence superiority over the viewer, immunity to the very thing designed to most engage the spectator."

In the next two chapters, Tessa Dwyer and Adrian Danks evoke Sconce's paracinematic framework more directly in discussions of inept examples of the pragmatic aesthetic strategies of subtitling and rear-projection. Dwyer's "B-Grade Subtitles" begins by showing how the celebration of translational errors affectionately known as "flubtitles" or "Engrish" fits clearly within the lexicon of paracinema. Linking the camp activity of reveling in the wrongness of these errors to both historical film criticism and contemporary Internet fandom, Dwyer demonstrates the place of careless subtitling and dubbing in the construction of the bad foreign-language film genre. This practice gives Dwyer the opportunity to move beyond traditional "badfilm" discourses to examine how translation and subtitling necessarily destabilize these in their capacity to transform "*any* film into *badfilm*." In this context, translation itself is discussed as a bad object: a "blind spot" that film culture either ignores or acknowledges as a "necessary evil" that routinely condenses and obliterates the effect of the original. Mobilizing the work of Jacques Derrida, and looking forward to the ideas on "BADaptation" advanced later in the collection by I. Q. Hunter and Constantine Verevis, Dwyer contests this overdetermined negativity by arguing that translation always *necessarily* fails. She builds upon this position to conclude that, if the process of translation expresses the instability that underlies all language (and thereby dismantles any notion of a stable point of origin for translation) then bad translations can constitute a platform for rethinking badness itself.

In "Being in Two Places at the Same Time," Adrian Danks identifies the device of rear-projection as another example of bad technique that has received inadequate critical attention. As he details, rear-projection developed historically in an effort to avoid the poor effects of location sound recording, but "the sometimes wildly disproportionate dimensions, movements and illumination" of the projection in relation to the primary image suggest the development of a new kind of bad cinema. While thus typically dismissed for its artificiality and disjunction, specific instances of rear-projection move Danks to consider how the technique can also give rise to uncanny effects felt directly at the level of spectatorship. In the extended example that is examined from *Marnie* (Alfred Hitchcock, 1964) this effect is understood as evidence of Hitchcock's "profoundly impure cinema that mixes and contrasts aspects of realism with a heightened but often meticulous artificiality." Danks argues that, in the sequence under consideration, *Marnie* mobilizes instances of repetition and redundancy to become a kind of experimental "installation," one that advances rear-projection "as both an anachronistic and visionary technique."

In a manner that continues this interest in the redemptive and revisionist tendency of auteur discourse (examined further in the chapters of part II), R. Barton Palmer next examines a "blind spot" in the reception of *Cruising*, William Friedkin's 1980 investigative thriller set in New York's gay bar scene. Turning directly to the *effects* of the type of judgment considered throughout the volume as a whole, Palmer discusses how the evaluative reception of Friedkin's film as a bad object—incoherent and offensive—has bypassed its radical representational program which, "dependent on a kind of taboo-challenging neorealism, has never since been repeated." Emphasizing the instrumental function of a bad nomination and reputation, Palmer traces the ways in which a perceived connection between homosexuality and violence in the film has contributed to it being seen as slanderous. His argument opens onto the issues suggested above, though, in considering the *usefulness* of this offensiveness to its cause. As he indicates, the ways in which *Cruising* became controversial "reflected the increasing fragmentation of national values and the emergence of powerful forms of identity politics." The value of the film is thus revealed not in a straightforward reversal of taste, but in identifying it as a site for ongoing debates around essentialist and nonessentialist forms of homosexuality, heteronormality, and other forms of sexual being.

Murray Pomerance's chapter, "The Villain We Love: Notes on the Dramaturgy of Screen Evil," addresses a very different strategy of "offense": the badness of the bad guy, or the presentational problems that narrative villainy poses for filmmaking. Here, Pomerance again evokes issues around the reception of "low" material by drawing an analogy between the spectacle of public execution and the screening of a film in which villainy is destroyed. Vividly evoking the "weird and phantasmal organization" of the hour of execution, Pomerance argues that neither of these spectacles entertains inadvertently, "but is designed as a mechanism to produce an affective discharge and moral instruction through the exhibition of isolation, denigration, pain, and finally—in a notable culmination—death." Through the examples of historical and filmic villains including Adolf Hitler, Gollum, Norman Bates, Hannibal Lecter, and the Joker, Pomerance demonstrates a dramaturgical point on the narrative orchestration of "screen badness." In connection with the hero's victory, he shows that the villain's degradation "fills in a central jurisprudential lack, offering excuses, rationale, and teleological outcome for acts of vicious destruction played out in the name of all that is orderly, civilized, lovable, and true." In interrogating how the familiar narrative trajectory of villainy and punishment makes certain ethical movements in this way, Pomerance's discussion of the *aesthetically bad*—the gory and sensationalist—simultaneously emphasizes the ideas of *moral* badness raised elsewhere in the volume.

In the final entry to part I, Jamie Sexton turns directly to the topic of cult film as an issue of taste and value that many contributors evoke in their discussions of bad cinema. Sexton's chapter, "From Bad to Good and Back to Bad Again? Cult Cinema and its Unstable Trajectory," takes cult cinema itself as an object that has moved between "good" and "bad" status from after World War I to the present-day. In a piece that contributes to a fuller understanding of the connection between cult and badness, Sexton advances a three-part argument in which the flexibility of the term "cult" is demonstrated in and through its reception and construction by critics and audiences alike. Moving from its (bad) connection to the social forces of religion and mysticism as imagined by Siegfried Kracauer, Walter Benjamin, and Harry A. Potamkin, through its (good) establishment as a critical term used in connection with both film culture and individual texts, and on to a more recent perception that its gradual mainstreaming has (badly) compromised its validity and led to a "post-cult" culture, Sexton shows how the aesthetic concepts of intertextuality, exploitation, irony, nostalgia, and transgression have mutated across historical contexts to authenticate the difficulty of actually pinpointing cinematic "cultism." To say that we are now living in a "post-cult" culture, he argues, is itself ultimately bad, "implicitly valuing the critic's own nostalgic perspective and devaluing the experiences of newer generations." In this argument, Sexton rounds out part I, drawing (implicit) connections to key works—Manny Farber's "White Elephant vs. Termite Art," Pauline Kael's "Trash, Art and the Movies," and Susan Sontag's "Notes on Camp"—and demonstrating precisely how the codes of judgment mobilized by audiences and critics work ceaselessly in their location and relocation of films, directors, and styles.

While the first part of the book deals principally with questions of aesthetics, chapters such as those by Danks and Palmer, in their discussion of auteurs Hitchcock and Friedkin, go some way towards introducing the issues examined in part II, "Authorship." As has already been signaled (through the work of Elsaesser), classical auteur theory plays a central role in broad historical estimations of cinematic value insofar as its principal contribution is to provide a framework for *redeeming* "bad" populist products as "good" aesthetic objects worthy of close consideration. For many contributors to the volume, this framework is evoked as a means of demonstrating how the critic is inserted into the field of value. In his introduction to the collection *Auteurs and Authorship*, Barry Keith Grant gives an overview of the discourse that emphasizes this dimension of judgment, detailing the trend practiced by the magazines *Cahiers du Cinéma*, *Movie* and *Film Culture* of ranking directors in a deliberate effort to "provoke established critical orthodoxy" (2). In a move illustrated by Peter Wollen's 1972 distinction between Howard Hawks, the biological person, and "Howard Hawks," the critical concept, this trend ultimately evolves into a "code" for organizing the reception of the films bearing a director's name (Grant 4).

In the chapters of part II, this code is interrogated as a tool for evaluating—and *re*-evaluating—what constitutes good and bad cinematic expression. These authors attend to the factors—textual, critical, and institutional—which contribute to a pervasive understanding that, in Grant's description of Andrew Sarris's position, "the least satisfying film of an auteur is better than the most interesting work by a director who isn't" (3). Tom Conley offers the most explicit examination of this issue in "Coffee in Paradise: *The Horn Blows at Midnight*," a chapter that reflects on how the discourse of authorship offers a particular way of construing bad cinema: specifically, "[how] its practice demands that a film attributed to a given director *must* be treated as a critical object, and rarely as a work whose worth is determined by the degree of pleasure or disquiet it affords." Conley's chapter provides a case study in this mode of investigation by demonstrating how the motif of coffee in Raoul Walsh's self-described "terrible" film opens up to "comedies of similar facture" (such as Preston Sturges's 1940 *Christmas in July*), and more broadly to both manifest and latent content concerning historical issues of cinema and war. In showing how authorship necessarily turns viewing into a critical operation, Conley redeems this film as something other than what its reception has made it out to be. Its "bad" assessment can only remain in quotation marks, insofar as "an *auteur*'s film cannot be bad simply because auteurs, at least those who have been or remain worthy of the name, cannot fail to make what seem to be bad movies."

In the next chapter, Adrian Martin draws on the concept of authorship to demonstrate how bad cinema should not be reduced to a specific type or kind. In this chapter, Martin considers the overreliance of film criticism on a type of codified analysis that gives rise to nonevaluative categories (see Grant 5), such as the "bad" tautological concept of authorship that Timothy Corrigan suggests the commerce of auteurism relies upon. In Jean-Claude Brisseau's decadent and unpredictable films, Martin sees an occasion to move beyond the choices and values that compel criticism to designate films "bad" or "good" as "the unacceptable ridiculous, or the acceptable ridiculous." In the aspects deemed risible by many of Brisseau's critics—the incongruity, the elision of narrative detail, and the earnestness of the works—Martin sees an audacity that demonstrates the "triumph" of bad cinema in a "single, implicit rider, which is quite simply: *take it or leave it*; enter right into the movie, or just walk away. To take it you have to take it all, engage with it all, not cherry-pick the acceptable elements from the unacceptable ones, which is what the act of criticism (consciously or not) does all the time." In making this argument, Martin more generally touches upon questions of critical orthodoxy: that is, whether there is an "objective" component to discussions of good or bad, or whether such judgments are so entirely "impressionistic" that critical ideals of impartiality are abandoned from the outset.

The notion of authorship is examined in a different manner in Kate Egan's chapter, "*The Evil Dead* DVD Commentaries, Amateurishness, and Bad Film Discourse." Commentaries on the historical transformations of the discourse of authorship often lead to the conclusion that the contemporary era marks the moment of the marketable "auteur star" who, in Corrigan's description, "is meaningful primarily as a promotion or recovery of a movie or group of movies, frequently regardless of the filmic text itself" (105). In this move, promotional technology serves a key function in disseminating the auteur "brand" as a code that organizes the reception of a director's work. In her chapter, Egan demonstrates the central place of the DVD director's commentary in this process.

Attending to the remarks from director Sam Raimi, producer Robert Tapert, and star Bruce Campbell on a 1999 DVD release of the original 1981 film in the series, Egan identifies a paracinematic engagement that foregrounds and celebrates the film's flaws, gaffes, and mistakes. While acknowledging that this "bad" approach initially appears to contradict the typical function of the DVD commentary (that is, to enhance the aesthetic or cultural value of a film), Egan's discussion ultimately shows how the good-natured error-spotting does contribute to the film's status and appeal as a cult "artifact" from a past, pre-video era of film consumption. In part, she suggests, it achieves this by foregrounding the idea of the auteur star where, through "self-deprecation" and "sustaining camaraderie," Raimi, together with Tapert and Campbell, offers a reflection on the low-budget adventures of their filmmaking history to feed into an admiration for *The Evil Dead*'s "authentically amateur" status.

In "Liking *The Magus*," I. Q. Hunter takes up the idea of a code for judging a film's worth in relation to adaptation studies, where the logic of comparison traditionally determines that a film is good or bad in direct proportion to its reproduction of an original text. Hunter's aim of detailing why he likes Guy Green's 1968 film of John Fowles's iconic novel directly addresses the key problems that arise from this singular logic, which include overlooking what the film is doing *beyond* imitating a single (often canonized) source text. Accordingly, Hunter attends to a range of symbols, themes, and intertexts in this "failed mainstream art film" without attempting to establish whether they derive or deviate from the meanings of the novel: this not only includes an excursion into the film's uniquely cinematic innovations of visual rhyming and repetition, but also to the "existentialist puzzle" structure that recalls both *L'avventura* (Michelangelo Antonioni, 1960) and *The Game* (David Fincher, 1997), the presence of Anna Karina as a marker of the French New Wave, and Michael Caine's performance as a "retread" of his lead role in *Alfie* (Lewis Gilbert, 1966). In this way, Hunter effectively allows Green's film to "own" its badness, rather than be received as such through the code of its adaptation from a reputable source. *The Magus* is analyzed as a meaningful textual object with its own concerns, "inspired and structured by the novel, perhaps, but [a film that also] exhibits its own integrity, significance and (alas) style of relative failure."

In the volume's final entry, Constantine Verevis takes up these issues on the function and pleasure of adaptations in a discussion of *Candy*, Christian Marquand's 1968 film adapted from Terry Southern and Mason Hoffenberg's 1958 satiric novel *Candy*, itself inspired by Voltaire's

1759 picaresque, *Candide*. Verevis's essay, "BADaptation: Is *Candy* Faithful?," interrogates the "bad" rhetoric that pervades adaptation studies in and through those analyses that regularly employ terms of "betrayal and degradation" to lament the "infidelity" of film adaptations to their idealized sources and perceived points of origin. Verevis seeks to disturb this framework by examining what happens when a "bad object"—here, a controversial sex novel that becomes a U.S. best-seller—is adapted, thus mobilizing "BADaptation" as a concept to engage with and examine both the mutable reputation of the source text and traditional approaches to adaptation. In a detailed account of the inception of Marquand's film, Verevis demonstrates how its failure was ascribed to its tampering with the excesses of the *Candy* novel (labeled "unfilmable" by *Life* magazine) in an effort to translate the book's "hip, porno-parody" into a certified, mainstream film. In an argument that links back to I. Q. Hunter's assessment of *The Magus*, Verevis concludes that the value of *Candy* lies in its *transformation* of the sexual themes of the novel and its *negotiation* of the surrounding social and cultural changes: *Candy* succeeds "not by attempting a film that [is] 'adequate' to the ideals of the counter-culture, but by incorporating (however incoherently) disparate cinematic practices—mainstream, art house, exploitation—into its own positively 'unoriginal' and fractured film production."

In his emphatic description of the positive, *redemptive* force of combining these diverse practices, Verevis's chapter precisely sums up this volume's key theme: the idea—described above—of bad cinema not as one (generic) mode but as a term with which to interrogate and disrupt the categories of film criticism and culture. While many of the essays deal with bad cinema as what Deleuze sees as the "figurative violence" of (Hollywood) representation, their authors also see "epiphanies" in these films that—elsewhere in the collection—are seen exclusively in the "visionary" works of trash and art cinema, such as is the case of *Holy Motors*. Deleuze's "sublime conception of cinema" is thus revealed not as a purely textual quality but as a reading protocol. All the essays that follow address the *mobility* of bad cinema in a way that most exactly positions the term as a description of the activity of tracing a text, figure, or tradition in motion between the good and bad status ascribed by critics and audiences in specific contexts. The films discussed here all *shock* insofar as they arouse us as thinkers, and are in this way also transposed—moved, imagined—by thought. In this way, bad cinema is always founded upon the movement that Deleuze sees to transcend representation. The "violence" of this concept lies not always in what is represented, but in the capacity for this to be embedded in—and wrenched from—a variety of positions that do ultimately lie within us.

Works Cited

Bourdieu, Pierre. *Distinction: A Social Critique of the Judgement of Taste*. Trans. Richard Nice. Cambridge: Harvard UP, 1984. Print.

Bradshaw, Peter. "Cannes 2012: *Holy Motors*." *The Guardian*. Web. 23 Dec. 2012. http://www.guardian.co.uk/film/2012/may/23/holy-motors-review

———. "Rev. of *Holy Motors*." *The Guardian*. Web. 23 Dec. 2012. http://www.guardian.co.uk/film/2012/sep/27/holy-motors-review

Collins, Robbie. "Cannes 2012: Kylie Minogue in *Holy Motors*." *The Telegraph*. Web. 23 Dec. 2012. http://www.telegraph.co.uk/culture/film/cannes-film-festival/9287402/Cannes-2012-Kylie-Minogue-in-Holy-Motors-review.html

Corrigan, Timothy. *A Cinema Without Walls: Movies and Culture After Vietnam*. New Brunswick, NJ: Rutgers UP, 1991. Print.

Cousins, Mark. "The Wild Bunch." *Sight and Sound* 19.9 (2009): 22–36. Print.

Deleuze, Gilles. *Cinema 2: The Time-Image*. Trans. Hugh Tomlinson and Robert Galeta. Minneapolis: U of Minnesota P, 1989. Print.

Ebiri, Bilge. "Kylie Minogue Takes an Art-House Vacation in *Holy Motors*." *New York Magazine*. Web. 23 Dec. 2012. http://www.vulture.com/2012/10/kylie-minogue-on-holy-motors.html

Elsaesser, Thomas. "Two Decades in Another Country: Hollywood and the Cinéphiles." *Superculture: American Popular Culture and Europe*. Ed. C. W. E. Bigsby. London: Paul Elek, 1975. Print.

Farber, Manny. "White Elephant Art vs. Termite Art." *Negative Space: Manny Farber on the Movies*. New York: Da Capo Press, 1998. 134–44. Print.

Frow, John. *Cultural Studies and Cultural Value*. Oxford: Clarendon, 1995. Print.

Grant, Barry Keith, ed. "Introduction." *Auteurs and Authorship: a Film Reader*. Oxford: Blackwell, 2008. Print.

Hawkins, Joan. *Cutting Edge: Art-horror and the Horrific Avant-garde*. Minneapolis: U of Minnesota P, 2000. Print.

Hillis, Aaron. "Fall Arts Guide 2012: Film." *Village Voice*. Web. 23 Dec. 2012. http://www.villagevoice.com/2012-09-05/film/fall-guide-2012-film/

Jagernauth. *Indiewire*. Web. 23 Dec. 2012. http://www.indiewire.com/article/cannes-review-with-holy-motors-leos-carax-makes-a-nutty-comeback-but-dont-expect-any-easy-answers

Kael, Pauline. "Trash, Art, and the Movies." *Going Steady: Film Writings, 1968–1969*. New York: Marion Boyars, 1994. Print.

Kohn, Eric. "Leos Carax Makes a Nutty Comeback With *Holy Motors*, But Don't Expect Easy Answers." *Indiewire*. Web. 23 Dec. 2012. http://www.

indiewire.com/article/cannes-review-with-holy-motors-leos-carax-makes-a-nutty-comeback-but-dont-expect-any-easy-answers

Lodge, Guy. Rev. of *Holy Motors*. *Time Out*. Web. 23 Dec. 2012. http://www.timeout.com/film/reviews/92787/holy-motors.html

Mathijs, Ernest, and Xavier Mendik, eds. *The Cult Film Reader*. Maidenhead, UK: Open UP, 2008. Print.

Mottram, James. "*Holy Motors*: A Parisian Picaresque." *Total Film*. Web. 23 Dec. 2012. http://www.totalfilm.com/reviews/cinema/holy-motors

Polan, Dana. "On the Bad Goodness of *Born to Be Bad*: Auteurism, Evaluation, and Nicholas Ray's Outsider Cinema." *Bad: Infamy, Darkness, Evil, and Slime on Screen*. Ed. Murray Pomerance. Albany: State U of New York P, 2004. 201–11. Print.

Powers, John. "Rising in Cannes: The 13 Standout Actors and Directors at the Film Festival." *Vogue*. Web. 23 Dec. 2012. http://www.vogue.com/culture/article/rising-in-cannes-the-13-standout-actors-and-directors-at-the-film-festival/#1

Romney, Jonathan. Rev. of *Holy Motors*. *Screen Daily*. Web. 23 Dec. 2012. http://www.screendaily.com/reviews/the-latest/holy-motors/5042521.article#

Rosenbaum, Jonathan. "A Note on *Holy Motors*." Web. 23 Dec. 2012. http://www.jonathanrosenbaum.com/?p=32287

Sconce, Jeffrey, ed. *Sleaze Artists: Cinema at the Margins of Taste, Style, and Politics*. Durham, Duke UP, 2007. Print.

———. "'Trashing' the Academy: Taste, Excess, and an Emerging Politics of Cinematic Style." *Screen* 36.4 (1995): 371–93. Print.

Smith, Jack. "Belated Appreciation of V.S." *Film Culture* 31 (Winter 1963–64): 4–5. Print.

———. "The Perfect Filmic Appositeness of Maria Montez." *Film Culture* 27 (Winter 1962–63): 28–36. Print.

Sontag, Susan. "Notes on Camp." *Against Interpretation and Other Essays*. New York: Farrar, Strauss and Giroux, 1964. 275–92. Print.

Vincendeau, Ginette. Rev. of *Holy Motors*. *Sight and Sound* 22.10 (2012): 89–90. Print.

Willemen, Paul. "Through the Glass Darkly: Cinephilia Reconsidered [interview by Noel King]." *Looks and Frictions: Essays in Cultural Studies and Film Theory*. London: British Film Institute, 1994. 223–57. Print.

Williams, Linda. "Film Bodies: Gender, Genre, and Excess." *Film Quarterly* 44.4 (1991): 2–13. Print.

Part I

AESTHETICS

2

Explosive Apathy

JEFFREY SCONCE

In the opening act of the 2005 political thriller *Syriana* (Stephen Gaghan), a scene unfolds that, upon subsequent reflection, would appear to make little to no sense. An as yet unnamed man (well, not just any man but George Clooney) meets with a group of Islamic radicals in an abandoned building in Tehran. The viewer will later learn that Clooney is in fact undercover CIA agent Bob Barnes, but for now, in this his first scene, Clooney appears to be a black-market arms dealer looking to sell weapons to what we must assume is a terrorist cell. After a few tense exchanges among the nervous circle of men—guns are pointed, Farsi is spoken—the deal is finalized. Clooney leaves the building and, once in the street, begins striding towards the camera in measured, purposeful steps. In the background of the shot, we see the band of terrorists hurriedly get into a small car. Suddenly, the car explodes into a giant fireball. But Clooney, now facing the camera in medium close-up so that we might better gauge his reaction, does not so much as even flinch as the explosion's shockwave rips through the narrow street. He quickly but calmly exits the frame.

As a commentary on big oil and U.S. intervention in the Middle East, *Syriana* strives to be an important film and a *realistic* examination of current geopolitical intrigue. Within the contemporary codes of Hollywood verisimilitude, this expository introduction to Clooney's character radiates both the gritty mise-en-scène and elliptical narration one associates with today's serious filmmaking. Clooney, we must surmise from the timely explosion, is in fact not an arms dealer but some type of undercover operative. His complete lack of response to the violent explosion, his utter impassivity, suggests that he is the architect of the car bomb; or at the very least, he knew it was coming. Even so, Clooney's Bob Barnes must be one tough son of a bitch. Who, after all, could completely suppress even his instinctual reflexes in the face of such a tremendous explosion? And here is where the logic of the scene begins to break down. In exiting this tense Iranian arms sting, one that culminates in the fiery assassination of a terrorist cell, Clooney/Barnes understandably wants to get away from the area as quickly as possible without drawing undue attention to himself. And yet, what could be more profoundly suspicious than the sight of the iconically American Clooney walking through Tehran in perilous proximity to a car bomb and *not* reacting to the explosion? One would imagine that the Iranian police, like the audience, have seen enough movies to know what it means to remain completely unmoved by the eruption of a thunderous fireball: *That was me! I did that!* Would not the more appropriately undercover response here be to at least feign shock that a bomb has detonated so close by? Shouldn't Clooney/Barnes pretend to be somewhat startled, if only to better motivate his fleeing into the back alleys of the city towards his escape? (See figure 2.1.)

Offered as efficient and exciting exposition torn from today's headlines, this curious choice in staging actually threatens to undermine *Syriana*'s bid for geopolitical verisimilitude. For this brief moment, at least, the film seems possessed by another logic, another sensibility, another cinema. For all its ambitious use of location shooting, multiprotagonist structure, and slowly braided narration, *Syriana* borrows here a device cultivated in the political thriller's more cartoonish, steroid-poppin' cousin: the blockbuster action spectacular. We might call the device itself "explosive apathy": the now prominent staging convention that frames a character walking towards the camera, wholly disengaged from a massive detonation that fills the background space with fire, smoke, and debris, refusing to glance backwards for even a second at the incredible spectacle unfolding behind him.

There are variations, of course, but all of them remain faithful to this basic architecture. Sometimes the camera remains stationary, allowing the advancing figure to grow in screen size until assuming a type of monumental indifference in close-up. In other versions, the camera tracks backwards in step with the actor to emphasize his confident,

Figure 2.1. George Clooney walks away from an explosion in *Syriana* (2005) Courtesy Warner Bros. / The Kobal Collection.

purposeful stride. The actor may walk away from a seemingly random explosion or take a few measured steps before hitting a tiny detonator concealed in the palm. Either way, there's no looking back. Operating with relative impunity over the past two decades, the blatant absurdity of this device has of late finally become a target of satiric ridicule. In 2007, publishers promoted not one but two books examining "insultingly stupid movie physics," including a variety of examples related to misunderstandings about explosive force (Rogers, Weiner). At the 2009 MTV Movie Awards, meanwhile, Andy Samberg and Will Ferrell produced a digital short titled "Cool Guys Don't Look at Explosions" featuring the lyric, "The more you ignore it, the cooler you look." Continuing with the gag, *The Other Guys* (Adam McKay, 2010) features Ferrell and his sidekick Mark Wahlberg knocked to the pavement by a fiery blast. Writhing on the ground in shock and awe, Ferrell observes that it would be humanly impossible to simply walk away from an explosion without flinching: "The movie industry is completely irresponsible for the way it portrays explosions," he says in agony.

Almost as long as there have been movies, there have been things blowing up in the movies. From Georges Méliès's magical puff-bombs to the destruction of the Death Star to the many protagonists now seemingly oblivious to the shockwaves of a blistering fireball, filmmakers have long recognized that stylized explosions are intrinsically fascinating, well suited to the cinema's characteristic binding of story and spectacle. As many elite critics have lamented, the collective firepower of the cinema has multiplied dramatically over the past quarter century, an escalation linked to both technological innovation and the action spectacular's ascendance in the marketplace as Hollywood's most prominent A-genre. Once the product of gunpowder, springboards, agile stunt players, and occasional photographic matting, explosive effects can now be safely rendered through digital compositing without so much as lighting a match. Within the more alarmist wings of the cinema is ill/dying/dead crowd, this increase in explosive force figures as a particularly noxious symptom of Hollywood's perceived decline from sophisticated storyteller to purveyor of mindless spectacle. Artful dramatic filmmaking, as many critics and some aging talent lament, is deader than a doornail, blown off the screen by a "blockbuster" logic that emphasizes the "rollercoaster ride" over the traditionally venerated qualities of character, depth, complexity, and coherence.

In his study of contemporary popular cinema, *The Way Hollywood Tells It*, David Bordwell argues this familiar critical tirade over spectacle's alleged victory over the subtle complexities of classical narration is often hyperbolic and born of selective amnesia. Critics upset over a perceived degeneration of film art, he argues, typically concentrate on "the tent pole films—typically action pictures and heroic fantasy—or on the acknowledged classics (*Chinatown, The Godfather*).... Perhaps our orthodox account of the industry's recent history, focusing on the rise of the megapicture, lets all the other films slip too far to the periphery" (10). With characteristic skepticism, Bordwell gently needles fellow critics and scholars who, looking at this limited subset of action megapictures, claim a systemic erosion of classical continuity, or worse yet (for neo-formalism's anti-interpretive agenda) that this decline, if it does exist, is somehow indicative of "contradictions in capitalism or the crisis of masculinity" (104). Bordwell continues, "Instead of interpreting these movies as symptoms of something, we can ask how much they stray from the norms of traditional filmmaking. Do they announce the breakdown of Hollywood storytelling?" (104).

Examining these films closely in terms of formal organization, he argues, demonstrates that even the most "incoherent" and spectacular megapictures of the past few decades are still dependent on the basic architecture of classical continuity and narration. Why, then, does the experience of *Casablanca* (Michael Curtiz, 1942) seem to be so qualitatively different than that of *Saw 3-D* (Kevin Greutert, 2010), even if one puts aside historical differences of taste and genre? Bordwell attributes the general perception of radical change in recent Hollywood product to the industry's gradual cultivation of what he terms "intensified continuity," a more "aggressive" stylistic lexicon that mobilizes four key devices: (1) faster editing, (2) greater variability in lens selection, (3) increasingly tighter framing, and (4) more and faster camera movement. Intensified continuity does not necessarily mean that spectacle has displaced narrative, Bordwell concludes, but rather that Hollywood's characteristic interweaving of story and spectacle through classical continuity has simply developed a style that places the image in a more consistent state of dynamic flux, even as it generally obeys the "rules" of classical story structure. *Judge Dredd* (Danny Cannon, 1995), *The Rock* (Michael Bay, 1996), *Armageddon* (Michael Bay, 1998), and the many other films seen by pessimists to be benchmarks in filmmaking's race to the spectacular bottom are thus still fundamentally classical in their narrative organization, demonstrating not the endpoint of the Hollywood model but rather its immense (and apparently infinite) flexibility.

This all seems quite reasonable. Few would argue that contemporary film production is anything other than diverse. "Tent pole" megapictures are not the only games in town, even in terms of releases backed by the major studios. One can still enjoy the romantic-like comedies of the inexplicably prolific Jennifer Aniston, the self-conscious stylistic play of the Coen Brothers, or even the continuing erosion of Woody Allen's own little stylistic island in the art cinema archipelago. Nor would many argue that even the most horrifyingly incoherent action pictures, like the now somewhat infamous *Transformers: Revenge of the Fallen* (Michael Bay, 2009), are completely without plot, nor that the plot—however minimal—retains some utility in making the genre's extended set pieces legible and, in theory at least, entertaining. But the critical alarm over the ascendance of the spectacular megapicture in the movie marketplace is not really a concern over formal definitions.

If one wants to posit and defend the integrity of a system that somehow links Michael Bay and D. W. Griffith in terms of formal practice, that certainly can be done, even if such a model of classical narration would appear so abstract as to obscure more than it clarifies. Moments of explosive apathy, for example, could certainly be explained as simply another possible strategy for binding narrative to spectacle in the remarkably flexible classical system, conveying information about plot and character even as they provide for a moment of spectacular indulgence (we learn simultaneously, after all, that something important has exploded and that the apathetic nonwitness has "nerves of steel"). But there is also a certain "excess" in the explosively apathetic, an element that goes beyond a purely functional explanation of how the formal device momentarily integrates registers of narrative and spectacle.[1] In this respect, we might say that explosive apathy is an extremely "self-conscious" moment of narration (to continue with Bordwell's terminology),[2] self-conscious to the point of being exhibitionist and exhibitionist to the point of demanding, rather rudely, attention and even respect.

After all, there is no reason to maintain a pretense of indifference in the face of a tremendous explosion unless one is certain an audience is watching. And as this audience is often not present within the diegesis itself, it is by default the spectator who is called to bear witness to the unflinching protagonist's performance of testicular fortitude. Indeed, aimed primarily at the cinema's fourth wall, explosive apathy is an almost reflexive device, a staging that verges on breaking frame by presenting a spectacle of indifference purely for the benefit of the acknowledged spectator. *I know you are watching me be cool*, announce the apathetic, *that's why I'm cool!* More than a neutral option in conveying story and character information, explosive apathy thus carries with it a certain tone, an attitude that goes beyond the actual character to pervade the narration itself.

When contemporary critics bemoan the death of classical filmmaking in today's blockbuster mentality, they are as upset with the mentality as with the formal organization of the blockbusters themselves. In this respect, claiming that spectacle has dissolved narrative or that incoherence has replaced continuity is not to say that all vestiges of classical continuity/narration have vanished, but rather that the blockbuster's new iterations of narrative and spectacle have become so extreme and tilted towards the showcasing of exhibitionist action (and, crucially, its techniques) as to shift the traditional classical commitment to internal logic and diegetic plausibility towards a more aggressive, narcissistic, and ultimately glib form of stylistic preening. *Transformers: Revenge of the Fallen*, for example, may still be putatively organized around a goal-oriented protagonist moving through a set of obstacles and complications, and it may generally respect the classical continuity system in doing so, but this architecture is more vestigial than vital, subordinate to film's more explicit goal of creating an ass-kicking impact. The cinema, at least at these thresholds of the blockbuster action mode, has become insufferably obnoxious. And no single device is more obnoxious than explosive apathy.

Explosions Are Awesome

The impact of explosive apathy depends on the juxtaposition of two radically incongruous elements: extreme detachment and spectacular violence. Understanding the history of this device thus requires some attention to the primary object of calculated disinterest: the explosion itself. Here parody once again provides a useful starting point. Smart satire possesses an almost uncanny ability to see into the future, its comic hyperbole divining emerging currents that will later dominate the cultural landscape.

So it was with "Farm Film Report," a recurring sketch featured on NBC television's comedy series of the early 1980s, *SCTV*. Each installment featured the characters Big Jim McBob and Billy Sol Hurok,

Figure 2.2. Megan Fox and Shia LaBeouf make their escape in *Transformers: Revenge of the Fallen* (2009). Courtesy Paramount / The Kobal Collection.

hayseed movie critics entrusted with their own pre-dawn "Siskel and Ebert" reviews. While other movie critics offer complex assessments of a film's merit and artistry, McBob and Hurok used a single, simple criterion: the presence or absence of explosions. Movies ranked a recommendation only if something or someone in the film "blew up real good." Antonioni's *Zabriskie Point* (1970) thus earns their approval, while *Blow-Up* (1966), with its lack of anything actually blowing up, confuses and disappoints them.

Eventually celebrities began appearing on "Farm Film Report" to discuss recent projects and, of course, to be exploded. Changing the name of their show to "Farm Film Celebrity Blow Up," Big Jim and Billy Sol made sure Brooke Shields, Dustin Hoffman, Meryl Streep, Bernadette Peters, and Neil Sedaka all "blew up real good." At its most obvious, this running gag was an insider joke about the tastes of hix in the stix for violent pix (to employ *Variety* speak). And yet, there was also a certain populist pleasure in seeing Meryl Streep, then the ascending queen of serious acting in serious cinema, blown to smithereens by redneck revolutionaries, a triumphant victory for lowbrow sensationalism over highbrow boredom, or even better, over midcult aspirations for highbrow importance.[3]

That the "Farm Film Report" should develop a fetish for explosions in the early 1980s is significant. Though dressed in rustic overalls and faded flannel, Big Jim and Billy Sol's enthusiasm for all things explosive was less a commentary on bumpkin taste than a window on Hollywood's then growing emphasis on the teenage market for the action blockbuster. Appearing in the relatively recent historical wake of *Jaws* (Steven Spielberg, 1975), *Star Wars* (George Lucas, 1977), and *Raiders of the Lost Ark* (Steven Spielberg, 1981) (traditional benchmarks in the blockbuster ethos), "Farm Film Report" anticipated a decade in the action blockbuster which would become pivotal to the film industry's portfolio, an era that also saw the increasing influence of what Geoff King has termed the "impact aesthetic." For King, the impact aesthetic depends on rapid editing and a consistent staging of action in such a way that bodies, vehicles, explosions, debris, and other projectiles hurtle towards the camera (and thus the viewer). The typical action sequence, he notes, alternates between shots emphasizing lateral movement and those showcasing a type of "in-your-face" blocking that pushes the action through the fourth wall and into the spectator's lap. Much of the impetus for "intensified continuity," as described by Bordwell, stems from this era's attempt to draw spectators ever closer to increasingly complex sequences of accelerated action, with editing, framing, and camera movement collaborating to provoke an almost involuntary bodily response from the viewer (a response, moreover, that stands in stark contrast to that of the explosively apathetic).

The art of the explosion made tremendous strides in the 1980s and 1990s, especially as digital technologies allowed for more control over their choreography. King argues that explosions have come to figure so prominently in the action film in that they offer "one of the easiest ways to render visible the kinetics out of which action sequences are constructed" (102). The fiery explosion is emblematic of the genre's overall stylistic design, compressing the percussive editing, blocking, and sound design of raw action into a singularly explosive release of kinetic/cinematic energy. The fireball thus presents "all the force and intensity of the ideal action sequence compressed and made manifestly visible" (102). A large fireball also allows for a certain elasticity in staging the action. "Fireballs can move quickly," King notes, "but can also be rendered convincingly at speeds that provide time for the action that often occurs in their glowing paths" (102). Although the physics police enjoy reminding us that it is simply impossible to outrun an explosion, the ability of actors and vehicles to outmaneuver advancing fireballs is an accepted convention of the action spectacular; indeed, in some movies, quick-thinking heroes are even able to avoid bullets, typically rendered in slow motion so that we might better appreciate the gymnastics (the emphasis on slow-moving bullets that "explode" when hitting a target, moreover, suggests a creative microvariation on the "impact aesthetic," the bullet providing its own "explosive" force in superslow motion and extreme close-up).

Given this emphasis on maximum impact in the impact aesthetic, explosive apathy would appear to be a somewhat counterintuitive strategy. In a style that typically emphasizes fast-moving action pitched directly towards the viewer and threatening to blast out the fourth wall, explosive apathy places a character—usually the major protagonist(s)—between the explosion and the spectator, in effect blocking or damping the actual "impact" of the fireball. Moreover, explosive apathy typically unfolds in slow motion. While this might seem to allow for more manipulation of actors and objects in the path of the fireball, in practice this slow motion actually foregrounds the static resolve and detachment of the explosively apathetic who coolly walk away from the massive impact behind them. Typically, the explosively apathetic characters "cap" a scene by conveying some form of victory in their nonchalance, a coda marked by a sudden deceleration of velocity and impact. Pursuing a functional explanation of explosive apathy, one might consider it as a by-product of the accelerated stylization within the "impact aesthetic" as a whole.

Examples of this staging certainly predate the move towards the action blockbuster, but the iconic rendering of the explosively apathetic—a hero (or at times villain) striding away in silent bravado—really only becomes codified across the 1980s and 1990s. Here, one could argue the more explosions came to dominate the cinema, the more filmmakers had to find new ways to make them stand out from the general rise in pyrotechnics. In this context, one might argue explosive apathy is simply a logical strategy for recalibrating the spectator's attention, a means of re-spectacularizing the spectacle of explosive cinema at a key plot point. *This one counts!* announces the explosively apathetic. This particular explosion actually means something, *precisely because we are not reacting to it*. In this respect, explosive apathy serves almost as a type of emphatic caesura that momentarily arrests the breakneck pacing of the "impact aesthetic."

But the performative coolness of the explosively apathetic and the strident exhibitionism of its staging complicates any purely functional explanation of narrative legibility within spectacular proliferation. Explosive apathy may put a certain climatic explosion into narrative relief, but the hyper-stylization of this device in its most extreme forms—a pushing at the very limits of verisimilitude by moving to superslow motion, addressing the spectator frontally to the point of hostile confrontation, and defying the basic laws of human reflexology—suggests that the function of explosive apathy goes beyond establishing narrative clarity or providing simple contrast within the overall attack of the impact aesthetic. As a marker of tone, as an attitude embedded in the actors and the action, explosive apathy generally transcends naturalist constraint to inhabit a stylistic realm that we might deem "the awesome." The awesome, obviously, is that which aspires to produce awe, a particularly intense subset of the impact aesthetic that consistently seeks to push spectacular possibility. As a growing and particularly aggressive school of action cinema, the awesome does not merely accelerate and stylize action for maximum impact, but also engages in an exhibitionist address that invites the spectator to alternate between visceral engagement and contemplative appreciation, attending not only to the awesome aspects of the action event, but also to the mechanics and theatrics that produce cinematic awesomeness.

Whereas the impact aesthetic, as King notes (93–104), generally depends on fast movement and fast editing, certain shots becoming almost illegible as their blurring and motion simply contribute to an overall perception of velocity, awesomeness attains in those privileged moments when the action is rendered manifestly visible, slowed down through camera speed and editing to encourage an almost obscene engagement of action technique in and of itself: a bullet slows to the point that we can see it pancake against its target; a martial arts fighter leaps, bends, or ducks in multiple angles to avoid a death blow; the apathetic slowly walk away from an explosion decompressed for maximum absorption. The awesome is a fleeting moment of spectacle frozen for more considered contemplation, a moment when the impact aesthetic caps its impact by breaking the lateral/frontal staging of action with an equally contrasting manipulation of time/movement, one that allows the viewer to shift from merely absorbing impacts, shocks, and attractions to instead study, in minute detail, the space and trajectory of the action. Massive explosions are awesome, of course, but so too is Spiderman vertiginously web-slinging his way across Manhattan or the Na'vi riding mountain banshees through the open sky. Warping space and time is awesome, as is the ability to watch a bullet in 360-degree slow motion (even more awesome if, as in *Wanted* [Timur Bekmambetov, 2008], said bullet can itself warp space and time). Acceleration is awesome, especially when the spectator is compelled to assume the G-forced perspective of the protagonist (a convention solidified to great effect by Luke Skywalker's final assault on the Death Star in *Star Wars*). A zeppelin exploding in a film from the 1930s is spectacular, realized through models, matte shots, and editing doing their best to approximate period codes of zeppelin-explosion verisimilitude. A zeppelin exploding in IMAX, each tendril of flame and smoke in crisp relief, the projectiles of debris spinning on the x, y, and z axes along perfectly delineated smoke trails, the framing made mobile by a "camera" swooping through the open sky to assume perspectives impossible to the human eye, the subwoofer thud in the gut of the initial explosion gently sweetened by sounds of breaking glass, screams, and tinkling metal, the entire conflagration seemingly hurdling through the fourth wall and into the face of the audience (and with the current expansion of 3-D, even more so): that is *awesome!*

More than merely an extra-impacted aesthetic or an overly intensified continuity, the awesome aspires to be so overwhelming as to verge on hostility for the spectator. And, as befitting such confrontational exhibitionism, the poetics of the awesome seemingly expect a form of tribute. To judge something awesome, as in *That's awesome!*, is to acknowledge one's subordination to the visceral power of the cinematic onslaught, to meet image and sound with wonder, respect, and maybe even fear (which, after all, is the original connotation of "awe"). It is a moment of double-coded reading. Even as the spectator processes the import of an awesome moment within the diegesis as a plot point, there is also an enthrallment to the artistry and power of the awesomely executed, an appreciation grounded in an odd mix of kinesthetic empathy and aestheticized contemplation. Linda Williams has famously identified melodrama, horror, and pornography as "body genres" in that each seeks to elicit a *physiological* response in the spectator. To this we might add the awesome as a form of film style that—if ideally realized—would compel the spectator to shit and/or piss his pants and, moreover, to be glad that his pants have been thus soiled.

Dada to Boom-boom

When did the cinema become so awesome? There is a temptation to locate the origins of awesomeness, rather deterministically, in the advent of the various digital technologies for dissecting sound and image that have allowed the cinema to engage action with such analytic precision, to break so decisively from the spatiotemporal constraints of analogue reality/recording. Going even further, there is perhaps a temptation to locate the origin point of awesomeness in a single film: *The Matrix* (Andy and Lana Wachowski, 1999). By introducing the technique of "bullet time," a multicamera digital effect that produced the illusion of a camera moving through frozen space and time, *The Matrix* (and its sequels) allowed complex points of action to appear as veritable tableaux of analytical spectacle.[4] In an industry looking to ever intensify the impact aesthetic, bullet time soon became a standard component within the action arsenal and perhaps the sine qua non of cinematic awesomeness.[5] But the awesome is not wholly reducible to technological possibility, just as explosive apathy did not begin only when certain optical effects made it possible to safely composite actors and explosions in the same shot. This device, now so indicative of the awesome sensibility, predates the revolution in sound and image afforded by digital rendering technologies, not to mention the advent of intensified continuity and the impact aesthetic as standard industry practice.

Surprisingly, an intriguing antecedent to the staging of explosive apathy can be found in Max Ernst's collage novel of 1929, *The Hundred Headless Woman* (*La femme 100 têtes*). Divided into nine chapters, this signature work of Surrealism presents 147 collage panels Ernst assembled from wood engravings gathered from nineteenth-century novels, magazines, and encyclopedias. A panel in chapter 5, "Drum-roll among the stones," features a well-dressed man advancing in the foreground, seemingly oblivious to a tremendous explosion in the streets behind him. As in so much other Surrealist work, the image invokes a type of dream logic (what André Breton describes, in the novel's foreword, as "the innumerable illusions of true recognition" (10). As befitting an image conjured by "the most magnificently haunted brain" of the Surrealist era (Breton's description of Ernst), "Drum-roll among the stones" is both complex and suggestive (10). At a most basic (perhaps "manifest") level, Ernst's affluent citizen strolling imperviously through a city of soldiers and explosions evokes the detached privilege of the bourgeoisie so irksome to modern artists over the past two centuries, a figure "floundering" along the border between Dadaist disgust and Surrealist sleepwalking. No matter how one ultimately cares to interpret the image in terms of allegory or politics, however, "Drum roll among the stones" is most assuredly a confrontation with illogic, an ironic juxtaposition mobilized to trigger the irrationality of the "marvelous."

It is unlikely, of course, that a direct lineage connects Ernst's explosive provocation with the hundreds of CGI artists who even now are rendering dozens of explosions soon to be ignored by top Hollywood talent. Still, one can only wonder how an image born of the modernist avant-garde could become so "naturalized" as to proliferate across popular filmmaking a half-century later. What in 1929 stood as a jolt to realism and rationality is now a banal device deemed reasonably plausible within a range of genres.

In the opening sequence of *Wild in the Streets* (Barry Shear, 1968), for example, explosive apathy signals the protagonist's comic departure for a story world in which newly enfranchised hippie-teenagers take over the United States government.[6] When teenager Max Flatow (Christopher Jones)—soon to be a rock star and President of the United States—decides he can no longer continue living in the stifling suburban world of his parents, he signals his departure by ceremonially torching the family car. Having ignited an oily rag stuffed into the gas tank, Flatow strides towards the camera smiling as the car erupts in flames. Here the disinterest in the explosion, played as comedy, has actual thematic value:

Flatow is leaving and he's not looking back, literally. This comic use of this device still appears in contemporary filmmaking, even as other genres ask viewers to take this staging more seriously.

Comic versions of this device are usually less about actual apathy or indifference, but instead highlight a gloating victory of extreme payback. This payback, in turn, often implies a winking bond between the comic arsonist and the spectator as they share in a victory of some sort. For teenagers watching *Wild in the Streets* in 1968, there was no doubt some solidarity in seeing a screen surrogate torching the family station wagon and heading for the coast, a generational bond reaffirmed by Jones maintaining his cheerful focus on the sympathetic audience beyond the fourth wall. The "chick flick" comedy *She-Devil* (Susan Seidelman, 1989) makes a similar comic use of the device. Playing a frumpy housewife deserted by her philandering husband, Ruth Patchett (Roseanne) burns down the family home, advancing towards the screen with a smile on her face as the house collapses behind her. She too is "not looking back," and does so in solidarity with an audience presumably primed to revel in the destruction of a cheating husband's property.

Today, of course, explosive apathy is most often associated with action cinema, heroes and villains vying for supremacy through exchanges of explosive firepower. An interesting antecedent here can be found in Francis Ford Coppola's *Apocalypse Now* (1979), a film that can also claim a rather explicit affinity for surrealist practices. A benchmark (if not the endpoint) of a particular school of modernist art cinema, Coppola's famously troubled project adapted Joseph Conrad's *Heart of Darkness* to the jungle warfare of Vietnam, making frequent recourse to avowedly absurdist scenarios to capture the hallucinatory illogic of what came to stand as America's most "senseless" war. In one particularly demented episode, Lt. Col. Bill Kilgore (Robert Duvall) leads an air offensive to "pacify" a Vietnamese village and take control of its beachhead. Kilgore's other (and we assume primary) motive in the mission is to introduce a new solider, formerly a champion surfer in the United States, to the excellent breakers off the Vietnamese coast. As the scene progresses, we see that years in the shit have made Kilgore completely oblivious to the mortar and small arms fire that continually erupt around him. While the surfer and his fellow grunts duck and cover at each blast and report, Kilgore strides confidently across the beach in search of good waves, completely unconcerned that the beachhead does not yet appear completely secured. In keeping with the overall design of the film, Kilgore's impassivity serves here as a sign of surreal insanity that echoes the illogic of U.S. foreign policy, a war psychosis culminating in Kilgore's famously professed love for the "smell of napalm in the morning." "Someday this will all be over," he muses wistfully. This explosive disconnect echoes in the film's famous opening as well, a protracted and wholly static shot of the jungle suddenly disrupted by a massive wall of flaming napalm. Impactful to be sure, the eerie silence of the composition (save for "The End" by The Doors, of course) is oddly distancing and arguably emblematic of the American public's relationship to the overall conflict: fascination at a safe distance.

Much like Ernst's oblivious flâneur, Lt. Col. Kilgore is somewhat demented, perhaps even wholly psychotic. In its contemporary iterations, explosive apathy remains a convenient device for underscoring a psychopathic character's singular focus on his modus operandi; indeed, this emphasis on focus and resolve makes for a point of contact between the comic and action deployments of this device. In more stylized renderings of action cinema, a character walks away from an explosion already pondering its impact on his or her adversaries (much as Roseanne imagines her husband's response in *She-Devil*). In *The Dark Knight* (Christopher Nolan, 2008), for example, the Joker (Heath Ledger) destroys an entire hospital through a series of detonations without turning to look back at his handiwork, his nihilistic insanity further underscored (and made perversely comic) by his trademark makeup and the donning of a nurse's uniform.

Joel and Ethan Coen, meanwhile, have put this device to work even within the somewhat more sober palette of cinematic naturalism. In *No Country for Old Men* (2007), villain Anton Chigurh (Javier Bardem) must treat a serious wound so that he might continue his obsessive pursuit of Llewelyn Moss (Josh Brolin). Unable to go to a hospital, Chigurh instead detonates a car in front of a pharmacy, blowing out its windows and creating the distraction he needs to steal the necessary medical supplies. By emphasizing Chigurh's utter indifference to his own decoy explosion, the shot emphasizes the singular focus of his criminal insanity. He is, in this moment, cinematic kin to Michael Myers of the *Halloween* series and Jason from the *Friday the 13th* franchise: an unstoppable force of pure evil that appears to be something other than human.

When used to suggest a sense of psychotic detachment in a character, explosive apathy can take on an aspect of the uncanny, casting doubt on whether "an apparently animate being is really alive; or conversely, whether a lifeless object might not be in fact animate" (Freud 226). Following Ernst Jentsch, Freud argued that epileptic fits and manifestations of insanity are uncanny in that they "excite in the spectator the impression of automatic, mechanical processes at work behind the ordinary appearance of mental activity" (226). In this respect, those who present "insane" versions of explosive apathy appear drained of normal affect, "inhuman" by virtue of an ability to suppress the seemingly reflexive instinct of the startle response.

Also uncanny, of course, are waxworks, dolls, mannequins, and automatons, the antecedents of the robots, cyborgs, and androids populating contemporary science fiction (and the action film). Here too are important ancestors to the explosively apathetic of today, variously mechanized characters that have helped codify the device's primary use as a means for projecting superhuman power. Paul Verhoeven's *Robocop* (1987), for example, centered on the existential and political questions attending the world's first cyborg police officer, half-man half-machine, working for the newly privatized police force of a decaying Detroit. Lauded by many as a "smart" action film, the movie also provoked concern and even outrage over what many perceived to be its extraordinary and "gratuitous" levels of violence. In a strategy that would typify Verhoeven's Hollywood career, the film operates in an ambiguous zone of excess somewhere between parody and exploitation. Was the film excessively violent, or was it trying to make a point about America's fascination with excessive violence? Always interested in the borderlands of fascism, Verhoeven achieved much of this shock effect by organizing the film's ultraviolent "justice" around the implacable indifference of its cybernetic lead. Of course, it is Robocop's last remaining shreds of human identity that provide the film with its central moral conflict, his human memories gradually interfering with his ability to mechanically administer the law. Before resolving this tension, however, the film revels in the spectacle of the Robocop—a cyborg who appears outwardly at least to be more man than machine—almost preternaturally oblivious to any and all threats to his body. In what itself has become a stock variation on explosive apathy, Robocop at one point emerges from a wall of flames, wholly unaffected by his brush with the conflagration.

This uncanny collision of the human form with extraordinary and typically lethal violence was also central to the *Terminator* series, the first two installments in particular pioneering many of the techniques and technologies of what would come to define the impact aesthetic. Again echoing the immortal logic of the slasher film, *The Terminator* (James Cameron, 1984) famously ends with the T-1 unit (played by the already somewhat uncanny Arnold Schwarzenegger) gradually stripped of its flesh to become pure exoskeleton, one also capable of walking through walls of fire in order execute its mission. The sequel, *Terminator 2: Judgment Day* (James Cameron, 1991), redoubled this uncanny effect by casting the formerly evil T-1 as the hero pitted against the even more uncanny T-1000, a robot-line now capable of shape-shifting and thus even more spectacular displays of a "human" body impervious to bullets, explosions, fire, and other usually deadly forms of violence. By pitting T-1 and T-1000 against one another, moreover, the film arguably narrates its own contribution to the industry's overall escalation of spectacle, the now obsolescent Schwarzenegger battling the consummately professional (and seemingly psychotic) impassivity of a wholly fluid T-1000, the latter's uncanny CGI shape-shifting abilities a harbinger of the cinema's ascension into even more spectacular awesomeness.

An extraordinarily expensive sequel to the sleeper success of the first film, *Terminator 2* serves even today as a working catalogue of devices for staging the professional discipline, singular narrative resolve, and protean indestructibility so crucial to both heroes and villains in the more extreme examples of the impact aesthetic. In the recombinatory logic of Hollywood, however, this extreme stoicism, an apathetic detachment once confined primarily to robots and the insane, has gradually migrated to the flesh-and-blood actants of the contemporary action spectacle who, while ostensibly still human, nevertheless replicate this alien logic of absolute invulnerability, able to suppress all signs of fear, pain, fatigue, and distraction. Much as a talent for the quick draw distinguished extraordinary status in the classical Western, the ability to walk away nonchalantly from a massive explosion has become perhaps the privileged marker of superhuman machismo among cinematic spies, assassins, vigilantes, enforcers, transporters, warriors, cops, bad dudes, and many others working the more awesome end of the action genre's trade in violence.

Blown Away

Forged in the industry's turn towards action blockbusters in the 1980s and proliferating across the 1990s, explosive apathy is now such a common staging device as to appear in many different arenas of popular culture. Whether played straight or put in ironic quotation marks, explosive apathy still figures prominently, not only in the cinema, but also in music videos, commercials, and quotidian television programming. Though explosive apathy first manifested among agents of extraordinary power at the edge of the human, now rappers walk away from exploding luxury cars and teenage geeks walk away from exploding gaming consoles. The Internet is rife with Photo Shop parodies of the explosively apathetic, drawing attention to the predictability of the convention as well as its fundamentally absurd illogic. After circulating widely for some twenty years, then, perhaps explosive apathy has finally lost the ability to elicit an awesome response. Like the iris wipe, zoom focus, and the spinning newspaper headline, it may well be that explosive apathy is nearing exhaustion, overexposure and parody defamiliarizing it to the point that it can no longer function "invisibly." Increasingly, even within the action cinema itself, the explosively apathetic appear more in quotation marks, still invoking the awesome, but a more self-aware, ironic form of awe.

Perhaps audiences have also begun to recognize just how truly insulting, obnoxious, and condescending this signifying convention actually is: at least when performed nonironically by mere mortals. Again, the explosively apathetic practically *demand* the attention and adulation of an audience, adopting a mannered posture that only makes sense in the presence of a witness to its awesomeness. Surrounded by awesome spectacle, they perform "coolness" by remaining aloof to the very spectacle the audience is presumably hoping to see. It is a device that is thus both narcissistic and obnoxious, especially when considered alongside its phylogenic siblings in staging movie explosions: what we can call *fireball fleeing* and *shockwave surfing*. As three highly stylized options in marrying story and spectacle, the devices comprise a sort of affective continuum of possible responses to the sudden intrusion of explosive spectacle.

Fireball fleeing presents the relatively neutral middle term, separating the extreme positions of shockwave surfing and explosive impassivity. Again, as King suggests, movie explosions operate in time and space in such a way that fleeing them remains a plausible (if improbable) option, even if that means little more than throwing oneself in a ditch to avoid the advancing wall of fire (102–3). Here we are encouraged to identify with the protagonist's plight as he or she struggles to remain one step ahead of the advancing blast: they share our healthy respect for the explosion's deadly force.

"Shockwave surfers," on the other hand, are caught in closer proximity to the fireball. While not necessarily vaporized, burned, or even singed by the encounter, they do find themselves caught up in the force of the shockwave as a human projectile. They are in this moment, quite literally blown away by the action, much as the ideal spectator of the ideal action film seeks to be blown away by the movie itself (Bruce Willis riding the ejection seat in *Die Hard 2* [Renny Harlin, 1990] comes to mind here). As detailed extensively above, finally, the explosively apathetic neither flee nor ride the spectacular blast, but instead remain resolutely unimpressed and unmoved by the irresistible force unfolding behind them.

To be blown away or not to be blown away? This would seem to be the question facing both filmmakers and audiences in these moments of explosive excess. And it is in this slippage between being blown away, as in literal displacement by an explosion, to being blown away as popular slang for a particularly dynamic entertainment experience, that the perversely dismissive logic of explosive apathy truly begins to emerge. As the third term in this continuum, the explosively apathetic quite clearly stand apart from those reduced to panicked fleeing or terrorized surfing. Again, whereas fireball fleeing and shockwave surfing both remain sealed within the story world, the exhibitionist quality of explosive apathy calls out its audience—be it diegetic, in the theater, or both—as a witness to the awesome power of the protagonist. Like rival bears meeting in the woods, the explosively apathetic look towards the viewer almost in provocation, amplifying a fleeting moment of flaming spectacle into a more aggressively narcissistic form of confrontation.

This is the attitude imparted by the explosively apathetic, one that inherently mocks the spectators who have come to see the film. By standing impassively between the spectator and the fiery spectacle he has paid admission to see, the explosively apathetic quite literally embody a condescending critique of the viewer's desire for witnessing the awesome. The explosively apathetic announce in their very silence superiority over the viewer, immunity to the very thing designed to most engage the spectator. Having mastered all modes of distraction, fear, pain, technology, and even spectacle itself, the explosively apathetic thus invite us to admire them for their utter disinterest in what is of great interest to us. Whereas fireball fleeing and shockwave surfing fully indulge our immersion in the thrill ride of spectacular action, the explosively apathetic remain performatively aloof. We are blown away. They most decidedly are not. Worse yet, they insist that we be impressed by the fact that they are so completely unimpressed.

Notes

1. "Excess" is a notoriously imprecise concept, of course. Here I am using it in the tradition of Roland Barthes's essay on "The Third Meaning," an approach later elaborated by Kristin Thompson in "The Concept of Cinematic Excess."
2. Bordwell elaborates on this concept in *Narration in the Fiction Film*.
3. Ever childlike in their enthusiasm for "real good" explosions, Big Jim and Billy Sol typified *SCTV*'s frequent jokes about quality cinema undercut by the increasingly juvenile demands of the movie marketplace. In a later episode, for example, an unscrupulous producer looks to make a sequel to Stanley Kubrick's *2001: A Space Odyssey* (1968), updating the film for the emerging teen slasher market by arming the famous monolith with a butcher knife and setting him loose on a spaceship full of co-eds. In an installment of Count Floyd's late-night *Monster Chiller Horror Theater*, meanwhile, the station accidentally orders Ingmar Bergman's *Hour of the Wolf* (1968), forcing Floyd to convince his viewers that the brooding art film is in fact "really scary."
4. "Bullet time" is in fact a registered trademark of Warner Brothers.
5. *The Matrix*, it should be noted, also features an interesting variation on explosive apathy—the now rather iconic tableau of Trinity, clad in her tight leather simulation suit, crouched in frozen contemplation of a massive firewall unfurling before her. While not a classic articulation of the device, Trinity remaining relatively "unmoved" by the immense spectacle of fire before her (admittedly, a wall of simulated fire), the shot nevertheless trades in the same cool detachment from spectacular impact so typical of this device.
6. Ratified on July 1, 1971, the Twenty-sixth Amendment lowered the voting age in the United States to 18.

Works Cited

Barthes, Roland. "The Third Meaning: Research Notes on Some Eisenstein Stills." *Image Music Text*. Trans. Stephen Heath. London: Fontana, 1977. Print.

Bordwell, David. *Narration in the Fiction Film*. Madison: U of Wisconsin P, 1985. Print.

———. *The Way Hollywood Tells It: Story and Style in Modern Movies*. Berkeley: U of California P, 2006. Print.

Ernst, Max. *The Hundred Headless Woman* (*La femme 100 têtes*). Foreword by André Breton. New York: G. Braziller, 1981. Print.

Freud, Sigmund. "The Uncanny." [1919] *The Complete Psychological Works of Sigmund Freud*. Vol. 17. Ed. and trans. James Strachey. London: Hogarth Press, 1963. Print.

King, Geoff. *Spectacular Narratives: Hollywood in the Age of the Blockbuster*. London: I. B. Tauris, 2001. Print.

Rogers, Tom. *Insultingly Stupid Movie Physics: Hollywood's Best Mistakes, Goofs and Flat-Out Destructions of the Basic Laws of the Universe*. Naperville: Sourcebooks Hysteria, 2007. Print.

Thompson, Kristin. "The Concept of Cinematic Excess." *Narrative, Apparatus, Ideology*. Ed. Philip Rosen. New York: Columbia UP, 1986 [1981]. 131–43. Print.

Weiner, Adam. *Don't Try This At Home!: The Physics of Hollywood Movies*. New York: Kaplan Publishing, 2007. Print.

Williams, Linda. "Film Bodies: Gender, Genre and Excess." *Film Quarterly* 44.4 (1991): 2–13. Print.

3

B-Grade Subtitles

Tessa Dwyer

The "bad" credentials of the subtitle reproduced in figure 3.1 are easy to spot. Sourced from a website that "celebrates the wonderful Engrish [sic] subtitles featured in an Asian bootleg DVD of Lord of The Rings: The Two Towers," this line of incomprehensible English appears on one of over eighty screen grabs lovingly collected from three hours of footage and displayed for the sole purpose of humorous revelry.[1] The original English dialogue is transcribed as follows: "Can you not see? Your uncle is wearied by your malcontent." No further details regarding the genesis of this pirated DVD are provided, and the viewer is left to wonder at the very inclusion of English subtitles on an English-language film.[2] The motivation likely rests with the predominance of English as a lingua franca throughout the Asian region and beyond. English as a second language is more accessible in written than spoken form, while English subtitles present a more cost-effective strategy than subtitles in local languages with limited appeal. Evidently, many geopolitical nuances of badness go unacknowledged in this entertaining exposé.

Nevertheless, this Internet homage to the translational errors of B-grade subtitling clearly fits within a "badfilm" or paracinema lexicon.[3] Noting the "camp attitude" driving such celebrations of mistranslation, Abe Mark Nornes traces "this fun back to the silent era when early film critics ridiculed sloppy intertitles," before linking it specifically "to the fandom surrounding Hong Kong cinema and its love of the

Figure 3.1. Bad subtitles for *The Lord of the Rings: The Two Towers* (2002). Source http://www.angelfire.com/rings/ttt-subtitles/000-020/index.html.

adolescent pratfalls, spectacular violence, and bathroom humour of the former colony's cinema" (16–17). In fact, sloppy subtitling and dubbing emerge as the hallmarks of many a "bad" foreign-language genre, from Hong Kong "chop-socky on late-night TV" (Chute 34) to Italy's typically out-of-synch spaghetti Westerns, termed a "bastard" genre by Geoffrey Nowell-Smith. Over two decades ago, for instance, John Powers glorified "bad" Hong Kong film translation in *Film Comment*, identifying it as one component of a delightfully flawed whole: "English-language viewers are even rewarded with scads of uproarious subtitles," he enthuses, "ranging from the cryptic minimalism of 'I'll' to the teasing ambiguity of 'You are a cunny'" (36).

Tapping into this form of subcultural pleasure, Quentin Tarantino announced in 2004 that he planned to follow up his two *Kill Bill* (2003, 2004) films with a kung fu feature shot entirely in Mandarin and released in two English-language versions, one subtitled and the other dubbed. "In homage to the often shakily-shot budget martial arts films of the era, the English dubbing will be deliberately out of synchronisation with the action," reported the *Sydney Morning Herald* in 2004. Although this Mandarin-language feature has not yet eventuated, the title of Tarantino's *Inglourious Basterds* (2009) exhibits a similar preoccupation with language difference and the errors of translation. A remake and deliberate mistranslation of the Italian-language war film *Quel maledetto treno blindato / The Inglorious Bastards* (Enzo Castellari, 1978), Tarantino's film contains French, German, English, and Russian language and employs subtitles throughout.

However, although substandard subtitles would seem to fit nicely into the bad film context, as simply another subgenre of paracinema activity (albeit one that is currently under-represented in the pages of *Zontar: The Magazine from Venus* or *Psychotronic Video*), it is my aim to demonstrate that the badness accrued by films *in-translation* is radically exponential and as such disrupts bad film discourse in significant, unpredictable ways. Humorously inept subtitles or "flubtitles" as they are referred to on a Hong Kong film fan website, do not simply delineate another genre of bad film production and appreciation.[4] Rather, they plainly testify to the significance of the intercultural within the bad film movement: a discourse that they also necessarily destabilize by potentially transforming *any* film into *bad film*. It is only through the prism of translation, for instance, that a successful Hollywood franchise like *Lord of the Rings: The Two Towers* (Peter Jackson, 2002) could ever be entertained as a paracinema artifact.

The intercultural slippage articulated by flubtitles does not only occur at the point of reception, but also actively intervenes within the production and performance of badness and film. As Lawrence Venuti ("Translating Derrida" 257) details, within Western society, translation tends to be viewed as a "second-order" mode that can never measure up to the primacy of the "original." For Jacques Derrida, this overdetermined negativity or failure activates translation's deconstructive effect. Derrida's conception of translation as "supplement" ("'Living On'" 75) is vital, I propose, to a consideration of the transnational within bad film, ultimately suggesting how B-grade subtitles might provide a means of reconceptualizing badness itself.

Intercultural Cult

Bad film and paracinema are traditionally areas that have welcomed foreign-language films, directors and genres. *Paracinema* magazine, for instance, features recent articles on the French-language sexploitation film *Emmanuelle* (Just Jaeckin, 1974); Italian cannibal films; Italian auteurs Pier Paolo Pasolini, Bernardo Bertolucci, and Dario Argento; Japan's Takeshi Miike; Austria's Michael Haneke, and Czech director Juraj Herz's *The Cremator / Spalovač mrtvol* (1969). Issue 9 of *Zontar* includes an article on Soviet TV personality Dr. Kashprovsky, while the *Zontar* website makes available for download the English subtitled Japanese-language version of *Gojira / Godzilla* (Ishiro Honda, 1954). From time to time, this overt courting of the foreign even goes so far as to detail various practicalities of language difference. Jayne Jain Kennedy's article on Dr. Kashprovsky, for instance, refers to the fact that the videotapes discussed are "fourth generation" copies brought to America by "a Russian woman" who provided informal, on-the-spot translations (39).[5]

Despite this active engagement with the foreign (along with the bizarre, the oppositional, and the culturally resistant), "badfilm" remains a largely Western, Anglo-American phenomenon or "reading protocol" (Sconce 372). Consequently, access to films, genres and directors from non–English-speaking contexts tends to depend upon the logistics of film translation, predominantly subtitling and dubbing. Although occasionally acknowledged, this fact is rarely considered in any depth.[6] Little to no mention is made of the influential role that language-difference plays in the appreciation and interpretation of these foreign products and their various "Bad-Truths" (Curran 41). How different translation strategies serve to frame, amplify, or even activate experiences of badness is largely overlooked, as is the manner in which subtitling and dubbing can function to signpost certain aesthetic positions, reinforcing the high/low cultural divide or taste wars that bad film potentially disrupts. While the bad film movement might not appear to suffer the same "monolingualism" that characterizes America's mainstream film audiences (see Rich), it continues nevertheless to refrain from any sustained or critical engagement with language difference and intercultural viewing. The politics of translation constitute a blind spot common to *both* bad film appreciation and mainstream movie-going alike.

Cult film practices, for instance, exemplify the ways in which translation is implicated within bad film discourse. Characterized as a market segment always seeking to discover new frontiers in the obscure and marginal, bizarre and exotic, cult film consumers seek out the unfamiliar and unusual in a "uniquely touristic" manner (Corrigan 26; see also Imanjaya 49). Consequently "the intersection between foreign-language film and 'cult' genre film" has been identified as a fertile ground for DVD distributors, as is demonstrated by the emergence of outfits such as Mondo Macabro and Tartan's "Asia Extreme" label.[7] Promising "the wild side of world cinema on DVD," Mondo Macabro's catalogue includes exploitation films from Argentina, Indonesia, and Pakistan while the "Asia Extreme" brand groups together "shocking" films from China, Japan, South Korea, and Thailand (Imanjaya 144; Shin 9).

Despite the celebratory tone of these distribution companies, the consumption of foreign-language films via Western cult readings can manifest as a form of cultural appropriation that obscures as much as brings to light the particularities of non–English speaking cultures. In his discussion of Indonesian New Order era exploitation films, for instance, Ekky Imanjaya notes how the English dubbing done by labels such as Mondo Macabro tends to alter dialogue in order to erase "spiritual Islamic elements" and identifies this tendency as part of a repeated, recognizable strategy to "adapt some Eastern features, making them more acceptable to Western taste" (151). For Imanjaya, the English-language version of a film like *Jaka Sembung / The Warrior* (Sisworo Gautama Putra, 1981) deliberately mistranslates or censors dialogue, subjecting the film to a "secularization process" aimed at "Western consumers" (152). At the same time, he notes "the mystic and supernatural is always highlighted" thereby emphasising the exotic, cultural "otherness" of Indonesian films (151). While New Order exploitation films are available to a limited extent within Indonesia and are starting to attract local "Jakarta cult-fan boys" (Imanjaya 149), Antonio Marcio de Silva notes that the Brazilian women-in-prison film *A Prisão / Bare Behind Bars* (Oswaldo de Oliveira, 1980) is currently only available as an English dub. With no Portuguese-language version currently in distribution, this film has been commandeered by Anglo-American "cultism" and remains inaccessible to domestic audiences (see Silva).

Philip Brophy draws attention to a more clandestine form of appropriation of the 1950s, which formalizes links between B-grade cinema, foreign-language films, and badness. Specifically, Brophy refers to "the post-war practice of importing so-called 'B-grade' foreign movies to be cut-up and repackaged as an American product" (233). In fact, as Brophy details, it was the unauthorized American re-mixes that more accurately fitted the B-grade mold. The original-language films from Russia and other Eastern European countries were often overtly artistic or political (233–34). For example, Aleksandr Ptushko's *Sadko* (1952) which won the Silver Lion award at the Venice Film Festival in 1953 was recomposed in the United States as James Landis's *The Magic Voyage of Sinbad* (1962), despite the fact that this ambitious adaptation of an epic Russian folk tale or heroic song (a *film-bylina*) bore no connection whatsoever to the Sinbad narrative (Brophy 233; Weldon 447; Upchurch 35).

Consequently, many of the B-grade sci-fi titles celebrated in the pages of *Zontar, Paracinema,* and *Psychotronic Video* could well have started life as popular, artful foreign-language fantasy films.[8] The "bowdlerized dubbed version" of *The Magic Voyage of Sinbad* was released by Roger Corman's Filmgroup (Upchurch 36). As producer/director for American

International Pictures, Corman also bought the rights to *Niebo Zowiet* (Mikhail Karzhukov and Aleksandr Kozyr, 1959), which was cut up to provide uncredited footage for *Battle Beyond the Sun* (1963) directed by Thomas Colchart—actually a pseudonym for Francis Ford Coppola (Weldon 38; Lentz 328). To complete the Americanization process of this film, Coppola rewrote the dialogue, enlisted voice dubbers, and shot new special effects sequences that included two monsters contrived to resemble male and female genitalia (Weldon 38). According to the website the Gods of Filmmaking, "*Battle Beyond the Sun* is exactly what it appears to be; a sci-fi action drama that plays itself so straight that it's hilarious. And all that with bad dubbing over Russian actors. . . . What more could you ask for?"

Corman also released two distinct English-dubbed reworkings of Pavel Klushantsev's Russian-language *Planeta Bur* (1962) as *Voyage to the Prehistoric Planet* (Curtis Harrington, 1965) and *Voyage to the Planet of Prehistoric Women* (Peter Bogdanovich, 1968), both of which also include footage from *Niebo Zowiet* (Charles 109–10). Both Harrington and Bogdanovich attempted to distance themselves for these productions credited to "John Sebastian" and "Derek Thomas" respectively (114, 116). According to Brophy, "the original language of these foreign films rendered them ripe for recoding and reformatting so as to make them 'suitable' for an American/Western understanding" (233). Charles notes, for instance, how in *Voyage to the Prehistoric Planet*, "references to socialist doctrine have been removed" (115). In this way, translation and intercultural appropriation reveal themselves to be built into the very fabric of the B-grade system.

Translation permeates the bad film movement in further ways still. In the Anglo-American context, dubbing and subtitling carry specific lowbrow/highbrow associations that are regularly exploited in order to cue audience expectations and shape patterns of reception.[9] In the United States, as in other Anglophone countries such as Canada, Australia, and the United Kingdom, subtitling tends to be equated with the art house circuit, and dubbing with popular fare such as animation, action, and exploitation (Betz 48; Nornes 12). For instance, the U.S. sexploitation film *Female Animal* (Jerry Gross, 1970) shot in Puerto Rico, masquerades itself as a European coproduction in order to capitalize on the licentious appeal of some European art films which, as Mark Betz, Joan Hawkins, and Eric Schaefer note, often teeter precariously between high and low exhibition contexts.[10] *Female Animal* includes fictitious Spanish-language credits and foreign production company names, seeking to create the illusion that it is a Spanish-language film that has been dubbed into English. In this instance, the specter of translation is deployed in order to profit from the exoticism of language difference. "Badness" is deliberately invoked through *Female Animal*'s pseudo-dubbing, which plays upon an expectation of cultural variance in moral codes. This dubbing pretense cues audiences to the film's low-brow sensibilities and, utilizing the levels of mediation built into translation processes, seeks to fabricate an eroticized distancing effect.[11]

From Indonesian exploitation to American B-grades to replica Euro-sleaze, translation has a multifaceted role to play in both the production and reception of bad film. As these diverse examples reveal, the intricacies of translation techniques and conventions provide a type of upside-down perspective on bad film and the intercultural. Strategies of exoticization and appropriation are reflected back at cult film audiences, who begin to catch a glimpse of themselves looking. Documented instances of censorship and cultural overwriting through dubbing function as a useful reminder to always consider the "productive effects" of reading and viewing practices (Cather 61), that is, how modes of film appreciation and analysis are produced (through what tools and technologies), and how they, in turn, are productive of new objects and texts.

Double Badness

A decade before the dizzying duplicitous dubbing of *Female Animal*, *New York Times* film critic Bosley Crowther envisioned a far more "authentic" potential in this technique. Following a dubbed screening of Ingmar Bergman's Swedish-language *Wild Strawberries* (1957), Crowther lambasted the then dominant practice within the United States of subtitling foreign art films. Pronouncing that "English subtitles affixed to foreign-language films are generally inadequate to communicate the increasingly complex and essential information contained in what the actors have to say," Crowther detailed how with "the addition of a few vivid words, conveyed with vocal expression," a new "logic and clarity" emerged from this "film loaded with verbal information and nuances" ("More on Dubbing"). "English subtitles really do not convey a great deal more of the characters conversation than did the subtitles on old silent films," he states (X9). Specifically, the dubbing of this film enabled Crowther to identify the "unmistakable intimation in the English dialogue that the old physician, years ago, had demanded—and perhaps even performed—

an abortion on his unfaithful wife" (X1). For Crowther, this "becomes the elusive key to the psychological syndrome in this picture" (X1).

Evidently, for Crowther, subtitling constitutes a "bad" method of film translation whereas dubbing, conversely, is positioned as "good." The badness that Crowther attributes to subtitles bears little resemblance to the playful and subversive attitude that tends to accompany the term within bad film discourse. There is no irony or countercultural sentiment in Crowther's bold demand that "subtitles must go!" However, this distinction does not delimit the relevance of Crowther's attack to the present discussion, for the badness that Crowther earnestly sought to expose during his anti-subtitling campaign is symptomatic of another, altogether different "bad" which film translation appears unable to shake. The motivation for introducing it here is to initiate a shift in focus from examining the role that translation plays in bad film discourse, to looking instead at the role that badness plays in translation discourse.

Despite the centrality of translation to film's emergence as one of the first truly global institutions, this medium developed hand in hand with a rhetoric emphasizing the "universal" nature of its image-based language (see Hanson 76–89). Hence, within film culture, the topic of translation tends to be ignored, denounced, or at best acknowledged as a necessary evil. Nornes comments, "it is likely that no one has ever come away from a foreign film admiring the translation" (11). He continues: "subtitling or dubbing attracts comment only when it inspires a desire for reciprocal violence, a revenge for the text in the face of its corruption; for . . . most spectators are quick to grudgingly champion one while disparaging the other" (11). In this underestimation of translation, film culture is by no means alone. As Venuti argues, the marginalization of translation as a second-order mode is systemic within Western society as a whole, a phenomenon he traces back to the prioritization of fluency or invisibility as its modus operandi whereby translations are judged most "successful" when unnoticeable: when they sound as though they are "originals" (*Translator's Invisibility* 1, 7).

The meager attention this subject has tended to attract within film culture has mainly come from nonacademic areas: in the odd review written by critics, fans, or buffs, and occasionally in commentary supplied by filmmakers and/or translators themselves. In such cases, the interest devoted to translation tends towards the subjective and remains couched in the negative. Even within this limited arena, most of the energy devoted to translation is preoccupied with deciding which of its two prevailing methods—subtitling or dubbing—represents the lesser of two evils. As Crowther's commentary demonstrates, in this context, invocations of malevolence are by no means restricted to examples of "bad" translation alone. In critiquing an entire *method*, rather than merely one or other particular instance of translation, Crowther effectively bypasses the issue of execution. How well the subtitles are rendered in any particular film hardly figures in his argument. Rather, Crowther posits the subtitle's badness as an unavoidable side effect of its form, which, he argues, necessarily condenses dialogue to an unsatisfactory degree while obliterating the expressive subtleties of tone, pitch, and delivery ("Subtitles Must Go").

While Crowther represented something of a maverick at the time, largely alone in his defense of dubbing among viewers of foreign art films, in other respects his stance was not atypical at all. His focus on method over execution epitomizes the manner in which film translation has been and continues to be approached within Anglo-American film criticism: as an all-subsuming polemic between subtitling and dubbing (Betz; Nornes). The ongoing debate between these two predominant methods of film translation has tended to obscure many of the intricacies involved, passing over both the minutiae of bad "flubtitles" and the overarching unequal power relations in which *good* and *bad* translations routinely partake, from the hegemony of Hollywood, for instance, to the increasing number of Anglicisms that surface in the subtitling and dubbing of countries such as Germany and Denmark (Gottlieb 224). In the context of these impassioned sub/dub wars, the category of badness becomes unwieldy and inescapable.

Two scenes from the French-language art house films *Vendredi Soir / Friday Night* (Claire Denis, 2002) and *Cléo de 5 à 7 / Cleo from 5 to 7* (Agnès Varda, 1962) serve to illustrate some of the multiple, slippery ways in which translation is routinely labeled as bad within film discourse. *Vendredi Soir*'s Valérie looks from her car into a café, watching some people inside. In the original French-language version, the dialogue of the characters inside the café is barely audible, whereas in the English-subtitled version, it is plainly transcribed in translation at the bottom of the screen. The effect is one of over-accentuation, with the subtitles annulling nuances in volume level. Denis reports that the subtitler refused her alternative suggestion to "print them with one letter missing or one word missing" and that she still regrets this particular translation decision (75). In *Cléo de 5 à 7*, Cléo and her housekeeper travel around the streets of Paris in a taxi. In one scene, the car radio commentary alludes to France's war with Algeria at the time. As is often the case, one English subtitled version leaves this background dialogue untranslated. Ella Shohat and Robert Stam comment that the lack of attention given to this radio coverage functions to censor or depoliticize the film (47–48). "Radio allusions to the war in Algeria . . . scandalised the partisans of L'Algérie Française," they write, "but went untranslated in the English version" (48).

In both these scenes, the badness of subtitling per se is demonstrated: in particular, its tendency to distort or imbalance a film's soundtrack by either prioritizing character dialogue above all other written and spoken messages, or by over-articulating the barely audible. However, these examples also show how issues of method and execution feed and bleed into one another, further complicating assignations of badness. Nornes argues, for instance, that subtitles are not intrinsically good or bad and that a creative, "abusive" approach, such as that suggested by Denis (yet refused by her translator), is always possible (182). Nornes suggests that shortcomings like those noted by Shohat and Stam are owing as much to the "corruptions" of convention as to the subtitling method itself (184). His aim is to denaturalize such institutionalized conventions and to instigate a shift in focus from mode to methodology, challenging "translators with attitude" to find new, creative approaches (27).

At this juncture, the notion of bad film translation introduced at the beginning of this chapter in relation to bootlegged DVDs no longer appears so straightforward. Subcultural celebrations of sloppy subtitling in some ways seem to miss the point. In Crowther's estimation, incompetence exists a priori within the superimposed text of the subtitle mechanism itself, whereas for Nornes, corruption results from the naturalized (and hence, invisible) domesticating tendencies of "quality" subtitling from which bootlegging operations fall noticeably short. Conspicuously inept subtitles draw attention to the very process of translation, thereby confounding the invisibility that characterizes the professional environment. Moreover, as Shohat and Stam note, translations are necessarily situated in specific, sociopolitical contexts, and attention must be paid to the "bad" acts of depoliticization or censorship that can occur as a result. From these diverse viewpoints, one begins to glimpse the multiple, concurrent layers of badness at work within all film translation processes.

These competing notions of badness are qualified even further when film translation is considered as merely one subset of audiovisual language transfer within the diversity of the translation field.[12] In comparison to literary translation, for instance, audiovisual translation tends to struggle for recognition. As Dirk Delabastita notes, "it is often thought more prestigious to study Shakespeare than to study popular literature or, for that matter, derivative phenomena such as translations. Those who do study translations would, therefore, rather study translations of Shakespeare than translations of TV soap operas" (97). In fact, many translation scholars do not consider either subtitling or dubbing to constitute translation "proper" (Gottlieb 219). Film translation is so reliant upon the constraints of text compression, time-space equations and lip-synchronicity that it is likened instead to a form of "adaptation" (Delabastita 99).

The relatively bad status of subtitling and dubbing within translation practice and discourse is reciprocated, in turn, by the ill repute in which they are regarded by film culture where they tend to be viewed in strictly postproduction terms, entirely secondary to the filmmaking process and the meanings it generates. A director like Denis, for instance, who was personally involved in the English subtitling of *Vendredi Soir*, represents the exception. Most directors afford this process little to no thought (Watt 5).[13] Film translation is beyond the confines of "'real' translation" (Gottlieb 219) just as films in translation lie outside the parameters of filmmaking proper. Here, we begin to surmise how irrespective of issues of competence, intent, form or context, translation constitutes a "bad" object for film culture *in general*, virtually elided from its composite strains of history, theory, and criticism (Nornes 18).

It would seem that film translation is at least doubly bad, besieged in every direction by notions of failure, error, inauthenticity, and impropriety. However, the innumerable charges leveled against subtitling and dubbing ultimately rebound to expose impurities at the heart of both the film medium itself and translation as a discipline. In respect to film, translation uncovers deep insecurities, exposing the artificial nature of the filmic apparatus in any number of ways. It has been suggested, for example, that dubbing unwittingly reinforces the inherent uncanniness of film sound and thereby uncovers anxieties already present (See Altman; Doane; Maurice; Spadoni).[14] To provide just a brief indication of the complexity into which translation potentially taps, Robert Spadoni notes how the technological advent of sound synchronization meant that viewers became more aware of film as a *manufactured* object (6), a fact that Alice Maurice relates back to the early sound era's investment in black performers as counteractive signs of the "real" and the "primitive" (49).

Failing Derrida

The disparagement of subtitling and dubbing is somewhat qualified and destabilized by the systemic undervaluation of translation *as a whole* within the Anglo-American context. Merging the empirical and the theoretical in a way that is perhaps emblematic of translation's unique potential, Venuti's detailed historical account of the second-order status of translation within the English-speaking world, owes a great debt to the philosophical schema of Derrida. Time and again within Derrida's writings, translation/untranslatability is established as a defining feature of both philosophy and deconstruction, with the "summons to translation" positioned "at the very threshold of all reading-writing" ("What is a 'Relevant' Translation?" 175). Translation acts as a type of leitmotif throughout Derrida's texts and provides an illuminating perspective from which to approach his work as a whole.[15] In this section, I examine Derrida's position on translation in some detail in order to suggest how it might offer a means of reconceptualizing the "bad" in relation to film. In doing so, I seek to outline some alternate ways in which comical "Engrish" subtitles intervene within the bad film landscape, beyond subcultural celebrations alone.

For Derrida, translation—that is, *all* translation—ultimately fails. Failure is inevitable because translation, put simply, constitutes an impossible task.[16] As he explains however, this impossibility in no way precludes translation's necessity. Rather, Derrida declares its "necessity as impossibility" ("Des Tours" 170–71), eruditely arguing that the impossibility of translation stems from the paradox of language itself. If language is a system of words taught to infants by others, it necessarily molds interiority (the self) into an externally imposed foreign framework. Once expressed, these words reenter the realm of the other, with meaning always as dependent upon circumstances of reception as production and hence, radically open, unpredictable and unstable.[17] Thus, despite its power-wielding capabilities, language also always implies a surrendering of control: an investment in the foreign and the unknown, existing midway between producer and receiver, self and other, specificity and universalism. For Derrida, it is translation that brings into relief this "double bind" or split consciousness inherent within all language.

Furthermore, all languages comprise elements that are *both* irreducibly specific or context-bound *and* universally transmissible. Derrida explains this concept in relation to the distinction between proper names and common nouns. He writes: "a proper name, in the proper sense, does not properly belong to the language; it does not belong there, although and because its call makes the language possible (what would a language be without the possibility of calling by a proper name?)" ("Des Tours" 172). The proper name of a specific place or person, for instance, is thought to have a "one-to-one correspondence with a referent that exists, as a 'real' presence, before and outside of language" (Davis 10). At the same time, it forms part of a repeatable language system functioning in relation to other signifiers of that larger system, and hence reveals its commonality with other nouns (which are themselves names). The proper name thus presents a limit case of the translatability *and* untranslatability that permeates all language (12), and hence accounts for the inevitability of *mis*translation. The necessary impossibility or failure of translation ultimately serves to expose the limitations and impurities that already inhabit the "original." Paul de Man's introduction of the term "disarticulation" provides an effective illustration of this concept. He states:

> the original is disarticulated, the original is reduced to the status of prose, is decanonized, all that by the process of translation, because the impossibility of translation is due to disruptions which are there in the original, but which the original managed to hide. (97–98)

For Derrida, as "one language licks another," translation forces upon words a level of self-reflexivity, an acknowledgement of their borders, contours, and restrictions (Venuti, "Translating Derrida" 175). Translation makes us aware of language *as language*, of language in abstraction or the "being-language of language" (Derrida, "Des Tours" 201). Ironically, translation draws attention to the ambiguities, impurities and instabilities of language through its very *inability* to reproduce them. This inability is crucial. Derrida writes: "at best, [translation] can get everything across except this: the fact that there are, in one linguistic system, perhaps several languages or tongues. Sometimes—I would even say always—several tongues" (*Ear of the Other* 100). Derrida argues that while a translation may attempt to represent a text's indeterminacy or linguistic play, it can only do so via a process of arrest that is both artificial and, to a degree, random. A translation may seek to express a word's implied as well as literal meaning, and yet in doing so, the "original" ambiguity of the word is lost. Meaning that had remained virtual or symbolic is concretized, spelled out. This supposed clarification inevitably constitutes an addition: an *interpretation* that selects and foregrounds certain words and meanings above others, altering the text and creating a whole additional set of ambiguities in the process.

Through translation, the ongoing interplay of multiple meanings generated by words in specific contexts, is necessarily halted. A translation is decided upon which arbitrarily freezes the meaning and movement of words. However, just as translation "brings the *arrêt* of everything, decides, suspends," it also "sets in motion" by providing a new momentum (Derrida, "'Living On'" 100). In selecting certain lines of interpretation, new meanings and connections are forged. For Derrida, while a translation may attempt—more or less successfully—to determine what a word means, it cannot help but fail to express that word's very imprecision, its open polysemia. Rather, translation forces words to change course. The "putting of something 'into other words' does not put the 'same thing' into other words. . . . The thing itself is necessarily altered" (75). Instead of "clarifying an ambiguous expression," translation amasses the powers of indecision," creating a "textual supplement" that is "overdetermining," "less controllable," and thus all the more "'powerful' than what it comments upon or translates" (75).

If translation necessarily fails in Derrida's estimation, it remains to be seen what the implications of such thinking might be in relation to paracinema and B-grade subtitles. To reiterate: Derrida's thoughts on translation function foremost to destabilize "origins." The demonstrable failure of translation serves to articulate the instability and untranslatability that underlies all language and as such effectively dismantles any notion of a stable or "pure" point of origin for translation (Venuti, "Introduction" 7). Hence, mistranslations need to be understood not as aberrations that lie outside language systems but rather as their core constituents. As Kathleen Davis suggests, for Derrida, "detours and multiple pathways *constitute* any system that enables meaning; they are not 'accidents' belonging to its outside, but are the conditions of possibility for signification" (34).

Derrida's take on translation offers a way to reconceptualize badness in general, whether attached to language systems, "Z-budget film" (Curran 41) or Hong Kong movie flubtitles. Most importantly, Derridean deconstruction provides a means to engage with badness in a way that does not simply aim to recuperate it, promoting "bad" as a new, alternate type of "good." This is a real danger to which many paracinema advocates succumb. *Zontar*'s Brian Curran, for instance, analyzes the common phenomenon of compiling definitive "bad classics" or 50 worst lists, such as that prepared by director Joe Dante for *Famous Monsters of Filmland* when he was just sixteen, published under the catchy title of "Dante's Inferno" (Curran 43). If bad film discourse (whether fan-based or academic) merely rehearses the "so-bad-it's-good" argument, it risks its own annulment. Bad film appreciation that simply replaces one good with another or flaunts a new aesthetic of "tasteless" taste effectively nullifies its own rebellious and subversive, nonhegemonic spirit, ultimately rendering a disservice to its disruptive potency and sense of play.

For Derrida, the failure of translation is not co-opted by any "good." Rather, this *necessary* failure points to underlying, fundamental layers of impossibility that ground all meaning making processes. The momentum of deconstruction seeks to disassemble wholes and undo structures, unloading terms precisely "to show what they have been doing all along" (Davis 50). Like the concept of "Bad-Truth" advanced by *Zontar* "which 'unravels itself' before the viewers startled eyes to reveal the poignant, unspeakable 'TRUTH' of the film's 'behind-the-scenes' 'REALITY,'" the fragmented whole that deconstruction reveals is inherently flawed (Curran 41). Furthermore, this "reality" does not describe an actual "presence," but rather, exists on the axis *between* the actual and the virtual. "Bad-Truth," Derrida-style, can never be pointed at, named, or affixed. A list of the greatest badfilms of all time only seeks to prescribe, contain, and ultimately canonize or "make good" that badness. Rather, for Derrida, invocations of "badness" (and indeed goodness) must remain nonprescriptive and abstract in order to stay attentive to the particularity and located nature of difference.

Unlike many bad film fans, Derrida never seems to promote badness for its own sake. Despite his deconstructive penchant, he never revels in the pleasures of trash aesthetics or "bad" taste. Derrida's inference that "the translator, per definition, fails" in no way seeks to promote bad translation (de Man 80). Nor does it mean that all translations are equally bad. Like Walter Benjamin, who provides the starting point for "Des Tours de Babel," Derrida still retains a working sense of the "good" and the "bad." In contrast to much translation theory and bad film critique however, he never attempts to set out or prescribe what does or does not constitute either category, and instead only invokes such values through recourse to the virtual. For Derrida, a "good" translation "only succeeds in *promising* success, in *promising* reconciliation" (*Ear of the Other* 123–24, emphasis added). Success is never present or actual, it remains virtual: intuited or anticipated, a future projection. He writes: "There are translations that don't even manage to promise, but a good translation is one that enacts that performative called a promise with the result that through the translation one sees the coming shape of a possible reconciliation among languages" (123–24).

Derrida's deployment of the actual/virtual nexus resonates in relation to the theory/practice tensions that animate academic approaches to trash aesthetics. The necessary imperfection of the concrete, Derrida reminds us, intimates a type of purity destined to remain abstract or virtual: to be forever *mis*translated. By coupling a deconstructive "bad" with translation, Derrida suggests how processes like subtitling and dubbing, termed "secondary," "derivative," or "supplementary," challenge notions of "first-ness." Filmmaking "proper," for instance, is called into question: the "original" language of film sound technology exposed as artificial and inauthentic, as a form of "ventriloquism" (Altman). Likewise, the secondary status of "bad film" is itself upturned. Translation proves capable of shifting center/periphery dynamics, exposing bad film's very own bad objects: its intercultural and theoretical blind spots.

Open Endings

As suggested at the start of this discussion, the overt badness of an unintelligible subtitle draws attention to the lack of quality control that often accompanies processes of translation. This level of uncontrollability immediately begins to intimate further connected layers of badness, highlighting the hegemony of English-language Hollywood fare throughout much of the world's film industries, for instance, and the proliferation of media piracy operations in response.[18] Similarly, for Derrida, the failures and limitations of translation manifest in both actual and virtual forms. Translation constantly pulls towards the concrete *and* the abstract, the irreducibly specific (of the *un*translatable) *and* the utterly transferable (*Ear of the Other* 102). Screen grabs of film subtitles provide a static visual demonstration of the tangible "badness" that translation can produce. Moreover, this actual blockage or mistranslation also provides a presentiment of absence, of something missing. Derrida approaches this absence through the abstract, noting the way in which the threshold between translation and untranslatability constitutes the precondition of all meaning-making. By exposing the concrete limits of language, translation engages with the virtual, serving to "re-mark the affinity among the languages, to exhibit its own possibility" ("Des Tours" 186).[19]

The incompetence of "Engrish" subtitling does not simply delineate another paracinematic genre. The comic ineptitude of such subtitles articulates points of untranslatability, leading onto multiple, crisscrossing paths of destabilization and deconstruction that ultimately prompt a reconsideration of both badness in general and the filmic medium itself. As a "bad" object of film culture and industry, omitted from historical accounts of the medium along with its critical appraisal and theorization, translation wields a disorientating power capable of turning *any* film into bad film. This transformative capacity is evidenced both in the bootleg translation of *Lord of Rings: The Two Towers* and in the way that dubbing recalls the technical artificiality at the basis of all sound film. Moreover, issues of translation prompt a thorough "unpacking" of badness. Bad film's virtual neglect to date of the multitude of issues raised by subtitling and dubbing (not to mention monotone voice-overs, irreverent fan subbing and playful linguistic hijacking), uncovers a blind spot shared by both mainstream and "niche" film culture. This systemic sidelining of translation is echoed in broader cultural terms by its marginalization throughout Anglo-American society since at least the seventeenth century (Venuti, *Translator's Invisibility* 47). The challenge today is to bring an awareness of language difference, intercultural dynamics and actual operations of language transfer to bear on Western critical paradigms. Most significantly, an awareness of translation directs bad film discourse to non-Western, non-English-speaking contexts and audiences. As the murky waters of the intercultural spill into the frame, we glimpse the uncontainable mass of badness lurking therein.

Notes

1. The website provides the following definition: "Engrish is a slang term which refers to an English language phrase that arose through poor translation of another language (usually Japanese) into English, or sometimes, poor translation of English into another language followed by good translation back into English. This used to be a frequent occurrence with product manuals, which might say something like 'to make speed up find up out document,' but it's less frequent today. Another source of poor translation is an unchecked machine-produced translation, such as that from the Babelfish service" (see Engrish Two Towers Subtitles).

2. This phenomenon is also documented by Pang on viewing a pirated DVD of *Kill Bill: Vol. 1* (Quentin Tarantino, 2003).

3. Sconce seems to adopt the term "badfilm" from the *Zontar* fanzine and provides the following explanation of paracinema: "In short, the explicit manifesto of paracinematic culture is to valorize all forms of cinematic 'trash,' whether such films have been either explicitly rejected or simply ignored by legitimate film culture" (371–72).

4. The Flubtitles website states: "As you can tell, we dig really funky, jacked-up subtitles. In looking around on the net, we've seen lists of bad subtitles floating around everywhere—always the same few. We wanted to spread the gospel about all the lesser-known horrible subtitles that were going unacknowledged—because heaven forbid a single flubtitle should slip through the cracks!"

5. In the introduction to a section exploring "National and International Cults," *The Cult Film Reader* provides a useful cataloguing of the foreign-language flavor of much cult experience. With the sole exception of Erdogan however, the texts within this section, characteristically, do not refer directly to any specifics of translation.

6. One exception is an essay by Fujiwara that considers the impact of dubbing on "badfilm" readings of the Italian horror genre.

7. Other similar distribution outfits include labels such as Optimum Asia, Eastern Cult, Eastern Edge, Dragon Dynasty, Premier Asia, and Dark Asia. See Shin (9) and Imanjaya (150).

8. According to Curran, "it is in the redoubtable HORROR/SCIENCE FICTION genre that the most profound 'BAD-STATEMENTS' have usually been made" (41).

9. Nornes notes that in countries where foreign-language fare is mainstream, such distinctions do not prevail to the same extent.

10. I wish to personally thank Eric Schaefer for drawing my attention to the dubbing masquerade effect in this film.

11. For an equally fascinating instance of faking it in relation to the translation of erotic material, see Lev on the English subtitling of *Querelle* (Rainer Werner Fassbinder, 1982) in the United States.

12. Venuti provides a far more comprehensive overview of translation as a discipline and details its distinct linguistic and cultural theory ("Translating Derrida").

13. As Watt mentions, Stanley Kubrick is another notable exception. The dubbing of Kubrick's *Full Metal Jacket* (1987) by Harada Masato is discussed in detail by Nornes (216–19).

14. See, e.g., Altman; Doane; Maurice; and Spadoni.

15. Philip E. Lewis suggests that translation constitutes a leitmotif for Derrida, while Louise Burchill comments on the general profitability of examining Derrida through his theorization of translation. These sentiments are echoed by Davis (1, 9) and provide the basis for the "Roundtable on Translation" in *The Ear of the Other*, a discussion between Derrida and an invited panel of scholars, which occurred at a colloquium held at the University of Montreal in 1979.

16. In making this declaration, Derrida retranslates the term *Aufgabe* from Walter Benjamin's seminal essay "The Task of the Translator" (1923), understanding it to mean not just "task" but also "duty" or "debt" ("Des Tours" 176). He states, "Benjamin says of the restitution that it could very well be impossible: insolvent debt within a genealogical scene" (176). Paul de Man adds that *Aufgabe* can also mean a defeat or a giving up (80).

17. Venuti writes, "the relation between the individual and the collective in language is never an equality, but always weighted towards the 'other' from which or whom one learns a language" ("Translating Derrida" 238).

18. As Venuti notes, "'English' is an idealist notion that conceals a panoply of Englishes ranged in a hierarchical order of value and power among themselves and over every other language in the world" ("Translating Derrida" 259). For a discussion of media piracy and global power relations, see Pang.

19. Interpreting Benjamin, Derrida states: "in a mode that is solely anticipatory, annunciatory, almost prophetic, translation renders present an affinity that is never present in this presentation" ("Des Tours" 187). Translation seeks this affinity or "the accord of tongues" which "lets the pure language and the being-language of the language, resonate, announcing it rather than presenting it" (202).

Works Cited

Altman, Rick. "Moving Lips: Cinema as Ventriloquism." *Yale French Studies* 60 (1980): 67–79. Print.

Betz, Mark. *Beyond the Subtitle: Remapping European Art Cinema*. Minneapolis: U of Minnesota P, 2009. Print.

Brophy, Philip. "Funny Accents: The Sound of Racism." *Cinesonic: Experiencing the Soundtrack*. Ed. Philip Brophy. Sydney: Australian Film, Television and Radio School, 2001. 226–37. Print.

Burchill, Louise. "Multiple Translations." Paper presented at *Translation/Transformation Seminar Series*, Victorian College of the Arts, Melbourne, 21 Sept. 2006.

Cather, Kirsten. "'I Know It When I Hear It': The Case of the Blind Film Censor." *The Velvet Light Trap* 63 (2009): 60–62. Print.

Charles, John. "Planeta Burbank: Domesticating *Planet of Storms*." *Video Watchdog Special Edition* 1 (1994): 108–19. Print.

Chute, David. "Made in Hong Kong: Editor's Note." *Film Comment* 24.3 (1988): 34–35. Print.

Corrigan, Timothy. "Film and the Culture of Cult." *The Cult Film Experience: Beyond All Reason*. Ed. J. P. Telotte. Austin: U of Texas P, 1991. 26–41. Print.

Crowther, Bosley. "Subtitles Must Go! Let's Have Dubbed English Dialogue on Foreign-Language Films." *New York Times*, 7 Aug. 1960. Print.

———. "More on Dubbing Films: Clarification of 'Wild Strawberries' Comes in English Dialogue." *New York Times*, 6 Nov. 1960: X1, X9. Print.

Curran, Brian. "Notes on the Great Bad Film Debate." *Zontar* 9 (n.d.): 40–44. <http://www.zontar.net/Z9-40.html>

Dante, Joe. Jr. "Dante's Inferno." *Famous Monsters of Filmland* 18 (July 1962): 14–23. Print.

Davis, Kathleen. *Deconstruction and Translation*. Manchester: St. Jerome Publishing, 2001. Print.

Delabastita, Dirk. "Translation and the Mass Media." *Translation, History and Culture*. Ed Susan Bassnett and André Lefevere. London: Pinter, 1990. 97–109.

de Man, Paul. *The Resistance to Theory*. Minneapolis: U of Minnesota P, 1986. Print.

Denis, Clair. "Outside Myself." Interview with Atom Egoyan. *Subtitles: on the Foreignness of Film*. Ed. Atom Egoyan and Ian Balfour. Cambridge: MIT Press, 2004. 69–78.

Derrida, Jacques. "'Living On' / Borderlines." Trans. by James Hulbert. *Deconstruction and Criticism* Ed. Harold Bloom et al. New York: Continuum, 1979. 75–176. Print.

———. *The Ear of the Other* [*L'oreille de l'autre*]. Trans. and ed. Peggy Kamuf. Lincoln: U of Nebraska P, 1985 [1982]. Print.

———. "Des Tours de Babel." Trans. Joseph F. Graham. *Difference in Translation*. Ed. Joseph F. Graham. Ithaca: Cornell UP, 1985. 165–207. Print.

———. "What is a 'Relevant' Translation? [*Qu'est-ce qu'une traduction 'relevante'?* (1998)]." Trans. Lawrence Venuti. *Critical Inquiry* 27.2 (2001): 174–200. Print.

Doane, Mary Ann. "The Voice in the Cinema: The Articulation of Body and Space." *Film Sound*. Ed. Elisabeth Weis and John Belton. New York: Colombia UP, 1985. 162–76. Print.

Engrish Two Towers Subtitles. Web. 14 Apr. 2009. <http://www.angelfire.com/rings/ttt-subtitles/>

Erdogan, Nezih. "Mute Bodies, Disembodied Voices: Notes on Sound in Turkish Popular Cinema." *The Cult Film Reader*. Ed. Ernest Mathijs and Xavier Mendik. Berkshire: Open UP, 2008. 349–59. Print.

Flubtitles. Web. <http://www.flubtitles.com/>

Fujiwara, Chris. "Boredom, *Spasmo* and Italian System." *Sleaze Artists: Cinema at the Margins of Taste, Style and Politics*. Ed. Jeffrey Sconce. Durham: Duke UP, 2007. 240–58. Print.

Gods of Filmmaking. "*Battle Beyond the Sun* (1962)." Web. 13 June 2010. <http://www.ambidextrouspics.com/>

Gottlieb, Henrik. "Subtitles and International Anglification." *Nordic Journal of English Studies* 3.1 (2004): 219–30. Print.

Hanson, Miriam. *Babel and Babylon: Spectatorship in American Silent Film*. Cambridge: Harvard UP, 1991. Print.
Hawkins, Joan. "Sleaze Mania, Euro-Trash, and High Art: The Place of European Art Films in American Low Culture." *Film Quarterly* 53.2 (1999–2000): 14–29. Print.
Imanjaya, Ekky. "The Other Side of Indonesia: New Order's Indonesian Exploitation Cinema as Cult Films." *Colloquy* 18 (2009). Web. <http://www.colloquy.monash.ed.au/issue18/imanjaya.pdf>
Kennedy, Jayne Jain. "Faith Healing: Russian Style." *Zontar* 9 (n.d.): 38–39. Web. 21 May 2010. <http://www.zontar.net/Z9-40.html>
Lentz, Harris M. *Science Fiction: Horror and Fantasy Film and Television Credits, Through 1987*. Jefferson: McFarland, 1989. Print.
Lewis, Philip E. "The Measure of Translation Effects." *Difference in Translation*. Ed. Joseph F. Graham. Ithaca: Cornell UP, 1985. 31–62. Print.
Lev, Peter. *The Euro-American Cinema*. Austin: U of Texas P, 1993. Print.
Maurice, Alice. "'Cinema at Its Source': Synchronising Race and Sound in the Early Talkies." *Camera Obscura* 17.1 (2002): 31–71. Print.
Nornes, Abe Mark. *Cinema Babel: Translating Global Cinema*. Minneapolis: U of Minnesota P, 2007. Print.
Nowell-Smith, Geoffrey. "Italy sotto voce." *Sight and Sound* 37.3 (1968): 145–47. Print.
Pang, Laikwan. "Copying *Kill Bill*." *Social Text* 23.2 (Summer 2005): 133–53. Print.
Powers, John. "Glimpse Eastward." *Film Comment* 24.3 (1988): 35–38. Print.
Rich, Ruby. "To Read or Not to Read: Subtitles, Trailers, and Monolingualism." *Subtitles: on the Foreignness of Film*. Ed. Atom Egoyan and Ian Balfour. Cambridge: MIT Press, 2004. 153–69. Print.
Schaefer, Eric. *"Bold! Daring! Shocking! True!": A History of Exploitation Films 1919–1959*. Durham: Duke UP, 1999. Print.
Sconce, Jeffrey. "'Trashing' the Academy: Taste, Excess, and an Emerging Politics of Cinematic Style." *Screen* 36.4 (1995): 371–93. Print.
Shin, Chi-Yun. "Art of Branding: Tartan 'Asia-Extreme' Films." *Jump Cut* 50 (2008): 1–17. Web. 21 May 2010. <http://www.ejumpcut.org/archive/jc50.2008/TartanDist/index.html>
Shohat, Ella and Robert Stam. "The Cinema after Babel: Language, Difference, Power." *Screen* 26.3–4 (1985): 35–58. Print.
Silva, Antonio Marcio de. "Brazilian Women Prison Films: A Gendered Reading." Paper presented at the *B for Bad Cinema: Aesthetics, Politics and Cultural Value* conference at Monash University, Melbourne, Australia, 15–17 April 2009.
Spadoni, Robert. "The Uncanny Body of Early Sound Film." *The Velvet Light Trap* 51 (2003): 4–16. Print.
"Tarantino's Next Film in Mandarin." *Sydney Morning Herald*, 2 Nov. 2004. Web. 6 June 2010. <http://www.smh.com.au/articles/2004/11/02/1099362127937.html>

Upchurch, Alan. "Russian Fantastika Part One: The Fairytale Landscapes of Aleksandr Ptushko." *Video Watchdog* 8 (1991): 24–37. Print.

Venuti, Lawrence. "Introduction." *Rethinking Translation: Discourse, Subjectivity, Ideology*. Ed. Lawrence Venuti. London: Routledge, 1992. 1–17. Print.

———. *The Translator's Invisibility: A History of Translation*. London: Routledge, 1995. Print.

———. "Translating Derrida on Translation: Relevance and Disciplinary Resistance." *The Yale Journal of Criticism* 16.2 (2003): 237–62. Print.

Watt, Michael. "'Do you speak Christian?' Dubbing and the Manipulation of the Cinematic Experience." *Bright Lights Film Journal* 29 (2000). Web. 4 Dec. 2005 <http://www.brightlightsfilm.com/29/dubbing1.html>

Weldon, Michael (with Charles Beesley, Bob Martin and Akira Fitton). *The Psychotronic Encyclopedia of Film*. New York: Ballantine Books, 1983. Print.

4

Being in Two Places at the Same Time
The Forgotten Geography of Rear-Projection

ADRIAN DANKS

> You should not be permitted to reason. Because the film should be stronger than reason.
>
> —Alfred Hitchcock (qtd. in Cameron and Jeffrey 21)

> For years, a cadre of Hitchcock's admirers (this author amongst the most defensive of them) concocted tortuous arguments more admirable for their ingenuity than consistent with the facts: to account for the sloppy technique of the film [*Marnie*], rationalizations were adduced to demonstrate that these aberrations were deliberate on Hitchcock's part, a conscious reversion to an expressionistic style that used artifice to represent a disordered psyche. But the real reason was simpler and sadder, and those reviewers who were critical, it should be admitted, were right: these moments [often featuring rear-projection] in *Marnie* are not emotionally disturbing, they are simply visually jarring; they mark not a deliberate use of unconventional means, but are simply unpleasant examples of the director's cavalier disinterest in the final product.
>
> —Donald Spoto (476)

In the late 1990s, while distractedly watching daytime television, I became fascinated with a scene from the 1947 film noir, *Dead Reckoning* (John Cromwell), an extraordinarily hermetic, slightly above average, and highly artificial example of the genre. The scene unfolding before me showed characters played by Humphrey Bogart and Lizabeth Scott driving through an expansive and very "open" exterior rear-projected setting in a convertible.[1] My heightened interest in this scene was probably encouraged and enabled by my distracted state. I was at once engaged by the film—its spatial and temporal manipulations and dislocations—and traversing another space altogether as I wandered around the house. This state seemed to mirror what I was watching on screen: a bifurcated temporal and spatial realm that seemed both here and there, now and then.

Rear-projection is a ubiquitous device that has not received its fair share of critical attention.[2] Although it has been discussed in a piecemeal fashion in relation to the work of Alfred Hitchcock (Païni; Fried; Carcassonne; Thomson, *Movie Man* 72–75), and alongside other technical and stylistic innovations of the 1930s more generally, it is more routinely relegated to the realm of the anachronistic and the technically and aesthetically suspect (or inept). In this respect it is a pertinent form or technique to analyze in relation to the question of what might constitute "bad cinema," particularly in an aesthetic sense. Rear-projection has often been singled out as a "bad" technique due to such factors as its self-consciousness, spatial and temporal discontinuity, artificiality, pictorial inability to adequately suggest appropriate lines of perspective, hermetic qualities, and imperialist and colonialist implications. For example, the artifice of rear-projection is highlighted and emphasized in the garish and dramatically unconvincing raft sequences that dominate Otto Preminger's *River of No Return* (1954), a film that particularly suffers from the alternation and fusion of location derived footage with unconvincing studio interiors. Therefore, the common dismissal of rear-projection as a dated and aesthetically suspect device predominantly relies upon a teleological understanding of film history that favors realism over a more constructivist and synthetic notion of cinematic form. Rear-projection is also criticized as part and parcel of a broader set of techniques, styles, and industrial processes that define the heightened artificiality of classical Hollywood as an outmoded form. This chapter will focus attention on many of these "bad" or negative elements while also examining how this technique can be read in more complex and sometimes contradictory ways.

Those writers who have attempted to sympathetically examine this technique and its common use have only ever done so in a piecemeal and overly conceptual manner, using it as a means to further explore specific ideas and approaches they have examined elsewhere. For example, Laura Mulvey, in a short and evocative discussion, overplays what she considers the poignant temporality of rear-projection, a form she also inaccurately and too enthusiastically describes as "an aesthetic emblem of a bygone studio era" ("Clumsy Sublime" 3). Mulvey's overly poetic approach to "rear-projection" is indebted to Dominique Païni's groundbreaking work on the use of the broader category of "transparencies" in Hitchcock's cinema. In so doing, Mulvey boldly restates Païni's view that such "transparencies," including rear-projection, "are all about time" (3). Mulvey's approach to the form is also deeply indebted to the work she had already completed on stillness, temporality, and the moving image (*Death Twenty-Four Times a Second*). As I will argue, although temporality is a crucial aspect and "affect" of rear-projection, it is rare for the different or contrasting planes of the image heightened through this technique to register as distinct—that is, past and present—time frames.

Although Mulvey is correct in identifying rear-projection as a potent symbol of the imperialist and combinatory nature of classical Hollywood cinema, and its proclivity for "representing the world," (an approach that David Thomson ["Driving"] has also flirted with in his more prosaic reading of the form in relation to the geography of Hollywood and California more generally) rear-projection is, in reality, a technique that is not isolated to Hollywood. It is, in fact, more routine than often suggested—both in terms of production and the impact it has on audiences—and has never completely gone away. It obviously "reappears" in the self-conscious deployment of the technique in such film history conscious, nostalgic and period set works as *Far from Heaven* (Todd Haynes, 2002), *The Good German* (Steven Soderbergh, 2006), *Pulp Fiction* (Quentin Tarantino, 1994), and *Shutter Island* (Martin Scorsese, 2010),[3] and still has a significant place, with various digital enhancements, in contemporary television, special effects–driven films and scenes where characters are shown traveling in vehicles.

Unconvincing too is Mulvey's claim that "with the passing of time" the "disappearance" of rear-projection "has given this once-despised technology new interest and poignancy" ("Clumsy Sublime" 3). Mulvey overstates the "punctum"-like[4] qualities of rear-projection, and the degree to which is was "despised" or even noticed by audiences and filmmakers of the time (and often now). As will be discussed, Hitchcock's long-term use of the technique, for example, is part of a broader combinatory and contrapuntal aesthetic found in his work. Nevertheless, it is true that by the early 1960s the technique of rear-projection was becoming somewhat anachronistic and jarring, particularly at the point where many films largely moved out of the studio and onto location. This dissatisfaction with rear-projection—a response that still underlines many accounts and discussions of films like *Marnie* (1964) and is exemplified by Spoto's confession (cited above)—seems mainly reserved for those instances where the technique becomes palpably, routinely, and even aggressively noticeable, working against particular cultural and historical conceptions of what constitutes cinematic realism. The patent "antirealism" of this technique was undoubtedly less apparent in the 1930s when rear-projection was initially introduced in a systemized fashion. Accordingly, it is a mistake to divorce or quarantine instances of this technique from the broader aesthetic, economic, stylistic, and formal regimes that characterize the full-scale introduction of truly revolutionary elements like sound and color cinematography.

For many critics—and possibly viewers—rear-projection becomes particularly problematic (or bad) within scenes and films that otherwise seem relatively objective. In this regard, the critique of Hitchcock's use of this device can seem somewhat misplaced. Films such as *Vertigo* (1958) and *Marnie* (1964) rely on the conflation and even confusion of subjectivity and objectivity, as well as various elements that draw attention to the crafted nature and form of the artistic creation we are watching. But it is also Hitchcock's attentiveness to the actuality of place that can make his use of rear-projection startling and jarring.

Rear-projection was a key technique that emerged within a range of technical developments that helped reaffirm control over almost all elements of production in the early years of sound. It was fully introduced by Fox Studios in 1930 in Frank Borzage's *Liliom*. Revealingly, Borzage's understandably tepid use of this technique was limited to a fantasy sequence set on a train hurtling towards the weigh-station between heaven and hell. It is placed alongside a barrage of other special effects including mattes and the extensive use of models, and demonstrates the technical limitations of this technique when it was first introduced. The fantasy setting of the sequence somewhat justified the muddy illumination and lack of focus. Although American filmmakers such as Norman Dawn had experimented with rear-projection much earlier,[5] it became a fairly ubiquitous technique by about 1933 and fully standardized by the late 1930s (see Bordwell and Thompson 131–34). Its widespread deployment in both largely urban set crime films and melodramas, as well as such special effects extravaganzas as *King Kong* (Merian C. Cooper and Ernest B. Schoedsack, 1933), consolidated its use as a means to represent a diverse geography—and to move characters within it—while controlling and streamlining production within the confines of the studio.

So rear-projection fully arrives around the same time as a range of other techniques and devices like the optical printer, sound, widescreen and large-gauge cinematography, more sensitive film stocks, brighter lamps for projectors, and such similarly transportive techniques as the wipe (Bordwell and Thompson 132). It is largely used, in early sound film at least, to help avoid the kind of "bad cinema" associated with location sound recording. Nevertheless, the sometimes wildly disproportionate dimensions, movements, and illumination of the rear-projection in relation to the "primary" image, as well as the curious attenuations of sound it entails, suggest the development of a new kind of bad cinema that places the potentially dislocating effect of editing within a single image. The cinema of the 1930s, in particular, is full of sequences that feature rear-projected shots that provide a jarring dislocation of action and image, to sometimes curiously hysterical effect. For example, an early car chase in Warner Bros. *The Beast of the City* (Charles Brabin, 1932) is a riot of spatial discontinuity and tonal disharmony.

What is specifically striking about the (abovementioned) scene from *Dead Reckoning*, a film made some time after the consolidation and integration of rear-projection techniques, is both its artificial nature (the characters are *and* are not moving) and the ways it suggests an enclosed *and* open space. In the process, it presents something that is most definitely a movie but also a movie within a movie (that the characters sometimes watch and interact with it but mostly don't). As a result, the background is also brought to the forefront of my perception. This element makes one aware of an aspect of the film, typically a little fogged and not very sharply focused, that one (I suppose) was meant to disregard. Like the other background sounds and effects, this "exterior" image, appearing behind and ultimately to the side of the characters, is plainly meant to have a more ambient atmospheric effect: acting to create a vaporous but pointedly artificial sense of freedom.

This sequence also has other functions and purposes. Once one becomes aware of the extreme artifice of what is being watched—an effect that is only very rarely strived for in rear-projection—other elements of the film start to fall away. This sequence in *Dead Reckoning* is integrated into a highly interior and studio-bound framework. It is one of numerous scenes throughout the film that use rear-projection in either a limited or more extended fashion. For example, an early train ride is backgrounded by rear-projected footage of the industrial hinterlands of Philadelphia that both passes by distractedly and helps to provide a degree of uneasiness to the conversation that is unfolding. Unsurprisingly, for a film of this period and genre, the moment under consideration is only one of numerous scenes that utilize rear-projection to simulate the forward momentum of driving. Its achievement in this regard is generally no better or worse, or more surprising, than hundreds of Hollywood films of this era. Nevertheless, there is something that is a little more self-conscious about its use in this sequence.

As in many examples of this trope—and car-bound rear-projection is the most common form of this technique—this scene uses rear-projection as a means to dynamize and "move" a conversation between two characters. It also works to transport these characters from one location to another and help establish their physical and gestural relationship. Nevertheless, it becomes difficult to hold onto or remember the airy conversation—or partial interrogation, I guess—that unfolds. The basic substance of this conversation highlights the chauvinistic qualities of Bogart's character, while showing Scott's character driving the car and responding to her companion's quizzical thoughts. Her gestures in this scene also consciously respond to the "outward" freedom that the closed-air of the rear-projection offers: she removes her hat and unfurls her hair in the artificial breeze that wafts by.

Apparent too when watching this scene is a keen sense of geographic or spatial dislocation, a reaction that is not uncommon when experiencing this broader class of elements called process cinematography. It is in this regard that the technique of rear-projection can evoke some of the common conceptions of modernity and how they have transformed our relation to space and time. This is, of course, a conscious effect that is not normally aimed at within the largely streamlined continuity of classical Hollywood cinema. But some films do make our apperception of these qualities much more likely or apparent. For example, a sequence from Max Ophuls's *Letter from an Unknown Woman* (1948) provides both a parody of and psychological justification for this technique. During the long night of seduction that occurs between Stefan (Louis Jourdan) and Lisa (Joan Fontaine), they venture into a fairground and take their place on a ride that simulates a train journey through

Europe by the use of a revolving background and various other artificial and "clumsy" effects of sound and image. Ophuls goes out of his way to show us—and the characters—the utter artifice of this illusion, while also suggesting its role in a process of seduction. Thus although Stefan and Lisa are consciously aware of the fakeness of their surroundings and how they are created—as well as the ridiculous condensation of space, place, and time that the ride and their conversation entails—they are nevertheless still caught up in the seduction. Despite its patently antiromantic trappings, this illusion actually works, and they are won over by the manipulations of a form that simulates elements of the act of moviegoing. This instance also self-consciously "points" to several other moments in the film where rear-projection is actually used without its concomitant artifice being emphasized.

In the case of Dead Reckoning, the scene or place being represented is fairly generic. But one quickly becomes aware of the power, possibilities, and limitations of the technique during the sequence, and the things it can tell us about cinema *as* modernity. This includes the streamlined nature of classical Hollywood production and the degree of synchronization required to fuse the projector with the camera, as well as the almost scientific precision required in gathering the background "plates": the qualities of rear-projection that might qualify it as bad cinema, and the colonial or global aspirations that such "symptoms" of the cinema might embody.[6] Thus it sits alongside a set of techniques designed to expand the range of Hollywood cinema *and* ground it, give it continuity. It also helped heighten, in tandem with the diverse geography of California, Hollywood's self-confident, and troubling ability to incorporate and "represent the world" within its increasingly streamlined productions. Even the nomenclature commonly used for this device—the "plate" when the background is in movement; a "stereo" if it involves the projection of a still image—points towards its industrialized, jigsawed-together qualities (see Fielding 259–305). These terms also situate the origins and form of the device within nineteenth-century photography and its associated forms like the stereoscope.

A key to the disjunctiveness of this technique, and its often perceived badness, lies in the degree of separation it creates between the foreground and background elements of the image. Thus, in the scene from Dead Reckoning specific characters are shown "within" an environment and absent-mindedly respond to the atmosphere of the moment and their surroundings. But one is not so easily convinced that they are truly there. This gulf between foreground and background is sometimes addressed by movies that attempt to get characters to "interact" with the rear-projection. Despite attempting to fuse the spatial and temporal presentness of the two images, these moments often come across as oddly and paradoxically artificial and self-conscious, arguably "bad" in terms of the spatial and aesthetic divide they attempt to bridge. A good (or bad) example of this occurs within the extraordinary battle sequence of Cecil B. DeMille's *The Plainsman* (1936). Using very large, multiple rear-projections onto huge screens, with cannily disguised masking lines, the film grandly struggles—and fails—to convince us of the spatial proximity of the soldiers and the American Indians they are fighting. This is despite the meticulous planning that went into matching the foreground action and background plates, and those specific moments when the firing of a gun in one plane has an appropriate effect in the other.[7] A similar effect can be noted in a film like Otto Preminger's highly interior *The Fan* (1949). An early street scene crowds its two central characters and a flower stand into the corner of the frame while rear-projected figures mill around them. This attempt to make the projection dominate the shot only acts to highlight its separation (and runs counter to the overridingly realistic and objective aesthetic developed by Preminger).

A more successful attempt to fashion such a connection can be found in Charles Laughton's *The Night of the Hunter* (1955). Laughton's film, like many of Hitchcock's, is an impure or hybrid work that fuses expressionistic techniques and Brechtian devices with a more lyrical, Griffith-like realism. In an early scene, Robert Mitchum's murderous preacher, Harry Powell, is shown "driving" an old jalopy through the countryside, the heightened artifice of the juxtaposed background plates and almost comically cutout shape of the car matched by Mitchum's over-the-top performance. But in this sequence he also casually refers to the graveyard and church that pass by ("Not that you mind the killin's. Your book is full of 'em."), and his distanciation from his surroundings seems curiously apt (even though contemporary audiences often laugh at these moments). He is an antisocial, overly inflated, and proto-cinematic figure who verges on the supernatural.

Dead Reckoning's use of rear-projection comes across as both intriguing and typical. Its impact—I imagine—has much to do with the broader spatiotemporal qualities of cinema and the specificity of an afternoon viewing. But my fixation also emerges out of an understanding of what rear-projection actually presents to the viewer. Therefore, like many other techniques that imbed one image or screen with another, it makes us more aware of the film we are watching and the circumstances of its viewing. But in comparison with, say, sequences in films where characters go to the movies, rear-projection has a more curious nature and ontology. What we are actually viewing are images that have been projected at us while we are watching an image being projected onto the screen. This notion or idea of projection, and how it enlarges, distorts, and separates out elements of the image, partly accounts for the uncanny quality of some examples of this form.

In the first part of this chapter I have attempted to provide some sense of what attracts me to rear-projection, as well as to introduce some reasons as to why it might commonly be considered "bad" or anachronistic. In this second part I move on to a more detailed analysis of a particular sequence from Hitchcock's *Marnie*, the film most widely criticized and analyzed for its use of this technique, as a means of further grounding the discussion and emphasizing notions of "badness" in particular kinds of cinema. Although the writing on this technique in general is quite limited and specific, it has, as already mentioned, been most thoroughly discussed in relation to the work of Hitchcock.[8] Although *Marnie* has long since entered the canon as one of Hitchcock's most oneiric and stylistically audacious films, its initial reception was considerably more hostile and often singled out the director's reliance upon what were considered defunct or hardly contemporary themes and techniques. For example, one of Hitchcock's most ardent supporters, Andrew Sarris, took exception to *Marnie*'s use of rear-projection and other related devices:

> His fake sets, particularly of dockside Baltimore, have never been more distracting, and the process shots of [Marnie] on horseback are appallingly dated. Again, the inability of the leads to hold the foreground imposes an extra burden on the background. Who cared if Rio were in process in *Notorious* when Bergman and Grant held the foreground? (143) (See figure 4.1.)

Sarris's disdain for and even resentment at Hitchcock's slipshod technique, and how it spurned him as a viewer, was reiterated by many of the initial reviewers of Hitchcock's film (See, e.g., Archer 3471–72). But as the film was released at close to the height of the initial auteurist appreciation of the director, various other writers including Peter

Figure 4.1. Cary Grant and Grace Kelly in rear-projection shot from *To Catch a Thief* (1954) Courtesy Paramount / The Kobal Collection.

Bogdanovich and Robin Wood (*Hitchcock's Films* 163–73) were quick to defend Hitchcock's specific use of rear-projection and background paintings on aesthetic and psychological grounds, arguing that they were totally in keeping with the director's use of such devices throughout his career (though neither bothered to ask whether they were "good" or "bad" examples in terms of how they were rendered and achieved). Nevertheless the power of these objections—understandably promoted by the muted excess of the film itself—has led many subsequent writers to feel that they need to further justify and explain these elements.

But Sarris's wounded critique does need to be further addressed. Although Hitchcock deploys rear-projection extensively in films such as *Vertigo* (1958), *North by Northwest* (1959), and *The Birds* (1963), there is something more unsettling and displeasing about its use in *Marnie*. Nevertheless, when watching *Marnie* afresh, and with an eye to its use of this device, one becomes aware, somewhat surprisingly, that its appearance is actually quite limited and that this relative scarcity might be part of the problem or difficulty that many critics have encountered.

One is compelled to ask why such a once ubiquitous technique as rear-projection—and specifically its use in *Marnie*—is considered bad, anachronistic, or simply inadequate. One of the reasons this Hitchcock example has been singled out is that he deployed it extensively and expressively throughout his work from the early 1930s onwards, alongside other formal elements of process cinematography and broader special effects.[9] Rear-projection was also positively received in his earlier American work as a sign of his control and expansive use of cinema's, and specifically Hollywood's, technical means, and of his take-up of new techniques and developments more generally. For example, an outstanding and innovative use of rear-projection occurs in one of Hitchcock's earliest American films, *Foreign Correspondent* (1940). Although rear-projection is utilized at various points in the film, the most notable instance occurs during the plane crash that provides its conclusion. As the plane hurtles towards the sea the quickly passing landscape glimpsed through each of the windows is created by rear-projection, the water bursting through these screens as the craft starts to sink. The effect is particularly remarkable when the water explodes through the screen and into the cockpit (Rickitt 83).

But by the time of *Marnie*'s release the use of rear-projection—and certainly examples as self-consciously artificial and disjunctive as Hitchcock's—had begun to wane (though it was still ubiquitous in Hollywood and international cinema for driving sequences). In some respects, Hitchcock's use of rear-projection and associated devices in his two subsequent films, *Torn Curtain* (1966) and *Topaz* (1969), is even more problematic and considerably less expressive (and defendable) than it is in *Marnie*. It is also much more difficult to read these elements in relation to the psychological states and motivations of their characters. A particularly static, garish, and nontransformative use of rear-projection occurs in *Torn Curtain*, in a dialogue scene between the protagonist played by Paul Newman and an undercover agent in a field in East Germany. This long, rather boring conversation takes place on a slowly moving tractor that is plainly disassociated from its gradually receding background. Whereas the artifice of many driving sequences is motivated by the speed of the car, the slowness of this transport makes the unmotivated artifice of the scene more apparent and distracting. When the agent finally says, "Well, mister, this is where you get off," it merely acts to reinforce the fact the characters haven't really gone anywhere and that we haven't been "transported" as an audience either.

This anachronistic, tired, or just plain "bad" deployment of rear-projection found in *Torn Curtain* comes much closer to exemplifying displeasure with the technique that Spoto ascribes to sequences in *Marnie*: "they mark not a deliberate use of unconventional means, but are simply unpleasant examples of the director's cavalier disinterest in the final product" (476). It is in *Torn Curtain* that this "cavalier disinterest" or disenchantment becomes truly apparent, and features several other scenes that are marked by an extraordinary degree of pictorial artificiality. For example, the key dialogue exchange between Newman's and Julie Andrews's characters—where he confesses that he is a double agent—is staged on an elaborate interior set that fails to register almost any sense of a real location.

By contrast, I will focus now upon on a less showy instance of Hitchcock's use of rear-projection: a long driving sequence situated almost half-way through *Marnie* that is *quietly* extraordinary (both hypnotic and extremely repetitious) and one that has been largely ignored in the piecemeal discussion of Hitchcock's use of this device. It is also one of the most extensive and sustained uses of rear-projection in Hitchcock's cinema and provides a set of interesting variations on the most common setting and justification for the use of this technique, namely, car travel. This extended sequence comes after several earlier appearances of self-consciously artificial rear-projection—particularly at the Atlantic City racetrack—painted backdrops and matte painting. It provides an important transition, in terms of power and control, between the central characters of Marnie (Tippi Hedren) and Mark (Sean Connery). The sense of entrapment that the rear-projection and contained settings communicate proves central to our understanding of Marnie's predicament—and sickness—and of the virtual blackmail that Mark is using to ensnare her.

The garish, combinatory, and audacious use of rear-projection in *Marnie*'s foxhunting sequence—which some consider a core instance of the director's powers to create "pure cinema" (Wood, "Looking" 84), and others (e.g., Spoto 476) of his loss of command of an evolving medium—is always singled out by those wishing to make an argument for or against the film, and the director's attachment to this technique. This sequence is often discussed alongside Hitchcock's use of the painted backdrop of a large ship at the end of the street in which Marnie's mother lives. For example, both Ken Mogg (166) and Robin Wood (*Hitchcock's Films* 163–65) open their discussions of the film with justifications and claims for the aesthetic and thematic significance and success of these elements.

One of the most interesting discussions of *Marnie*'s use of this technique appears in David Thomson's *Movie Man* (73–74). He compares Hitchcock's use of rear-projection to Michelangelo Antonioni's contemporaneous studies of alienation and spatial disorientation. Whereas Antonioni in *La notte* (1962) creates this sense of alienation (and even isolation) largely within the directly filmed space—so it is a function of the ways characters interact with their environment as much as the camera (and soundtrack)—in *Marnie* and other Hitchcock films, this sense of dislocation, of being divorced or separated from the environment, is created by such elements as the layers and dimensions of the image itself, as well as its lack of realistic depth and off-kilter sense of perspective. Therefore, one of the reasons that the use of rear-projection can often seem so frustrating, restricting, or bad, is that the cinema, or what we often champion as such, seems to be occurring elsewhere in these sequences.

Despite the fact that the sequence in question is broken into three parts—two set in a car, the other in a diner—it represents a continuous eleven-minute conversation between Marnie and Mark. Therefore, this conversation and sequence appears to be in real time, but the background plates of the projection highlight a different temporality and spatiality than that contained in the largely "hermetic" foreground. So this is an extraordinarily static section of the film that mainly alternates between the two characters' talking heads and that therefore uses rear-projection as a means to animate and mobilize what is basically a long discussion or interrogation. In this sequence, Hitchcock's use of the technique is both extremely conventional, even mundane—this is precisely how rear-projection is commonly used, as a means to move or animate a static conversation needed for plot development or explanation—and oddly hypnotic. It thus combines the banal with the strange.

However, what is most commonly unsettling about rear-projection is its impurity. It can be argued, as Thomson and Mulvey have, that rear-projection draws together different regimes or forms of cinema, most particularly fiction and documentary. In this respect, the rear-projection in this scene from *Marnie* is almost, or in a definitional sense actually is, a documentary of the movement of cars on particular streets in a specific place and time. This is a quality that Thomson poetically and even concretely discusses in his analysis of rear-projection and its relation to the image factories of Hollywood and a broader California in his essay, "Driving in a Back Projection." Thomson argues for the documentary dimensions of this "generic" and sometimes recycled footage and the value it could provide to future historians: "As evidence, I think, it is all the more appealing in that it is so casual, so devoid of intent" ("Driving" 24).

Nevertheless, what is most remarkable about the sequence from *Marnie* involves the ways in which Hitchcock deliberately counters the common rules of rear-projection's use, particularly in driving sequences. Most examples of this form rely heavily upon two-shots when filming characters in front of the rear window of the car. This helps to unify their relationship but also avoids the difficulty of matching single, intercut shots of individual characters with roughly the same rear-projection plate. For similar reasons, these sequences and shots are often held for shorter periods than others. In essence, they want to produce an *effect* rather than make us aware of the spatially and temporally disorientating qualities they also entertain. Hitchcock's and his cinematographer Robert Burks's approach in this scene is quietly and consistently willful. They constantly shoot the characters straight on in front of the rear-projection screen, whereas commonly these shots would frame characters against the side windows (and, of course, there are some of these shots too).

In the process, *Marnie* almost becomes a kind of installation in this sequence, utilizing the notions of repetition and redundancy more commonly characteristic of experimental cinema (though these are elements that can also be found in a film like *Psycho* [1960]). Alongside the other, more conventional transformations of temporality, where an unbroken eleven-minute conversation traverses more territory than is possible or logical, Hitchcock produces a hypnotic and disjointed sense of time, place, and space *in* the rear-projections. So in the process of editing between shots of Marnie and Mark, there is often an overlap where the vehicle we see in one shot minutely—or sometimes more extensively—returns to an earlier position on the road in the next.

This could be read in a number of ways. For instance, the sequence can make us aware of the cinematic apparatus. In this respect, the rear-projection—particularly when characters face it—simulates our position when watching the film, while the slippage of the rear-projected road sequences mime, ever so slightly, the reverse and forward motion of editing. But the overwhelming effect, I think, is something else. Once one becomes focused on these rear-projections, which, oddly, is more likely due to Hitchcock's relentlessness in this sequence, they almost take on a life of their own. Therefore, counter to Sarris's argument about the distraction created by these moments, I would argue that Hitchcock's use of rear-projection in this scene and elsewhere in the film makes us aware of the isolated world that "crowds" the central character, and the sense of dislocation that she herself feels. In a conventional sense this rear-projection can indeed become distracting or, more accurately, the main subject of the film that we are watching.

The colonialist or imperialist dimensions of many of the rear-projections discussed, including Hitchcock's, are built into the technique. Such a reading or understanding focuses critically on Hollywood's ability (or that of equivalent cinemas elsewhere) to represent almost any place in the world while maintaining strict controls over the core of production and where it occurs: of essentially indulging in a means of *showing* time while saving time (see Vasey). One of the reasons why rear-projection is sometimes looked on with suspicion and scorn is because of its ability to distance the core participants in and elements of a film's production from the hardships and realities of setting and location. For example, this was a key motivation for the development of what was called the Independent Frame Process by the Rank Organisation in Britain in the late 1940s (see Dixon). Although ultimately unsuccessful, this process was designed to create a template or "frame" that would enable producers in colonial countries to film their own version of the story, complete with many of the props, backgrounds, and other production elements that would be shipped to them. A principal element of this system was a series of rear-projection plates.

But these qualities and tendencies can also be read in other ways. For example, Thomson claims that something has been lost in a contemporary cinema that much more heavily relies upon the greater fusion of actor, action, and location: "Today, pictures can go to Casablanca and Shanghai; they are ablaze with the real thing. But they miss the point, the imperial, storytelling confidence that staged far away places in Los Angeles" (Thomson "Driving" 24). But Thomson's reverie for the hermetic utopia of old Hollywood overstates the degree to which contemporary cinema relies on the copresence of actor and location[10] and doesn't quite account for the full realities of rear-projection itself. Although the Hollywood studios routinely produced films in which the key actors hardly stepped outside of the studio's walls, someone still had to capture the background plates that enabled this illusion of relative global ubiquity.

The case of Hitchcock complicates, yet again, such simple hierarchical distinctions between artifice and realism, set and actual location, the primary production crew and the second unit. Although Hitchcock's films are full of process shots that place an actor against a projected background plate or matte created elsewhere and some time before, they often intercut such close images with shots of the same actors in the actual locations. Hitchcock's is a profoundly impure cinema that mixes and contrasts aspects of realism with a heightened but often meticulous artificiality. As Joe McElhaney argues:

> Realism itself is not by any means antithetical to Hitchcock. If contrast is arguably the fundamental structuring element to Hitchcock's work, then every drive towards artifice, the "slice of cake" that Hitchcock sometimes called his cinema, will invariably be countered with a drive towards realism, the "slice of life." (78)

As my discussion of the central driving sequence in *Marnie* attests, such a contrast or fusion between artifice and realism can even be ascertained within a single shot.

As anyone who has even a passing interest in Hitchcock's work would know (or could have sensed), the specificity of place plays an absolutely central role in the director's work. For example, in the "Muir Woods" sequence of *Vertigo*, Hitchcock creates a romantic, dream-like atmosphere that both transforms the location and merges with it. This sequence also cuts together a series of shots that show the actors on location and in the studio in a meticulous reconstruction of their surroundings. As is common in Hitchcock's work, he mostly uses the studio to shoot close-ups, medium close-ups and some mid-shots of characters and to stage much of the dialogue (though even these are not hard-and-fast rules).

But such locations as the Santa Rosa of *Shadow of a Doubt* (1943) or the Muir Woods (both near San Francisco) are not the only terrains that Hitchcock's films explore. A film like *Notorious* (1946) uses rear-projection plates shot by the prominent cinematographer Gregg Toland to place its characters (but never actors) in Rio de Janeiro, while the opening sections of the remake of *The Man Who Knew Too Much* (1956) place the central characters in Morocco, alternating between shots on location and in the studio. The shift between these two films is a significant one for Hitchcock. Although he does use numerous actual locations in films like *Saboteur* (1942) and *Shadow of a Doubt* such films as *Rebecca* (1940), *Foreign Correspondent*, *Spellbound* (1945), and *Notorious* largely use rear-projection, matte paintings, models, and Californian locations to represent overseas locations. Specific sequences in these films attain a high level of artificiality that is derived from their attempts to fuse actual locations with studio-shot interiors. This reaches a preposterous or almost delirious level in the climactic skiing sequence from *Spellbound*, where the "realism" of the characters' actions in front of a rear-projection screen is almost totally subsumed by the heightened dramatic and psychological requirements of the moment.

Hitchcock's films of the 1950s are more clearly marked by the spectacle of the actors actually appearing in foreign locations. In the process, such films as *The Man Who Knew Too Much* (1955) and *To Catch a Thief* (1955) also act as touristic spectacles. Nevertheless, the controlled tension between those shots that feature rear-projection and those that don't is still evident. One would assume that part of the attraction of taking the main actors on location would be to further fuse their performances to their surroundings. Despite its highly constructed nature, rear-projection does allow actors to respond to a "physical" image apparent to them during the process of filming; this connection is perhaps heightened when the actor is familiar with and has visited the location unfolding behind them.

The use of rear-projection also becomes—though not in a uniform manner—more self-conscious in Hitchcock's later work.[11] This is plainly evident in my discussion of *Marnie*, but also playfully highlighted by some of the dialogue in the first scene of *The Man Who Knew Too Much*. As the characters ride at the back of the bus on the road to Marrakech, the young boy (Christopher Olsen) comments on the rear-projected scenery: "You sure I've never been to Africa before? It looks familiar." His mother (Doris Day) quickly replies: "We saw the same scenery last summer drivin' to Las Vegas."

In conclusion, it needs to be acknowledged that this is a slightly odd discussion of rear-projection within the framework of ideas of bad cinema, as I plainly do not regard the technique *per se* in such pejorative terms. In many of the examples I've described here, rear-projection emerges as both an anachronistic and visionary technique—proof of what Thomson argues is "both the mechanical ingenuity and the imaginative power of the film industry" (*Movie Man* 72). The conceptualization of rear-projection as a form or element of bad cinema, ultimately centers upon the mechanical and imaginative failure of this technique where, as Raymond Spottiswoode argues, "all the great explosive forces of life . . . must be shrunk into unreality to fit the back-projection screen" (349). Nevertheless, although such "failure" or "shrinkage" is a common critique of rear-projection, alongside its imperialist or colonialist implications, this negative approach only tells part of the broader and more complex story.

Notes

1. I use the expression "rear-projection" throughout this chapter, which is the most common name for this technique, particularly in the United States. It is interchangeable with "back-projection" and is included within the more encompassing term "process cinematography."

2. Critical discussion of rear-projection has mainly been restricted to the analysis of the work of Alfred Hitchcock and within the more general categories of cinematography and special effects. Writers such as Laura Mulvey, David Thomson, and (much earlier) Raymond Spottiswoode have begun the process of more fully conceptualizing this technique.

3. Rear-projection has also been used in a more experimental and self-conscious fashion by various filmmakers including Mark Rappaport, Guy Maddin, Philippe Garrel, and Jean-Marie Straub and Danièle Huillet.

4. The "punctum" is a term popularized by Roland Barthes in his book, *Camera Lucida: Reflections on Photography*. In regard to rear-projection, the "punctum"—essentially a particular quality that "punctures" the composition of the image—might refer to the technique's ability to make us aware of the "pastness" of the moving image when one "film" is placed within another.

5. Dawn supposedly experimented with very primitive rear-projection in two scenes from his now lost 1913 film, *The Drifter* (see Fielding 261).

6. Rear-projection systems start to be used in Europe from the early 1930s, and in a country like Australia from the middle part of the decade. It is generally argued that non-Hollywood systems were inferior in this earlier period, but by the time of a "colonially" themed and set film like *Pépé le Moko* (Julien Duvivier, 1937), the practical and expressive use of rear-projection was well established in Europe (see Salt 210).

7. One of the most interesting early articles on rear-projection is DeMille's account of the economic and aesthetic advantages of the technique in relation to *The Plainsman* (DeMille 458–59).

8. One of the most interesting discussions of Hitchcock's use of this technique is found in Jacobs (45–48). Jacobs argues that Hitchcock's use of rear-projection should be placed alongside other techniques, choices, and motifs that contribute to the director's "creative geography."

9. Hitchcock's use of rear-projection dates back to at least 1932 with his very limited exploration of the technique in *Rich and Strange*. Several of the director's later British films, such as *Young and Innocent* (1937) and *The Lady Vanishes* (1938), make extensive use of rear-projection for their journey-driven plots.

10. Thomson's argument is somewhat undermined by the widespread contemporary use of such devices as blue screen, computer animation, and digital matting.

11. This is even reflected in Hitchcock's cameo appearances in *Foreign Correspondent* and *To Catch a Thief*. In both films he appears in front of a rear-projection screen.

Works Cited

Archer, Eugene. "Marnie." *The New York Times Film Reviews, 1913–1968.* Vol. 5. New York: The New York Times and Arno Press, 1970. Print.
Barthes, Roland. *Camera Lucida: Reflections on Photography.* Trans. Richard Howard. London: Flamingo, 1984. Print.
Bogdanovich, Peter. "Marnie." *Cinema* 2.3 (1964): 49. Print.
Bordwell, David, and Kristin Thompson. "Technological Change and Classical Film Style." *Grand Design: Hollywood as a Modern Business Enterprise, 1930–1939.* Ed. Tino Balio. Berkeley: U of California P, 1993. 109–41. Print.
Cameron, Ian, and Richard Jeffrey. "The Universal Hitchcock." *Movie* 12 (Spring 1965): 21–24. Print.
Carcassonne, Philippe. "L'ordre et l'insécurité du monde." *Cinématographe* 59 (July–Aug. 1980): 13–16. Print.
DeMille, Cecil B. "A Director Looks at 'Process Shots.'" *American Cinematographer* 17.11 (1936): 45859. Print.
Dixon, Wheeler Winston. "The Doubled Image: Montgomery Tully's *Boys in Brown* and the Independent Frame Process." *Film Criticism* 16.1–2 (1991–92): 18–32. Print.
Fielding, Raymond. *The Technique of Special Effects.* London: Focal Press, 1965. Print.
Fried, Debra. "Love, American Style: Hitchcock's Hollywood." *Hitchcock's America.* Ed. Jonathan Freedman and Richard Millington. Oxford: Oxford UP, 1999. 15–28. Print.
Jacobs, Steven. *The Wrong House: The Architecture of Alfred Hitchcock.* Rotterdam: 010 Publishers, 2007. Print.
McElhaney, Joe. "The Object and the Face: *Notorious*, Bergman and the Close-up." *Hitchcock: Past and Future.* Ed. Richard Allen and Sam Ishii-Gonzáles. London: Routledge, 2004. 64–84. Print.
Mogg, Ken. *The Alfred Hitchcock Story.* Rev. ed. London: Titan Books, 2008. Print.
Mulvey, Laura. *Death Twenty-Four Times a Second: Stillness and the Moving Image.* London: Reaktion Books, 2006. Print.
———. "A Clumsy Sublime." *Film Quarterly* 60.3 (2007): 3. Print.
Païni, Dominique. "Les égarements du regard (à propos des *transparences* chez Hitchcock)." *Hitchcock et l'art: coïncidences fatales.* Ed. Dominique Païni and Guy Cogeral. Montréal: Musée des Beaux-Arts de Montréal, 2000. 51–78. Print.
Rickitt, Richard. *Special Effects: The History and Technique.* London: Aurum, 2006. Print.
Salt, Barry. *Film Style and Technology: History and Analysis.* 2nd ed. London: Starwood, 1992. Print.
Sarris, Andrew. *Confessions of a Cultist: On the Cinema, 1955–1969.* New York: Simon and Schuster, 1971. Print.

Spoto, Donald. *The Dark Side of Genius: The Art of Alfred Hitchcock*. London: Collins, 1983. Print.
Spottiswoode, Raymond. *Film and Its Technique*. London: Faber and Faber, 1951. Print.
Thomson, David. *Movie Man*. London: Secker and Warburg, 1967. Print.
———. "Driving in a Back Projection." *West of the West: Imagining California*. Ed. Leonard Michaels, David Reid, and Raquel Scherr. Berkeley: U of California P, 1989. 23–29. Print.
Vasey, Ruth. *The World According to Hollywood, 1918–1939*. Exeter: U of Exeter P, 1997. Print.
Wood, Robin. *Hitchcock's Films*. New York: Paperback Library, 1969. Print.
———. "Looking at *The Birds* and *Marnie* Through the *Rear Window*." *Cineaction* 50 (1999): 80–85. Print.

5

Redeeming *Cruising*

Tendentiously Offensive, Coherently Incoherent, Strangely Pleasurable

R. BARTON PALMER

In the Eyes of Beholders

"In cinema," Dana Polan suggests, "the concept of badness covers at least two ideas," roughly spanning the time-honored distinction between form and content (202). In Polan's view, the most often discussed and applied of these is aesthetic or artistic badness, while the second is moral, which involves not only questions of right and wrong but also those pertaining to intellectual quality as well, where judgments of interest and banality are at stake. Both aspects of badness as applied to individual cases involve the invocation of values and also, of course, the choice of which values to invoke. The difference is that aesthetic questions, unless linked directly to social praxis (for example, the proscription of formalism in Stalin's Soviet Union) are usually less compelling in a cultural sense. No group is likely to feel itself offended by a poorly made film; protesters are unlikely to picket a release because of clumsy acting, confusing editing, or a sloppily recorded sound track.

Moral badness, in contrast, cannot so easily be ignored and imposes an unusual, if not extraordinary, burden on critics. Inexpertly made films are hardly dangerous, but those that express or exemplify ideas, practices, values and so on that are thought bad or, to use a more dramatic term, evil, are a different matter entirely. Determinations of moral badness are notoriously debatable, and when the issues involved have a purchase in the larger culture, such judgments often open up controversies of some sort. The most important reason is that badness, like goodness, as a relational term usually connects to instrumentality in some sense. For example, something is bad for something or seems good to someone in respect to some interest, and such contingent evaluations identify particular elements of a text and the context of its reception, in the process providing a kind of public "reading." But films can be imagined, somewhat anthropomorphically, as issuing appeals of various kinds that can be judged morally, of which offensiveness, that is, some challenge to conventional sensibilities or accepted notions of good taste, seems the most common and significant category.

As the well-known history of modernism establishes, however, offensiveness as a rhetorical effect is a highly uncertain quality, more a matter of cultural politics (that is, a question of the values held by viewers) than a sure and certain consequence of a film's purveyance of themes or representations. The moral badness of cultural objects is best judged transactionally, a matter of reception history rather than a matter of fact. It is even sometimes the case that issues of moral badness that might seem inevitably to come into play simply do not. Indeed, the moral condemnation that is not made is often the most revealing, for it constitutes a silence that begs for explication. The power of silence, as Michel Foucault emphasizes, cannot be underestimated because questions of power and practice are ultimately at stake:

> Silence itself—the things one declines to say, or is forbidden to name, the discretion that is required between different speakers—is less the absolute limit of discourse . . . than an element that functions alongside the things said, with them and in relation to them within over-all strategies. (27)

Offensiveness might be a strategy to contest customary social categories, making some political point that is positive rather than negative, good rather than bad. However it is understood, offensiveness (a projection of a definitionally problematic psychological reaction onto its presumed inciting cause) is always a social question in the broadest sense to which determinative answers are inevitably difficult to provide. Consider the well-known case of *Miller v. California*. Attempting to provide a mechanism for determining the badness of films purported to be obscene, the U.S. Supreme Court decided that lower courts should make judgments of this kind based on "community standards" that can be offended against. A film not judged obscene, even if filled with sexual representations, would according to this standard have artistic, scientific, or social qualities redeeming what would otherwise be offensive or prurient, turning the supposed bad into the acknowledged good. Or to be more precise, the film might be acknowledged as good by those who have accepted the redemption principle, which is itself a matter of cultural politics.

And yet the court's move in *Miller* was, in effect, no more than a fainthearted transference of an intractable definitional problem from inevitably elusive abstractions to a cultural chimera, the reassuring but patently self-deceptive notion that any community of reasonable size is sufficiently unified ideologically to possesses and justly apply agreed-upon ethical standards. The court had already rejected the possibility that a national community might make such judgments, and that difficulty was not bypassed by a simple change of scale. Prurience, derived from a Latin root that means "to itch," denotes an appetitive eagerness that is tied inextricably to lust. Lust depends on a typology of objects, pleasures, and gestures that displays a complexity and variety not easy to anatomize and demanding a persistent Linnaeus just to make sense of their uniqueness.[1] Different folks really do have different strokes, as the aphorism suggests. Would it be surprising then that a given film might contest the conventional understanding of prurience? Here would be a case in which offensiveness could be truly illuminating in a self-reflexive fashion, offering a comment on its own hitherto unnoticed limitations and exclusions; offensiveness in this sense would be artistically justified according to the *Miller* standard. But falling outside customary understandings, this challenge might not be easily readable. In fact, it might not even surface sufficiently to prompt a legal challenge, constituting therefore another form of significant silence in a film's reception history.

A potentially endless exchange of opinion also looms on the horizon when the other idea of badness comes into play. This is the question, as Polan frames it, of whether a given film "seems to offer unsuccessful style" or is considered to be "bereft of beauty or related values" (202). Such films "look, feel, and are . . . bad," and such aesthetic failure, like moral impropriety, is clearly and customarily an object of critical analysis, so much so that artistic "defenses" of films that have been denigrated for one reason or another are a staple genre of cinema criticism. In fact, Polan usefully explains how the advent of auteurism has continued to prompt aesthetic revisionism of this kind. In his auteurist study of Nicholas Ray's *Born to Be Bad* (1950), Polan in fact finds himself untangling and explicating conflicting judgments of badness based on contrasting aesthetics (203).

Thus *Born to Be Bad* is bad for good reasons, failing to achieve, as these terms of approval/disapproval shift, the "bad goodness" that auteurist critics have found in the director's more personal, that is, artistically idiosyncratic productions. But Polan's recalibration of the badness of this film is of interest only to critics. His revisionism does not otherwise make cultural news. Context and utility are all, it seems, in any determination, either moral or aesthetic, of what bad cinema might be.

Cruising into Controversy

A more powerfully instructive case of a film judged bad on both aesthetic and moral grounds is William Friedkin's *Cruising* (1980), an investigative thriller set in New York's gay community. Here is a film that occasioned both intense debate about its cultural politics, even as it was widely viewed as poorly made, a judgment that, especially of late, has become a minor controversy in the manner of the revisionism to which Polan subjects *Born to Be Bad*. Critics are now more moved to praise the director's artistry than to rail against his creative fecklessness. Interestingly, however, the debate over the alleged moral badness of *Cruising* has bypassed how the film constructs an erotics that is unique for a mainstream Hollywood release. Its representational program, dependent on a kind of taboo-challenging neorealism, has rarely since been repeated. But this radicalism was not perceived as such upon the film's initial release, largely because judgments of badness, moral and aesthetic, shaped its reception.

And this blind spot in the film's reception, as well as the resulting silence, is especially surprising because throughout the 1970s intense legal scrutiny was given to cultural materials thought obscene, as the movie business responded to the so-called *Roth* test. In *Roth v. United States* (1957) Justice William Brennan, who wrote for the majority, declared that "sex, a great and mysterious motive force in human life," had been found of interest by "mankind through the ages" and was therefore a proper subject for an art that did not cater to "morbid interests." As we have seen in regard to the *Miller* decision, the problem then became to distinguish between pornography (which is bad because prurient) and art (which is good because it engages a legitimate interest of producers and consumers alike in exploring life's truths).

The impossible implication of this distinction, of course, is that sex conceived as an intellectualized theme would, could, and should be disconnected from the arousing power of its conversion into images and dramatic action, as if the truth of sex in some sense could be divorced from the stimulating power it wields. And it seems that this culturally specific blockage connects directly to one of the moral charges commonly made against *Cruising*, specifically that in it Friedkin offers a "sensationalized" account of gay sexual practices, eroticizing an interest in truth.

In any case, what is ultimately most intriguing about *Cruising* is that, presumably because its often graphic sexual representations are largely (if not completely) homosexual, the film calls into question whether prurience *sensu stricto* as measured physiologically constituted the film's appeal to an overwhelmingly heteronormal viewership. Is *Cruising*, in other words, arguably obscene, its prurience simply of a different order than that of other films in this era such as *Carnal Knowledge* (Mike Nichols, 1971), exhibitors of which were prosecuted for obscenity in Georgia (all sex in that film was heterosexual) but then exculpated by a famous Supreme Court review?[2] Was the sexual material in *Cruising* meant to be a turn-on for straight viewers—and, if so, in what sense could that be? Meriting extended discussion to be sure, such questions were never taken up within the culture at the time of the film's release. More surprising, perhaps, they continue to be passed over in silence, even as *Cruising* has in the last five years enjoyed a noteworthy revival of viewer interest and critical approval. It is easy enough now, in fact, to redeem the supposed badness of *Cruising* through further analysis of those judgments made in the early 1980s.

Early on (during location shooting in fact, after a shooting script was leaked to influential members of New York City's gay community), *Cruising* was identified as morally bad because it was supposed to be hostile towards and defamatory of homosexuality, even though large numbers of the patrons of the "leather bars" featured in the film appeared in it as enthusiastic extras. The film was supposed to establish a direct connection between gayness and violence, its slander otherwise thought to stem from a partial, demeaning, and exotic depiction of gay life. A number of gay activist groups organized protests to disrupt the film's shooting at a New York City meatpacking district gay bar, and pressure was put on the filmmakers and distributors to abandon production and, later, to abort the film's exhibition. Friedkin's problems did not end when production wrapped. Upon release, *Cruising* was judged to be bad because it did not make sense in the way that mainstream films usually do, directing viewers towards some point that they can take away. The film quickly made its way onto worst film lists, where, in a more limited way, it continues to languish.[3] At the time, the widespread and well-publicized protests soon made *Cruising* into one of Hollywood's most notorious releases since *The Birth of a Nation* (D. W. Griffith, 1915).

Cruising's production, in fact, speaks to the substantial artistic and thematic freedom given to successful Hollywood filmmakers in the immediate post-studio era before the pronounced turn to the right symbolized by the election to the American presidency of Ronald Reagan that same year. It was these rapidly changing conditions of production and reception, in fact, that made possible the very badness of which the film was eventually accused, as previously stringent rules about sexual representation as well as industry standards of narrative construction were then quickly losing purchase.

The exotic, perhaps *outré* nature of these scenes from *Cruising*, in fact, would likely elicit today even more widespread condemnation since nothing like them has since appeared in a mainstream release. For example, at one point the camera focuses on an ecstatic patron in bondage being fistfucked while interested onlookers gather and the film's main character gazes upon the proceedings with rapt attention, his growing excitement communicated to viewers by a series of POV sequences. It is an interesting fact that this sequence was allowed to remain in the film by the apparently bewildered Classification and Ratings Administration (CARA), which, inconsistently enough, ordered removed a scene briefly and none too clearly depicting two men engaged in fellatio. With that scene cut, the film received its R rating.

Such potentially controversial elements have in recent years not prevented a thorough re-evaluation of Friedkin's efforts. At the 2007 Cannes Film Festival, a retrospective screening was received with several standing ovations, while careful (and expensive) restoration of *Cruising*, overseen by Friedkin, ended that same year in a much-praised DVD release. Obviously, the widespread judgment of badness that had been passed on *Cruising* in 1980 had in some important ways been reversed. This was the result of a changed political climate in the new millennium (gay activist organizations were no longer as outraged by the film's portrayal of the homosexual community). But it was also that American film culture, now thoroughly postmodernized, was more accepting of substantial deviations from classic studio-era narrative norms.

At the end of the liberated 1970s, the screen acknowledgement of gayness was not an issue and was in fact increasingly a subject for Hollywood (Wilson 100), however exoticized and marred by one-dimensionality the relevant films might seem in retrospect (see Russo 182–245). Thus *Cruising* was not judged bad (at least in an organized, public fashion) because it was supposed to violate traditional moral protocols. Instead the ways in which *Cruising* did become controversial reflected the increasing fragmentation of national values and the emergence of powerful forms of identity politics. But the reaction of gay activists to the film was then, and continues to be, polarized, as the issue of its offensiveness (useful or not useful to the cause) is hotly debated.

On the one hand, it seems unfair, as gay activist Alexander Wilson does, to complain that Friedkin "trades on ignorance about homosexuality" because the film suggests that the "cruising" which provides it with a title is "principally an activity of men dressed in leather" (105). The film business, we might remember, is not journalism, and directors are not constrained by protocols requiring "fair and balanced" reporting, and in any case the "men dressed in leather" customarily dress in that fashion, and cruising is a form of what we might now call "social networking." On the other hand, as Wilson himself reports, "it was widely felt among the extras interviewed that the demonstrators didn't want the leather world to be seen by straight people," on the theory, one supposes, that this "truth" about the gay life might be harmful to the consciousness-raising campaign then being conducted by organizations such as the Gay Activists Alliance (105).

One of the extras interviewed about the film offered a quite different perspective: "On the set of *Cruising* there were men. This movie is going to destroy stereotypes, and even if it creates other stereotypes, it's positive" (qtd. in Wilson 105). Offensive in some eyes to be sure, *Cruising* could be seen as either calumny or liberation, an "outing" that offered an easily sensationalized and therefore damagingly partial view of gay life or one that, in contesting received views, themselves derogatory, told a shocking, but necessary truth, one that underlined the uniqueness of a lifestyle demanding recognition for what those who lived it actually did, having so long pretended otherwise.

Needless to say, Friedkin and the other filmmakers did not anticipate that *Cruising* would spark this kind of controversy, feeding into arguments within the gay community itself over promiscuity and the leather scene, especially, as Wilson points out, in the way these practices raised questions about the "connections between power relations and desire itself" (106). This seems, in fact, to be part of Friedkin's larger thematic interest in the project, but he did not think it in terms of identity politics. One of the film's first scenes involves two NYC policemen, ostensibly heterosexual (their dialogue reveals them as archly misogynist) and themselves ensconced in a "cruiser," accosting two transvestite prostitutes working the bars and forcing them to either deliver oral sex or go to jail on a soliciting charge. Here the distinction between queer and straight worlds blurs, making a central point about rigid cultural assumptions of "homosexuality" (itself a relatively modern invention).

It should be remarked that promoting the socially constructed nature of sexual identities has been a *desideratum* for gay film theorists such as Robin Wood, who argues that films about gayness should make "the acknowledgement that gayness is not a thing apart—that everyone is potentially gay or has potential gay proclivities" (54). Though it is debatable whether this point is useful for a political identity movement committed to an essentialist position on sexual identities (that is, pro-homosexual), *Cruising* clearly stages the permeability of the boundaries between heteronormality and other forms of sexual being, rejecting or, perhaps better, dialogizing customary gender and sexualities and interrogating heterosexuality and homosexuality as fixed forms of identity. In this reading, Friedkin's point would then be broadly humanist, disconnected from the more restrictive agendas of identity politics.

Who in fact could have predicted that a project designed as a kind of sequel to two wildly popular and successful action thrillers would become, to some degree because of Friedkin's handling, one of the most controversial films of the last half century? This was a film designed to sell theater seats, not score political points or outrage sensibilities. It was the brainchild of producer Philip D'Antoni to make a film version of Gerald Walker's reportage novel *Cruising*. In sensationalized, pseudo-modernist form, the novel offers the parallel stories, based loosely on some real cases, of a serial killer stalking New York's S&M bar scene and the detective who, going undercover into that nighttime world, poses as a potential victim in order to trap and capture him. A refugee from earlier success promoting glamorous television specials, D'Antoni had developed a yen to make gritty urban action neo-noir stories after his work with director Peter Yates on the highly successful *Bullitt* (1968). His partnership with director William Friedkin on a similar project, *The French Connection* (1971), brought him even greater popular success and critical acclaim, which he was determined to repeat.

Like the other D'Antoni neo-noirs, *Cruising* was originally meant, it seems, to limn a morally ambiguous cityscape that would be energized by a thrilling investigation and suspenseful chases.[4] It was not a picture designed to deliver a message of any kind. This time, however, the film would not center on pursuits that led, Hitchcock-fashion, through well-known public spaces—LAX in *Bullitt* (1968), the New York Transit System in *The French Connection* (1971), or New York's Pelham Parkway in *The Seven-Ups* (1973): with the real star of these three films in some sense being stunt driver Bill Hickman—but rather different episodes of cruising through an underground scene seldom glimpsed by outsiders that would be featured prominently. Former cultural editor at the *New York Times*, Walker was a highly qualified guide to the demimonde of meat-packing district bars that catered to a certain gay clientele cultivating a hypermasculine Hell's Angel look and manner, and conforming to novelist John Rechy's widely publicized ideas about "the new homosexual."

A film version would be energized more by a representational adventurism (taking the vast majority of viewers, including many gays, where they literally had never been before) than by its somewhat pedestrian plotting. The killer is identified from the outset, and his eventual capture seems a foregone conclusion untroubled by anything in the way of surprising twists and turns, beyond the way in which the undercover detective finds himself increasingly entangled in the world he has come to surveil and drawn to an erotic life previously unknown to him. It is unclear at the end whether, in addition, he may fall victim to the violent homophobia that motivates the killer, perhaps becoming his Secret Sharer. What is clear is that the detective finds this particular cruising scene more attractive the longer and deeper he immerses himself into it.

However the film's point is not that homosexuality is the cause of violence (none of the gay characters are violent except in the playacting sense that S&M is violent), but rather that homosexuals are the victims of a homophobia that has its roots in the repression of homosexual urges. The depiction of violence against gay men, then, can be seen as either morally insupportable (if it were interpreted as an encouragement for others to do the same, though victims are by no means seen as "deserving" of their fate) or as morally laudable (if the violence were seen as socially condemned, the object of a police investigation into crimes against despised victims that had, if ignored in the past, are now receiving the deployment of considerable official resources). The strident anti-establishment gay activism at the time likely ensured that it would be the first of these understandings of that film that would shape reception in that community.

D'Antoni had William Friedkin in mind to direct *Cruising* from the beginning, not only, it seems likely, because Friedkin had shown a talent like Yates for mounting compelling action sequences. A few years before, for whatever reason, Friedkin had agreed to mount a screen version of Mart Crowley's successful Off-Broadway play about middle-class New York gay life. His adaptation of *The Boys in the Band* (1970) was hailed by *Time* as "a landslide of truths" (qtd. in Russo 174), and even the somewhat cynical Vito Russo has stressed the importance of that film in the immediate post-Stonewall era. Here was a film that addressed aspects of gay life that had never previously appeared on celluloid, based on a play that is substantially autobiographical, which guaranteed its authenticity and cultural force, as Russo admits: "the internalized guilt and self-hatred of eight gay men at a Manhattan birthday formed the best and most potent argument for gay liberation ever offered in a popular art form" (176–77).

Boys in the Band drew considerable unfriendly fire, especially from the nascent gay liberation movement (the film was released barely a year after the famous Stonewall protests in New York). Some objected that the film's emphasis on gay self-loathing and maladjustment, though constituting a potent brief for greater social acceptance of gayness, also seemed to offer little in the way of positive images that might be useful in the ongoing struggle to depathologize homosexuality. The film's most sympathetic character, an anguished Catholic, proclaims at one point: "Show me a happy homosexual, and I'll show you a gay corpse." *Boys in the Band* deals, as Richard Dyer has documented, in "stereotyping through iconography," establishing the one-dimensional queerness of the partygoers by their dress (pants a bit too ironed, shirts a bit too crisp, jewelry a bit too prominent) and manner (a "mincing walk," exaggerated gestures, and a nervously effusive volubility) (32). In this case, Friedkin was willing to take on a project that would inevitably receive contrasting political readings. Though considered by many to be "the pinnacle of Hollywood's commitment to the exploration of such 'adult' themes," *Boys in the Band*, Russo suggests, "was in fact a freak show" (178). A harsh judgment, but not entirely off the mark.

Impenetrable Subterranean Basements

Friedkin seems to have been determined that *Cruising* would not be vitiated by the one-dimensional stereotypes that had dominated in *Boys in the Band*. The latter was a release committed to limning a world unknown to and, given the cultural politics of the time, presumably interesting to mainstream, heterosexual viewers, who could be reassured that homosexuality was somehow a resistible condition. The straight, but questioning, friend of the host who crashes the party concludes by film's end to go back to his wife. He decides after that angst-filled evening that the gay life is not for him.

The substantially more pointed unconventionality of *Cruising* can be measured by the similar libidinal journey of its main character, John Burns (Al Pacino), the undercover detective who identifies and captures the psychopath responsible for most—but certainly not all—the murders and yet another heterosexual visitor to an unknown world. Burns returns to his girlfriend Nancy (Karen Allen) after having embraced, with some relish it seems, an identity (including perhaps some sexual encounters) as a gay man and experiencing for a time a crisis in his desire for Nancy.

But in one of the film's most enigmatic scenes, their reunion is interestingly problematized by her donning of the motorcycle cap that had been part of his undercover costume: an item of dress that the film suggests is standard wear for habitués of the leather bars. Though the meaning of her gesture is far from clear, the possibility is at least raised that Nancy—perhaps intuitively, or as a result of her own curiosity—has reconfigured herself as a more complex sexual object, providing John two contrasting but now complementary appeals, one in which clothing of a certain kind figures prominently. Is she thinking that so costumed she might make it possible for John to satisfy with one partner a newly expanded desire, one whose dimensions she barely glimpses? No matter what the precise meaning of Nancy's gesture, here is certainly no "stereotyping through iconography," but the kind of progressive contestation of "heterosexual relations under patriarchy" advocated by Wood, as the film in some fashion "attempts to construct new ways of relating" or, at least, to suggest their possibility (54).

Friedkin makes it clear that he never thought of *Cruising* in any sense as political: "It never occurred to me that the film would be interpreted in a political context" (qtd. in Simon). And yet, from an auteurist perspective, it could be said that Friedkin's handling of gay themes is more sophisticated and progressive than had been the case with *Boys in the Band*, where he was dependent more on Crowley's play and less on his own artistic decisions (he took a strong role in the screenwriting chores for *Cruising*, producing five drafts of the script before shooting started).

Approached by D'Antoni to direct *Cruising*, Friedkin read Walker's novel carefully, but initially decided against participating, for reasons he has never made clear but which seem from his later comments to be largely artistic rather than practical. After D'Antoni returned to television, producer Jerry Weintraub acquired the rights to *Cruising* and talked to Steven Spielberg about directing. The project went nowhere in this form and then, more than five years after D'Antoni had originally approached him, the project was revived and Friedkin was invited again to direct. This time he accepted, persuaded that the story had become very timely. Burns would be the protagonist and the film would trace his experience of being "a stranger in a strange land," and the film would be about a "crisis of identity":

> Several things happened: there were a series of unsolved killings in New York in the leather bars on the lower west side. The mysterious deaths that were taking place in the gay community, that later turned out to be AIDS, but really didn't have a name then. And the fact that my friend Randy Jurgensen, of the New York police department, had been assigned to go undercover into some of the bars, because he resembled some of the victims. (Simon)

The film would thus offer a revelation of how "human nature has a great many dark passages and impenetrable subterranean basements" (Simon), a project that by its very nature could prove offensive. Yet *Cruising* depicts a subculture with vitality and rules of its own that owes nothing to the straight life and the then widely accepted stereotypes passing for knowledge of gay culture in the broader community.

Explaining the film's narrative incoherence compared to the standard industry product, Wood argues that like similar productions of the period (especially *Looking for Mr. Goodbar*, Richard Brooks, 1977), *Cruising* could only make sense were it possible to adopt a thoroughly transformed position on sexual identity, which was then (as, of course, now) simply impossible, for "the radical alternatives remain taboo" (61). What is more complex, but perfectly explicable in terms of context, is that the film would be viewed as a dangerous defamation of homosexuals by some members of the gay community, despite the fact that the sexual lives of gay men are presented in more *vérité* than any commercial film had previously thought or dared to do, with perhaps as many as five hundred patrons of the bars where the film was shot employed by Friedkin as extras and paid more if they agreed to appear more or less nude and engage in customary sexual acts, which apparently were not scripted (see Wilson 98–109). No one should be surprised that *Cruis-*

ing would be defended by academic and intellectual admirers, including some prominent gay commentators, as strangely if disturbingly progressive because of its compelling engagement with, among other dangers facing the gay community, the pressing issue of violent homophobia.

And yet other readings were possible. Simon Watney, for example, observes that the film "willfully position[s] homosexuality within a dense and mystifying field of associations with terror, violence, self-hatred and psychological disorder" (qtd. in Medhurst 61). As Andy Medhurst sensibly points out, however, such criticism usually fails to take into account the "merits" of films like *Cruising* as films, with Watney ignoring that *Cruising* is an action thriller in which terror and violence are essential atmospherics (61). It might further be noted that self-hatred and psychological disorder are the dark energies that motivate the film's serial killer, who is not gay. At one point, to be sure, he engages as the "top" in anal intercourse with one of the victims, but in American culture this practice, which retains the male prerogative of penetration, is not necessarily coded as gay.

In any event, the killer's maladjustments are clearly not shared by the gays sympathetically (if exotically, it is true) depicted in the film; these men are shown as contented (if eager for satisfying connections) in the bar scenes and as otherwise productive, law-abiding citizens (one of the slain is a prominent and wealthy member of the city's artistic community who hooks up with the killer in a porno arcade, where the sex act that the killer contemplates—accepting fellatio—once again does not necessarily code as gay in American culture). It is the gay characters who are the victims of violence in different forms (which is perpetrated by the killer and also by the police against them). If other films of the period with gay themes such as *Making Love* (Arthur Hiller, 1982) struck many gay activists as offering a "pallid celebration of bourgeois monogamy," then *Cruising* should perhaps be acknowledged as a significant advance because it emphatically does not attempt to accommodate gayness "within the dominant regime of sexual ideologies" (Medhurst 61).

In its carefully orchestrated and reality-based display of the meatpacking district scene, *Cruising*, as has been charged, does take a voyeuristic approach to its subject matter. These sequences are characteristically constructed through POV sequences anchored to the visions and interests of the undercover detective to whom this way of life was hitherto completely unknown, as it was for the anticipated viewer (figure 5.1). It is important to note, however, that Friedkin, though attacked on a number of grounds, has not been accused of distorting an aspect of gay life that flourished in the period after the Stonewall protests and before the advent of the AIDS epidemic in the 1980s.

If his somewhat scrupulous documentarianism is offensive because it appeals to viewers' desire to see and experience vicariously, this is a strange charge for it is only to say, in the end, that *Cruising* is a film like many others, exploiting no more, it could be argued, than the medium's capacity and affinity for evoking a world, one that in this instance exists prior to the crew setting up their cameras. Furthermore, if the film tells the truth, so to speak, how can that be a bad thing for an identity politics, which is, as Medhurst suggests, eager to "throw off the shackles of negative stereotyping" (61)? Dyer maintains that a gay identity politics should contest the attempt of "heterosexual society to define us for ourselves," and it might be said that Friedkin's neorealist deployment of real locations and nonactors recreating their accustomed roles allows that to happen in ways never before seen in a mainstream Hollywood production (31).

Figure 5.1. Undercover cop Steve Burns (Al Pacino) in *Cruising* (1980). Courtesy Lorimar / The Kobal Collection.

Divided Artistic Judgments

There is no doubt that, as Wood scrupulously details, *Cruising* is characterized by undeniable deep and pervasive incoherence that does not allow the narrative to make the kind of sense commercial films at the time usually did (especially in terms of re-establishing a conventional social order, as the reunion of Burns with his girlfriend does not resolve important questions concerning his involvement in the murders and his sexual identity). This central element of the film can be explained as a surprisingly effective postmodernist strategy, with Friedkin participating, as Adrian Martin maintains, in a key development within early New Hollywood filmmaking, the emergence of a "cinema of hysteria" that "actively cultivates incoherence" and is structured on "moment-to-moment spectacular effect" designed for maximum viewer affect. Filmmakers who worked in this vein at the time, such as Oliver Stone, Adrian Lyne, Tony Scott, Mike Figgis, and pre-eminently Friedkin, aimed to elicit "the sudden gasp, the revelatory dramatic frisson . . . the disorienting gear-change into high comedy or gross tragedy." Supporting this view with a painstaking and persuasive analysis of the film's use of diegetic/nondiegetic music and postsynchronized dialogue, Martin concludes that Friedkin achieves a "substantial artistic success" by deploying a "highly coherent incoherence," making the film a "masterpiece of 80s cinema."

And yet what Martin considers a "good badness" can also be interpreted as an unintended failing on the director's part, with a particularly complex production history, perhaps, preventing him from imposing a structure on its materials that is not riven with false leads, ambiguous images (even on the level of casting), and an ending that is manifestly "impossible" in realist terms. In this view, *Cruising* would be an eminently forgettable, flawed production, a thriller that betrays at every turn what the genre and, for that matter, all Hollywood genres require: a solid story clearly told, making points that entertain and engage. Generally sympathetic to auteurist releases (Friedkin then enjoyed a substantial reputation among the arty set in the wake of the gritty and innovative *French Connection* [1971] and *Exorcist* [1973]), Andrew Sarris termed his bitterly negative review "Cruising into Confusion." Alexander Wilson, writing in *Social Text*, echoed the views of the mainstream critics in terming the film "an unremarkable and muddled detective thriller . . . an aesthetically shoddy product" in which "the lifeless and insipid dialogue is worsened by mediocre acting" (98).

Martin, among others, would put a finer point on the film's critique, which he views as worthier of praise: "the film is not about an individual killer or his string of victims, but an entire social system running on sexual repression and twisted, murderous impulses." Friedkin, in other words, would in effect be saying: "We have met the enemy and he is us." Bill Krohn's thoroughgoing study of the film's production history confirms that the incoherence is in fact intentional, as changes were made to the shooting script to create precisely the undecidability about which some critics have complained.

The film's admirers argue that this undecidability is the formal reflex of its politics. Friedkin is imagined as refusing that most basic of generic conventions, narrative closure (in this case the clear identification and capture of all those responsible for the killings) in order to suggest a more pervasive, ultimately unlocalizable link between sexual difference and violent reaction in contemporary society. Thus Friedkin's film would not be "about" the gay community but the larger culture, which turns out to be attracted to an erotics linked to the experience of power wielding and being wielded. Such an indictment, it hardly needs emphasizing, would also reasonably cover viewers, who are clearly enlisted in Burns's project of going undercover in every sense and, vicariously, invited to experience the pleasure he eventually discovers in what Thomas D. Clagett, comparing *Cruising* to Pier Paolo Pasolini's even more controversial *Salò* (1975), terms "nightmare visions of sexual and emotional excess" (262). For the film's defenders, *Cruising*'s formal and moral offensiveness would be redeemed by its representation, but then indictment of what Martin terms "twisted, murderous impulses."

Scientia Sexualis

What this loud and passionate debate about goodness and badness, both aesthetic and political, has ignored is *Cruising*'s unusual form of representational pleasure, a significant variation on the appeal to prurient interest that characterized the debate about pornography and artistic freedom in the post-PCA era, as the advent and installation in Hollywood of CARA in 1968 made possible more broadly different forms of sexual representation. It seems remarkable, for example, that *Cruising*'s groundbreaking engagement with gay sexuality (other films with "gay themes" seem by contrast marked by a kind of almost Victorian reticence) has not been taken up by historians of the era; there is not even a brief discussion of the film, for example, in *Hollywood vs. Hard Core*, Jon Lewis's otherwise comprehensive account of a decade that witnessed the possibility that witty, sophisticated pornography geared for heterosexual viewers might go mainstream.[5] It seems undeniably significant that the kind of sexual display previously seen only in gay stag films suddenly was at the representational center of a major Hollywood release. But histories of the period do not make this seemingly obvious point.

Why did the erotic life of a persecuted minority forced into shadowy denial for centuries suddenly become the subject matter of a film designed to entertain an audience whose experience of sexuality was radically other? This question was raised only haltingly at the time by a handful of commentators. After arguing that the film was perhaps not the proper place for an "investigation" of the place of S&M culture within the gay community (as if the filmmaking community was moved by sociological curiosity), Alexander Wilson, for example, seems surprised by his own recognition of the fact that "gay culture is something that Hollywood seems increasingly to be fascinated with," even as he recalls that Jerry Weintraub, the film's producer, once proclaimed that what Wilson calls "our ghetto" is "visually exciting, erotic, sensual, horrifying, electric, and imaginative. It has a life of its own" (109).

Wilson, in disgust, terms the filmmakers' interest in the gay community "fatuous voyeurism," a phrase that, if he thought about it deeply, could legitimately characterize Hollywood filmmaking in general. Similarly, in his detailed and fair-minded explication, Wood proceeds from the assumption that *Cruising* is characterized essentially by the production of meaning, whether imparted to its materials by the director and other creative personnel or, more impersonally, through the way in which its context speaks through it. *Cruising*, he observes, "testifies eloquent to the logical necessity for radicalism" as the "issues and conflicts" that the film "dramatize[s] can no longer even appear to be resolvable within the system" (61–62). At the same time, he admits to another kind of appreciation of the film, one less intellectual and politically engaged, and more connected to its capacity to entertain through a peculiarly unstable form of affect. This is a film, Wood says, that has "occasioned me a great deal of pleasure and disturbance, in roughly equal measure." His reaction to the world that *Cruising* both represents and stylizes is exactly what Weintraub predicted; the film's images produced in him an energized oscillation between arousal and horror, a form of affect characteristic of its era, precisely what Martin terms a "cinema of hysteria."

To understand this pleasure properly, I believe, it is necessary to place *Cruising* within that general development within modern Western culture, which has witnessed not the gradual abandonment of the repression of sexuality but rather the "proliferation of specific pleasures and the multiplication of disparate sexualities" (Foucault 71), a cultural trend that catches up William Friedkin as much as it more famously does the Marquis de Sade. To repeat an earlier point, our culture rejects an *ars erotica* in which what Justice William Brennan terms "the great and mysterious force in human life" might be acknowledged as inextricably coupled to the "itching" of prurience. As a result, we remain fascinated by the other of what Foucault terms "the two great procedures for producing the truth of sex," a *scientia sexualis* in which we "find pleasure in the truth of pleasure, the pleasure of knowing the truth, of discovering and exposing it, the fascination of seeing and telling it, of captivating and capturing others by it" (57).

Our erotic art thus consists precisely in the "multiplication and intensification of pleasures connected to the production of the truth about sex" (71). And yet the intensified pleasure produced by the representation of hitherto unglimpsed forms of the erotic that *Cruising* offered viewers at the time could only haltingly be spoken of and was likely to be condemned as a side effect of the "fatuous voyeurism" supposedly motivating the filmmakers. Our guide to this world is a detective committed to discovering one form of truth (the identity of the serial killer stalking this cultural scene). John Burns, however, finds that his professionally motivated abandonment of identity and his calculated adoption of another produce an enduring fascination that cannot be divorced from his own experience of desire. Seeking to understand, he finds himself caught within a web of unanticipated pleasures.

Friedkin, it seems, intuitively understood better than many of this era how impossibly compromised is the supposedly detached position of the observer who has motives other than finding pleasure in viewing a highly charged sexual display. Initiated into a world whose appeal he is ill-prepared to resist, the detective models for the viewer not only the breakdown of scientific objectivity but what discontents that might entail, such as the contrasting transformations of homophobia and homosexuality. His shaky return to normality is unexpectedly dialogized, with its previous foundational assumption of heteronormality now called into question.

In this way, *Cruising* dramatizes an involuntary fall into prurience that mocks the era's desperate and inevitably failed attempts to redeem the cultural attraction to a *scientia sexualis* by insisting on the chasteness of this pursuit of truth, by somehow distinguishing between the offensiveness of obscenity, on the one hand, and the clarifying transcendence of art, on the other. In its deconstruction of this foundational binary, confounding easy judgments of good and bad, *Cruising* finds a value beyond both the identity politics in which it was initially swept up and also the negative reactions of reviewers at the time to its purveyance of a striking form of cinematic postmodernism.

Notes

1. One legal website offers this unhelpful definition: "A morbid, degrading and unhealthy interest in sex, as distinguished from a mere candid interest in sex" (http://www.lectlaw.com/def2/p106.htm). But does a "candid" interest in sex mean beyond lust in the sense that Christian theologians imagined prelapsarian relations between Adam and Eve, with his erections "automatic" and not generated by any imaginings?

2. The Supreme Court's review of *Jenkins v. Georgia*, reversing the lower court decision, found that the film was not "patently offensive" because even though it did depict "ultimate sex acts" the camera did not focus closely on these scenes or show genitals. The representations of sexual activity in *Cruising* make nonsense of the idea of "ultimate sex acts" (which seems a very Kinsey-oriented orgasmic criterion) and, though not showing genitals, definitely focus strongly on sexual activity, especially through POV sequences. See http://www.law.umkc.edu/faculty/projects/ftrials/conlaw/jenkins.html for the majority opinion, from which the above quotations are taken.

3. Where it persists to this day. See, for example, http://www.afterelton.com/askmonkey/uncaged-ten-worst-gay-films-ever?page=0,1

4. Upon reading Walker's novel, D'Antoni is reported to have said: "It was the spookiest book I'd ever read. It terrified me" (qtd. in Clagett 237). The producer immediately contacted the young director Steven Spielberg, who, in his noted TV project, *Duel* (1971), had shown the ability to create an attractively terrifying film, a talent he would put to even greater use in his break-out film, *Jaws* (1975).

5. While a thorough chronicle of the era's several films—*Deep Throat, A Clockwork Orange*, and *Carnal Knowledge* prominent among them—that almost transformed mainstream filmmaking during the 1970s, Lewis offers no discussion of those releases with gay themes that also challenged conventional sensibilities and, all things being equal, should have attracted more general public notice and perhaps legal challenges.

Works Cited

Clagett, Thomas D. *William Friedkin: Films of Aberration, Obsession and Reality*. Los Angeles: Silman-James Press, 2003. Print.

Dyer, Richard. "Stereotyping." *Gays and Film*. Ed. Richard Dyer. New York: New York Zoetrope, 1984. Print.

Foucault, Michel. *The History of Sexuality: Volume 1: An Introduction*. Trans. Robert Hurley. New York: Random House, 1978. Print.

Krohn, Bill. "Friedkin Out." *Rouge* 3 (2004). Web. <http://www.rouge.com.au/3/friedkin.html>

Lewis, Jon. *Hollywood v. Hard Core: How the Struggle over Censorship Saved the Modern Film Industry*. New York: New York UP, 2000. Print.

Martin, Adrian. "*Cruising*: The Sound of Violence." *FIPRESCI* 4 Oct. 2008. Web. www.fipresci.org/undercurrent/issue_0407/martin_cruising.htm

Medhurst, Andy. "Notes on Recent Gay Film Criticism." *Gays and Film*. Ed. Richard Dyer. New York: New York Zoetrope, 1984. Print.

Miller v. California, 413 US 15 (1973). *FindLaw*. Web. 28 Dec. 2010. <http://caselaw.lp.findlaw.com/cgi-bin/getcase.pl?court=us&vol=413&invol=15>

Polan, Dana. "On the Bad Goodness of *Born to Be Bad*." *Bad: Infamy, Darkness, Evil, and Slime on Screen*. Ed. Murray Pomerance. New York: State U of New York P, 2004. Print.

Rechy, John. *City of Night*. New York: Grove Press, 1963. Print.

Russo, Vito. *The Celluloid Closet: Homosexuality in the Movies*. New York: Harper & Row, 1987 [1985]. Print.

Sarris, Andrew. "Cruising into Confusion." *The Village Voice* (18 February 1980). Print.

Simon, Alex. "Cruising with Billy. William Friedkin Interview." *The Hollywood Interview*. Web. 28 Dec. 2010. http://thehollywoodinterview.blogspot.com/2008/01/cruising-with-billy.html

Wilson, Alexander. "Friedkin's *Cruising*, Ghetto Politics, and Gay Sexuality." *Social Text* 4 (Autumn 1981): 98–109. Print.

Wood, Robin. *Hollywood from Vietnam to Reagan*. New York: Columbia UP, 2003. Print.

6

The Villain We Love

Notes on the Dramaturgy of Screen Evil

Murray Pomerance

> In nature there's no blemish but the mind.
> —*Twelfth Night* III.iv.367

Abysmal Pleasures

There is a rich history, in both Europe and America, of public entertainment by capital punishment. Indeed, the public execution was originary to the society of the spectacle. "By the spectacle that accompanies it," writes Foucault, "torture does not reconcile; it traces around or, rather, on the very body of the condemned man signs that must not be effaced; in any case, men will remember public exhibition, the pillory, torture and pain duly observed. And, from the point of view of the law that imposes it, public torture and execution must be spectacular" (34).

Beyond demonstrating morally dramatic contingencies in such a way as to elicit the engagement, participation, and pleasure of a wide, often untutored audience, it partook of the essential nature of theatricality in its design. As a form of play, it suspended time (see Agamben 75–76). "The engine of death," writes Peter Ackroyd of activities in early

London, "which was transportable, was dragged by horses into grooves marked upon Newgate Street itself. It consisted of a *stage* upon which were constructed three parallel beams. The part of the stage next to the gaol had a covered platform" (296, emphasis added). He quotes Johnson to Boswell: "Executions are *intended* to draw spectators. If they don't draw spectators, they don't answer their purpose."

Nor in its complexity and density was the entertainment of public death always salutary. "Look," writes Christopher Hitchens,

> at the history of capital punishment in Britain and you will find all the ancestors of the pornography of lynching. "Hanging, drawing, and quartering"—the procedure whereby a half-strangled convict is cut down, eviscerated, and castrated alive, and then dismembered and burned—was the big attraction at what is now Marble Arch on the northeastern corner of Hyde Park, then called Tyburn. Grisly keepsakes were commonplace. Favorable vantage points were for sale. Ministers of religion (usually Protestant) were on hand. Executioners were celebrities. The free availability of strong drink, loose women, and a generalized atmosphere of *fiesta* were of the essence. (qtd. in Duff vi)

Randall McGowen points out that "in mid-eighteenth-century London . . . hangings lacked dignity. They were poorly staged, too much like carnival rather than solemn and frightening. The condemned became objects of admiration for their boldness in the face of death" (259). Foucault notes how executions became carnivalesque: "rules were inverted, authority mocked and criminals transformed into heroes" (61). That the thrill of execution might well be dark and chilling, a shock of terror, is recounted by William Makepeace Thackeray:

> After Thistlewood and his companions were hanged, their heads were taken off according to the sentence; and the executioner, as he severed each, held it up to the crowd in the proper orthodox way, saying, "Here is the head of a traitor!" At the sight of the first ghastly head the people were struck with terror, and a general expression of disgust and fear broke from them. The second head was looked at also with much interest, but the excitement regarding the third head diminished. When the executioner had come to the last of the

heads, he lifted it up; but, by some clumsiness, allowed it to drop. At this the crowd yelled out, "Ah, *Butter-fingers!*"—the excitement had passed entirely away. The punishment had grown to be a joke. (155)

At the hour of execution, Thackeray writes, "an immense sway and movement swept over the whole of that vast dense crowd. They were all uncovered directly, and a great murmur arose, more awful, *bizarre*, and undescribable than any sound I had ever before heard. Women and children began to shriek horridly" (156). All this was part of a melee with its own weird and phantasmal organization:

> Forty thousand persons (say the sheriffs), of all ranks and degrees—mechanics, gentlemen, pickpockets, members of both houses of parliament, street-walkers, newspaper-writers—gather together before Newgate at a very early hour; the most part of them give up their natural quiet night's rest, in order to partake of this hideous debauchery, which is more exciting than sleep, or than wine, or the last new ballet. (156)

Charles Dickens, writing about an execution in Horsemonger Lane in November of 1849, moaned that "a sight so inconceivably awful as the wickedness and levity of the immense crowd collected at that execution this morning could be imagined by no man and could be presented in no heathen land under the sun." As to the site of execution, an early eighteenth-century medical observer wrote that "there is always at that place ['ordinarily the central public location in the city' (Berthelot 930)]—such a mixture of oddnesses and hurry that from what passes, the best disposed spectator seldom can pick out anything that is edifying or moving" (Mandeville 25).

In cases of public execution, the condemned—a complete and spectacular exemplar of evil ("badness"), as it is contemporaneously understood—is thoroughly vilified as a monster existing outside the moral order, incorrigible, perduringly threatening, and the perpetrator of deeds so hideous or outrageous that they can be nullified, so to speak, only through an elaborate and grotesque death that causes dramatic excesses of torment and pain. "The aim," Foucault tells us, "was to make an example, not only by making people aware that the slightest offence was likely to be punished but by arousing feelings of terror by the spectacle of power letting its anger fall upon the guilty person" (58). Beyond the death, the treatment of the body of the victim is itself congruent with his definition as abject and excommunicate. James Ray wrote of the treatment of the corpse of a hanged spy in the mid-eighteenth century:

> An apothecary [sic] and surgeon . . . [intended] to anatomize [the] carcase [sic], and expected to have had leather of the skin (worth his money) which he accordingly gave to a tanner to dress; but the Miracle Mongers said, that the hide was of so holy a nature, that it would not tan, nor be confined to lie under water, by any weight that could be put upon it; so that the tanner, after much labor lost, was obliged to take his holy hide and bury it. . . . If this skin had been preserved and well managed, by a skilful priest, there might have been as many miracles wrought by it, as any holy relic brought from Rome. (197–98)

In the sixteenth century it had been believed that the condemned in public executions had been subjected to a "curse," and many considered "what a vengeable dangerous matter it were to eat and drink with us that were accursed, or to give us anything, for all that so did should be partakers of the same great curse" (Foxe 1030).

Cinema, too, is play and ceremonial, and the abject image of death and disfigurement is hardly foreign to it. If in a similarly religious and dramatic spirit of concern for the body of the accused and its transformation as pleasurable entertainment for the masses, William Wallace was hanged, drawn, and quartered for treason against the English crown in 1305: this is to say, he was subjected to the gibbet or gallows until he was *almost* dead, then removed to a table in public view where his genitals were sliced off and his intestines drawn out, these organs to be either burned or cooked in front of his eyes, at which point he was beheaded and his body sliced into four pieces to be dispersed according to the will of the Sovereign. Six hundred and ninety years later, but with no less relish for its audience and in a purely virtual manner, his execution was carried out onscreen, through the agency of Mel Gibson's performance in *Braveheart* (Mel Gibson, 1995).

That in 1606, Guy Fawkes and his Gunpowder Plotters, who had wanted to do away with James I, were hanged, drawn, and quartered, after a public trial that was so popular people paid more than ten shillings for entry is hinted at, although not very meticulously replicated, in James McTeigue's *V for Vendetta* (2005). The exploits of the assiduous highwayman Dick Turpin, who was dropped from the gallows publicly in April 1739, were brought to life again more than once onscreen, with Percy Moran in 1912, Tom Mix in 1925, Victor McLaglen in 1933, and Philip Friend in 1956 among his reincarnators.

Hawley Harvey Crippen was hanged in 1910 for murdering his wife: an execution that, if it was not carried out in a public square, was so substantially reported that readers around the world could feel they were watching; Donald Pleasence recreated him in *Dr. Crippen* (Robert Lynn, 1962) as Rudolf Fernau had done twenty years earlier in *Dr. Crippen an Bord* (Erich Engels, 1942). Witnessed directly or enjoyed vicariously through media reportage, at any rate, the termination in the state's (or the monarch's) name of prisoners deemed to be embodiments of evil has been both a spectacle and a source of intense pleasure for audiences for at least hundreds of years.

As to the spectacular nature of executions and their inherent appeal to the eye: perhaps no writer has captured the complex tensions implicit in viewing a villain's demise better than Alexandre Dumas, who in *The Black Tulip* describes the awful fates of Johan and Cornelius De Witt:

> A third assassin fired a pistol at point-blank range. This time, the gun did go off and blew out Jan's brains. This time he fell and did not get up. At that, each of the wretches, emboldened by his fall, tried to fire his weapon into the body. And everyone wanted to strike a blow with a hammer, a sword or a knife, everyone wanted to have his drop of blood and tear off his scrap of clothing.
>
> When the two bodies were thoroughly beaten, thoroughly dismembered, and thoroughly stripped, the mob dragged them, naked and bleeding, to an improvised gibbet, where amateur executioners hung them up by the feet.
>
> At this point, the most cowardly of all arrived and, not having dared to strike the living flesh, cut the dead flesh to pieces and went round the town selling small fragments of Johan and Cornelius at ten *sous* each. (36–37)

In *The Count of Monte Cristo*, Dumas brings us to watch this summary business in Italy:

> Twenty thousand voices were crying, "Death! Death!" [. . .] Franz was, as it were, mesmerized by the horrible scene. The

two assistants had carried the condemned man on to the scaffold and there, despite his efforts, his bites and his cries, they had forced him to his knees. Meanwhile the executioner had taken up his position on one side and raised the mace. Then, on a sign, the two assistants stepped aside. The prisoner wanted to get to his feet but, before he had time to do so, the club struck him on the left temple. There was a dull, muffled sound, the victim fell like a stricken bull, face downwards, then on the rebound turned over on his back. At this the executioner dropped his mace, pulled the knife out of his belt, cut open his throat with a single stroke and, immediately stepping on his belly, began as it were to knead the body with his feet. At each stamping of the foot, a jet of blood spurted from the condemned man's neck. (395)

Dumas' careful attention to the value of these proceedings as pleasurable engagement for a substantial public crowd is what I would like to especially emphasize. The author is aware not only that the crowd he is describing—the one including our character Franz—is raptly fixed upon the proceedings on the scaffold, but also that his readers—an even more important crowd—are: that every word of the fiction brings the hungry consumer closer and closer to a thrill that has been paid for and is contractually to be delivered. With cinema the effect is even more pungent: "not only must people know," Foucault warns, "they must see with their own eyes" (58).

Motion Pictures and Official Slaughter

We might consider that although in most Western countries public executions are now a thing of the past[1]—notwithstanding the audience of official witnesses who must watch the employment of the electric chair, the gas chamber, or the syringe in American death chambers today—the motion picture industry has persistently capitalized on a generally repressed hunger for blood, hidden beneath the mantle of the demand for public justice, that can be found among movie-goers around the world. "To unite the ideas of death and shame is not so easy as may be imagined. I will appeal to any man who hath seen an execution . . . whether the idea of shame hath ever intruded on his mind?" (Henry Fielding, qtd. in Foucault 61). While in cinema public denigration and termination of villains often takes place independently of systematized justice, justice of some rational or perverse kind is nevertheless always implicit, the mechanism of the plot functioning as its own rationalizing system with the audience dragooned as a jury of interested parties. In a way, the cinematic dramatization of villainy's demise, focused on the climactic, dramatic dispatch of the villain, are tantamount to public execution; indeed, the cinematic portrayal of a villain's death may be seen to serve many of the same moral, educational, and cathartic purposes as public executions—by and large carried on before the advent of cinema—did.

This linkage between public executions and cinematic narratives might seem strange if the fundamental motive for motion pictures and the purpose of the public execution were further removed, but they are in fact akin, and remarkably so. The public execution, like the public screening of films in which villainy is established and destroyed, does not entertain inadvertently but is designed as a mechanism to produce an affective discharge and moral instruction through the exhibition of isolation, denigration, pain, and finally—in a notable culmination—death. (Tom Gunning points to the legal regulation of film in terms of its nature, "its relation to audiences, its unique power of attraction," noting a "deep-rooted suspicion of the nature of cinema and spectacle itself" [22, 25].)

It is also hardly irrelevant that formal executions have become a staple of Western dramatic film, with such fare as *True Grit* (Henry Hathaway, 1969), which opens with a hanging in a public park circa 1880, a crowd happily chanting "Amazing Grace" and a kid selling peanuts all through it, and playful children swinging back and forth from a tall tree. Or such treatments as the electric chair in *The Postman Always Rings Twice* (Tay Garnett, 1946; Bob Rafelson, 1981); the gas chamber in *I Want to Live!* (Robert Wise, 1958); the guillotine in *The Battle of Algiers* (Gillo Pontecorvo, 1966); the gallows in *10 Rillington Place* (Richard Fleischer, 1971); the firing squad in *The Executioner's Song* (Lawrence Schiller, 1982); the lethal injection gurney in *Dead Man Walking* (Tim Robbins, 1995) and *True Crime* (Clint Eastwood, 1999); the gas chamber in *The Chamber* (James Foley, 1996); and the electric chair in *The Green Mile* (Frank Darabont, 1999), *The Man Who Wasn't There* (Joel and Ethan Coen, 2001), and *Monster's Ball* (Marc Foster, 2001). There are also parodic genre pieces—like the electric chair in *The Phantom Speaks* (John English, 1945) or *Alive* (Ryûhei Kitamura, 2002)—in which bad, bad people manage to escape their executions and return in a state of heightened malevolence.

Quite as frequently as miscreants are caught, tried, sentenced, and officially done away with onscreen, however, they manage to elude the formal clutches of justice only to be confronted with vigilante avengers, those vivacious, talented, clear-eyed, incessantly purposeful action-hero types who mobilize the blockbuster economy (Bruce Willis, Harrison Ford, Arnold Schwarzenegger, Sylvester Stallone, Jean-Claude Van Damme, Steven Seagal, Tom Cruise, Clive Owen, Daniel Craig, or—in the case of the Wicked Witch of the West—Judy Garland) who spare nothing in their pursuit of nefariousness and an ultimate—by which I mean, quasi-orgasmic—meting out of "appropriate" death. In *Lord of the Rings: The Return of the King* (Peter Jackson, 2003), a cinematic apotheosis of this heroic triumph, innocent Frodo with his sparkling eyes and pure soul, battles and then participates in dispatching the ugly and utterly malevolent Gollum, a slimy and traitorous killer who finally plummets into a river of molten lava. The hero need not be alive, technically speaking: in George A. Romero's *Land of the Dead* (2005), a malevolent capitalist (Dennis Hopper) is devoured by a purposeful zombie (John Leguizamo). And righteous termination of the insufficiently righteous can be not only patterned but archetypal, as in westerns: for instance, the vile Gene Hackman brutally slain by Clint Eastwood in *Unforgiven* (Clint Eastwood, 1995) and again—because truly evil characters can never really die—by Sharon Stone in *The Quick and the Dead* (Sam Raimi, 1995). Nor must heroic retribution be either modest or nice: in *Raiders of the Lost Ark* (Steven Spielberg, 1981), Indiana Jones backs a Nazi thug into the whirling propeller of an aircraft and later acts as witness while a cadre of Nazi militia and intelligence operatives are eaten alive by supernatural forces released from the Ark of the Covenant. Even animated villains can be disanimated: the villainous toon (Christopher Lloyd) who is the spirit of darkness in *Who Framed Roger Rabbit* (Robert Zemeckis, 1988) is tossed into a vat of lime-green chemicals that will erase him.

In films, the logic of the narrative fills in a central jurisprudential lack, offering excuses, rationale, and teleological outcome for acts of vicious destruction played out in the name of all that is orderly, civilized, lovable, and true. In Clint Eastwood's *Changeling* (2009), a kidnapper and murderer of children is put to death on the gallows in a scene of notable prolongation, focus, and discomfort for all who watch, yet in the name of vengeance and social probity that accord with the turns of a story that is both chilling and morally disruptive: the formal death of the killer is intended to set the balance aright. This is a somewhat complicated resolution, nicely in tune with the problematics of capital punishment more broadly. While the needs of the story for resolution and purification are directly and fully addressed, the character who has lost the most because of this killer's depravity finds no resolution at all in his death, nor even hope that resolution will ever come.

Anticipation and Delay

Regardless of the manner and degree in which the so-called bad guy—he is not invariably male, as Robert Benton's *Still of the Night* (1982) makes far too clear, but usually is—meets his end in movies, the logic of narrative exploitation requires that he should first survive as long as possible, certainly long enough to produce an attenuated threat for the hero and to provide the audience with an opportunity for thrillingly anticipating the schadenfreude that will be theirs at the releasing moment later, when in noble but resentful fury (and in the name of all that is just and good) he is eliminated.

Often one's anticipation is as great as, or greater than, one's thrill at the kill, this being a feature of screen violence in general that makes it pornographic. Our imagination lives in a hypothetical topography free from the stifling limits of social organization and the everyday. Regardless of the fact that the death of the villain seems morally justified; regardless of the fact that killing him is a principal aim of the hero (indeed, diegetically speaking, the hero's overriding and obsessive purpose, so that therefore the hero's vindication and fulfillment require this death); regardless of the fact that the villain's corrupt and unconscionable acts jar and affront our sensibilities to such an extent that we crave his demise (if only that we may escape more of his apparently boundless torment), still, no dramatic film will seem successful that shows the punishment of the villain too early.

George Bernard Shaw remarks in his introduction to *Caesar and Cleopatra* that when the gods wish to cause a man to fall, they first raise him to a great height; we might add, dramaturgically speaking, that they raise him slowly, so that our hunger that he might lose his balance can be whetted before being sated. Since screen events are all concoctions—since nothing that appears to be happening onscreen is actually happening in the world where the screen stands—what is at issue in this delayed gratification is a set of structural arrangements and configurations that fall not to agents of justice and the police, that is, not to the legal or jurisprudential system, but to experts in staging for camera: the writer, the director, the cinematographer, the actor, the designer, and even the composer who scribbles the tune that sings along with the villain's death.

There are a number of technical problems that confront filmmakers when evil is to be personified. What are they, and how may they be addressed? The filmic transformations and outplayings that we watch are formed in response to these technical demands, and therefore our pleasures and responses are based not in our personalities as viewers, nor even simply in the social reality of the theatrical scene (which applies across all stories, regardless of their characters), but in the architecture of narrative—this need to stretch screen badness to its full potential before arriving at the limiting moment when it can be made to disappear.

A Characterological Type

A notable and limiting case is the characterization onscreen of Adolf Hitler, especially as it has been managed in Bryan Singer's *Valkyrie* (2008). There are well over a hundred performances of this person, effected by such luminaries as Armin Mueller-Stahl, Günter Meisner, and Martin Wuttke (all German); Derek Jacobi, Alec Guinness, John Cleese, and Steven Berkoff (all British); Anthony Hopkins (Welsh); Bruno Ganz (Swiss); Ian Bannen (Scots), and Luther Adler (American). By comparison with the screen time taken up in their performances, the scenes showing Hitler in *Valkyrie* are relatively few in number and, for the most part, brief. But the performative work by David Bamber as Hitler beautifully illustrates the difficulties in this particular role and in the general problem of screening evil, not to mention some professional approaches to those problems. An especially interesting feature of the Hitler in this film, as I hope to show, is that by contrast with his model in real life, he must almost always be manifestly unreal.

It is public knowledge that Hitler committed suicide at the end of the war. Therefore, filmgoers watching any realistic narrative of the Third Reich (that perforce takes place during wartime) know they are unlikely to see him dying onscreen by other people's hands, this notwithstanding his extreme malevolence that might reasonably provoke audiences to yearn for his death. The frenzied scene in Quentin Tarantino's *Inglourious Basterds* (2009) in which two Jewish American soldiers go berserk machine-gunning Hitler in his private box at a theater is thus little more than a conceit. Furthermore, as Führer, Hitler would understandably have been protected by legion soldiers and heavy architecture, no less than with any Allied leader at the time. A filmmaker wishing to tantalize his audience with the prospect of Hitler's assassination must thus find a way to separate his narrative from historical reality, knowledge of which viewers import to the theater, all the while invoking this history as décor. Viewers must expect that villainy will come to punishment directly in front of their eyes, regardless of what really happened. It is also possible to rationalize the failure of the assassination strategy planned in the narrative—planned against this abject evil that, of all evils ever filmed, deserves punishment—by warming the target to our sensibilities. We become willing to see him live on while, by his command, so many innocents die. One solution, then, is to *separate the character from (historical) reality*; the other is to *separate him from his model's manifest wickedness*. In Valkyrie, both strategies are in use.

Abstraction from History

Diegetic Hitler is here abstracted from historical Hitler by Christopher McQuarrie and Nathan Alexander's screenplay, which through exaggeration of detail, intensification of focus, and star casting valorizes the attempt of Col. Claus Von Stauffenberg (the film's marquee attraction, Tom Cruise) and his colleagues (including noted British character players Kenneth Branagh, Terence Stamp, and Bill Nighy) to plant a bomb beneath the table where he is engaged in a comparatively dull military briefing. The film spends almost all of its considerable energies of scripting, casting, staging, and scoring to heighten our attention to: the philosophical commitments of the plotters; their building sense of purpose conflicted against various manifestations of cowardice and double-thinking; and the intricate design of their elaborate plot, which involves hundreds of people many of whom—entertainingly for us—do not recognize the help they are giving. Emphasized throughout is the would-be assassins' self-proclaimed legitimacy in the face of a regime only too clearly depicted as totally evil, and that they see as militarily inept.

If our concerns are to be riveted to the machinery of the assassination plot, that plot must be progressively reified in the context of the narrative. Thus, to understand the film as a whole, and to raptly watch it, one is forced to be as committed to the plot as the hero is— to believe in its underlying principle—and even to progress through the film with a hope that expands with one's commitment. Necessarily for the drama, this hope must be mitigated (yet not quite punctured) with rhythmic interruption, by mounting fears that something will cause the arrangements to collapse. From the writers' point of view: since in their finale the assassination must be foiled (so that the "Hitler" of the tale may proceed to his "bunker" and "kill himself" sometime after the credits), the audience must be kept from this foiling as long as possible, embedded in a plan and wish system they do not consider baseless. Shot after shot must carefully show how, against all odds, the conspiracy is being effected phase by phase, and with each accomplishment we must feel satisfaction and closure.

As to the actual culminating failure, it should be elided if possible, indeed swiftly removed from the narrative flow. Thanks to the miracle of communications technology—since it is by telephone that our plotters learn they have failed and by radio that Hitler's triumphant voice is heard by the German people—and with its characteristic turnabout instantaneity, the conspiracy comes apart (although we never learn exactly how or why), the ogre we had hoped to see destroyed is found to be alive and well—too alive! too well!—and our friendly conspirators are now lined up perfunctorily and shot. The entire project of *Valkyrie* is a voyage away from the historical reality with which this finale is so gravely infused, virtually lunging towards what we retrospectively invest in as hypothetical possibility, the termination of Hitler; the facts as historians know them can take precedence onscreen only at the conclusion, when all the audience's projection of fantasy has been lost. If Hitler himself is not ghostly in this film, the idea of him being put to death in a "public execution" is.

In *Valkyrie*, Hitler avoids the onscreen punishment we feel appropriate for him through the method of a realignment of the camera's eye. This is not a realignment towards Hitler's political achievement (such as we see, for instance, in Spielberg's *Schindler's List* [1993]) but a reframing upon the figurehead Stauffenberg—noble, wounded, liberal, feelingful, paternal, handsome, and committed—who, acting in the belief that he can slay a monster, mobilizes our engagement to share his motives and moves. As a narrative construct here, "Hitler" finally comes under the aegis of "those who would kill Hitler," and to the extent that they seem likely to be successful—thrillingly likely, indeed—Hitler their target is, and must be, preserved onscreen until the vital moment (that we so cherish) when they are. As "plotters," McQuarrie and Alexander are in conversation with their own creations, the plotters in the diegesis. No matter how enthusiastic and excited the diegetic plotters may become, if Stauffenberg and his colleagues are to accomplish their assassination they must not succeed early enough in the film that our building excitement dissolves. And so Hitler lives. Given this narrative, the failure of the conspiracy runs against logic; the diegesis must quickly metamorphose into history. For as long as this paradox can be kept from viewers (Hitler's suicide is casually announced on one of the last title cards before the end credits), our villain can survive as a fictional construct. Looked at either diegetically or historically, he is the abject criminal we have gathered in our dark public place to see executed, a fantastic project on our part, worth stretching to maximize our excitement at its action.

Characterological Separation

The separation of the dramaturgical Hitler from the irremediable negativity we normally attribute to him (else the assassination plot makes little cultural or historical sense) is accomplished through various production techniques. While the real Hitler was monstrous, the filmic Hitler cannot be such that our sense of sanity and security depend on him being squashed the instant we see him. The actor must act to humanize the reprobate. Posture must relax: rather than being styled as an aggressive brute, Hitler is made to seem frail and vulnerable, possibly arthritic. Bamber gives him a stooped back and a tentative loping gait: marching to his aircraft early in the film, he must get up steam and forge ahead, as though any sudden stop would jolt his frail skeleton. In his Berghof study, we see him glide around with minimal exertion, *à la manière de* Walter Matthau, as though his powers are dilute. Not only vulnerable—even in comparison with the grievously wounded Stauffenberg, an amputee from the African front—he is genteel. Hitler is the only person in the film—including Stauffenberg's wife—who shows even a moment of genuine sympathy for the younger man's physical pain, actually reaching out to affectionately touch the arm where a hand once was attached. His voice is low and confiding, grandfatherly, and his language is cultured, even Wagnerian. (In reality, Adolf Hitler did not come from the cultured classes and would have had hardly more exposure to, say, Richard Wagner than Stauffenberg's children, who in one scene play at being Valkyries while a phonograph record spins in front of them.)

Hitler has a wound of his own, a physical, perhaps neurasthenic, weakness; and he is agonized, perhaps a migraineur. In 1944, the year in which this film is set, he was fifty-five years old, hardly aged, although he had suffered wounds in World War I (wounds to which no reference is made in this performance). Costumer Joanna Johnston assists Bamber in tenderizing the characterization by clothing Hitler in slightly oversized garments, so that he seems diminished, passive, and timid in his direct presentations of self. The Berghof scene is our only opportunity to meet the character backstage of his military life and here Bamber's Hitler seems sociable, if withdrawn; entirely civil; affectionate to his dog. In general, then, this historically verified epitome of loathsomeness, this political threat to Germany (as Stauffenberg casts him) and to the rest of the world, never actually moves the audience to long for his demise *with urgency*, let alone to hunger for the pleasures of a gruesome punishment.

I bring the Bamber performance forward for discussion, among all those powerful evocations of Hitler that are part of film history—in *Inglourious Basterds*, he is diminished to a screaming lunatic—not at all to indicate that Singer has made a bizarre film about Nazi Germany, as, perhaps, he has, but to illustrate, by way of the limiting case of a man who may be expected to seem limitlessly bad, what must happen to evil characters onscreen in order that films might succeed with audiences. Movies about evil are ultimately movies. The reality of evil must be eclipsed by a dream, and this is a procedure in which not only history but also the real drama of human consequences is abated and finally erased. The death of the real Hitler at the end of the war was linked to the defeat, and the utter destruction, of Germany itself, a punishment even grander than public executions. This cataclysm involved bombings and firestorms in which, as W. G. Sebald tells us the author Hans Erich Nossack wrote, "[one found] objects lost forever, the rubble burying them and the dreadful new life moving beneath it, people's sudden craving for perfume" (51).

Film is less horrid and more euphemistic than this, of necessity. Audiences can be moved to want vengeance, retribution, or even simply pain and torment for screen characters, but as filmic narrative collapses around the production of this "justice," justice must not be delivered before a film is ready to collapse. Thus, what we can learn watching Bamber's performance of Hitler we can learn as well from countless other films involving villains, namely, that narrative villainy poses certain presentational problems, call them technical challenges to filmmaking. Like the condemned in public torments of old, the bad guy who merits punishment must above all seem watchable, since watching is what filmmaking is aimed at and being watchable is the cardinal virtue of all filmic characters. So that he may be watchable yet also credibly worth destroying, the villain's nefarious activity must be sufficiently and visibly negative that it arouses our disgust and moves us to identify with the hero who will bring him to task, yet at the same time not so negative as to force our withdrawal from the narrative in an aesthetic revolt. I should add that the endurance of the villain onscreen is also produced through the ineffectuality, incompetence, weakness, distraction, or clumsiness of the hero, but we must be willing to find the hero's incapacity entirely bearable, even a delight, because it prolongs a state of affairs that gives us fundamental pleasure, the ongoing battle between a force of good who means well and intends ultimately to succeed and a force of evil who is just attractive enough that we could wait to see him die *another* day.

But can the elasticity of this formula be stretched too far? At the end of *Star Wars* (George Lucas, 1977), should Darth Vader die outright, rather than escaping into the future? Ditto the sickening invader in Ridley Scott's *Alien* (1979), who, finally cast out into space, moves off screen without being discernibly dead. If, dramaturgically, the longer Saint George must dance before netting his dragon the greater our pleasure promises to be when defeat is gloriously produced. If the audience is kept in anticipation of the coup de grâce, and thus imagines it growing through the time of the delay, then might it be that a sort of contract is violated when at the end of a film the villain actually doesn't get punished at all? Is there a problem when, in *Valkyrie*—instead of being compelled to stand witness while his countrymen suffer (as Sebald describes it) a fire that "now rising two thousand meters into the sky, snatched oxygen to itself so violently that the air currents reached hurricane force . . . and drove human beings before it like living torches" while "the glass in the tram car windows melted" and "stocks of sugar boiled in the bakery cellars" and "those who had fled from their air-raid shelters sank, with grotesque contortions in the thick bubbles thrown up by the melting asphalt" (27)—Adolf Hitler, as we are informed, merely killed himself one day? Is not this bald information a brilliant defusion of desire, a blurring of the image we longed to see, that will never come? Is not the audience's agreement to enjoy the negativity of the immoral, the ugly, the antihuman, and the satanic offered on the basis of the provision that some suitable punishment will finally, really, definitively be meted out in accordance with prevailing codes, when what can be called the "right moment" has come?

Pure Screen Villainy

Any characterization of Hitler onscreen or onstage has a basis in historical fact. But we can also consider screen characterizations that do not, that are embedded only and wholly in film. Such bad characters have a history within a particular narrative—their action is caught up in the present, past, and future of the story—and a history in film, one that places them in a tradition of screen villains; but otherwise they exist only in our memories. As with all filmic villainies, their negativity must appeal to the audience: it is for the hero that they must be darkest, and so we must dis-identify with him to some degree, question his motives and regard the "bad guy" affectionately if the story is to expand with our approval.

So it is that in Hitchcock's *Psycho* (1960) we rebel, to the last moment, against accepting the true identity and nature of the villain, choosing instead a complex psychoanalytical invocation of a kind of cannibalistic dualism rather than simply confronting evil as such. In *North by Northwest* (Alfred Hitchcock, 1959), we find the malevolent Vandamm charming, even delicate, a paragon of civility, high culture, good manners, excellent wit, even erudition through all but a single moment of his screen presence: his chilling admission that he plans to drop Eve Kendal out of an airplane over the ocean. In another actor's hands, the Hannibal Lecter of *The Silence of the Lambs* (Jonathan Demme, 1991) might have crumbled into shards of moral deformity, but instead we are treated to Anthony Hopkins's sonorous voice as he enunciates a mocking wisdom, a fountainhead of forensic knowledge, a sense of right and wrong that shame the heroine's, and a poetic sensibility that comes through in his soft, even musical speech (figure 6.1).

As played by both Charles Laughton and Trevor Howard, Captain Bly in *Mutiny on the Bounty* (Frank Lloyd, 1935; Lewis Milestone, 1962) is only a festering pouch of weaknesses, so that finally when Fletcher Christian sets him to sea we pity him, fearful that his brittle sense of order and his high-strung psychology will split him. Further, in action films and high dramas, it has long been the convention to lard the story with dispensable minor flunkies—associates, kinsmen, or moral copies of the villain—who act and die in his place so that as the story advances the audience is offered a guarantee that the right side is winning and reason to hold off the villain's personal death for a pleasurable and remote future moment. Think of Peter Lorre's unctuous Joel Cairo in *The Maltese Falcon* (John Huston, 1941) or his weaselly little Ugarte in *Casablanca* (Michael Curtiz, 1942); or the dozens of underlit, expendable, myopic hunks who must be shot or exploded by Arnold Schwarzenegger in *Commando* (Michael L. Lester, 1985) before he manages a one-on-one with the viperous Aussie villain, Bennet (Vernon Wells); or the myriad uniformed myrmidons in virtually all James Bond films, who are shot from heights or sunk in the sea before the cryptic, contorted, evil genius

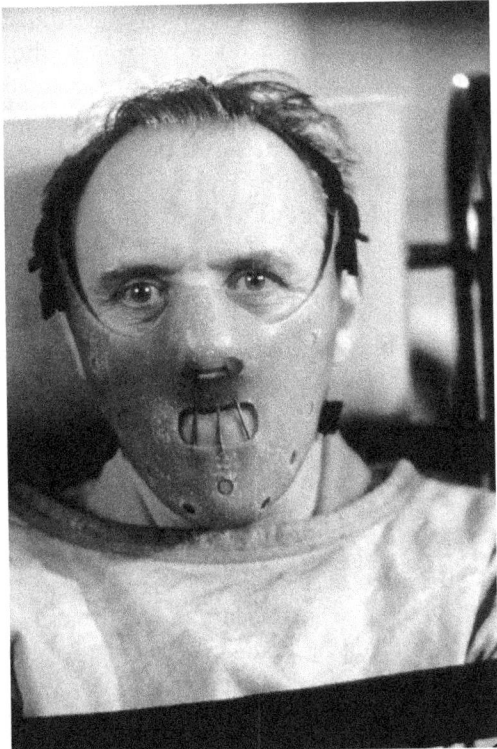

Figure 6.1. Anthony Hopkins as the villain Hannibal Lecter in *The Silence of the Lambs* (1991). Courtesy Orion / The Kobal Collection.

who is their leader, and Bond's true match, finally finds his—typically not sufficiently ceremonial—death.

Transfiguration

There is, to be sure, a ceremonial action involving the filmic villain, an action that almost always incorporates death with transfiguration. He finally—at the end of this film or the next, or the last in a sequence—meets an end that seems justified, wholly merited, and designed so as to be appropriate, an end that can be witnessed by all of us in this wholly theatrical environment of fiesta that is the public screening of a film: and that recalls, with its graphic horror and general festivity, the public execution. Since we have been loathe to release our emotional hold on the villain (and on his warped but addicting bond to the hero) some formal conversion is necessary, whereby he can be made utterly and wholly negative in our eyes, *negative and only negative*, the object of a kind of redeeming execration on our part. And at the same time, the hero, who has until now been holding back on purely moral grounds from accomplishing the final relieving and sanctifying act, must himself be changed into a person who has no inhibiting sense of propriety, who will do anything to rid the world of villainy in a forthright, dramatic way.

The systematic transformation I am invoking was labeled in 1956, by the sociologist Harold Garfinkel, as a "degradation ceremony." For Garfinkel, degradation ceremonies are inherently part of all societies, because in their routine features all societies provide the necessary conditions for them. And degradation, more than a mere change of status, is a material feature of the moral indignation to which as audiences we must be aroused before any filmic narrative, acting to produce such a ceremonial moment, can support "public denunciation," the requisite paradigm. We, of course, are the "public" implied here, since narratively speaking the hero can commit only the actions of which we tacitly approve. If we think of cinema as a modern replacement of the seventeenth- and eighteenth-century public space, the audience's moral evaluation of heroic and villainous action and its spectatorial presence now transpose the embodiment of the public execution into a purely mimetic affair. Symbols replace bodies, pictures of marks and degradations replace marks and degradations themselves. Of the actual transformation, Garfinkel writes:

> Destruction is intended literally. The transformation of identities is the destruction of one social object and the constitution of another. The transformation does not involve the substitution of one identity for another, with the terms of the old one loitering about like the overlooked parts of a fresh assembly, any more than the woman we see in the department-store window that turns out to be a dummy carries with it the possibilities of a woman. It is not that the old object has been overhauled; rather it is replaced by another. One declares, "*Now*, it was otherwise in the first place." (252)

A successful degradation requires both of the following elements: that the villain and what he does be removed from the everyday, rendered "out of the ordinary"; and that both perpetrator and event be typed, that is, made members of categories for which preferences can be demonstrated.

To demonstrate, let me take a signal case, Ridley Scott's *Hannibal* (2001). Near the conclusion, the clear-cut villain, Hannibal Lecter (Anthony Hopkins, in a trademark performance), having saved an eager young female FBI agent, Clarice Starling (Julianne Moore, assuming a role originated by Jodie Foster) from being mauled by wild boars, has brought her secretly to the lake house of one of her FBI colleagues, the slimy and abusive Paul Krendler (Ray Liotta), a man who has compromised Clarice's reputation and personal safety in order to use her as bait to catch Lecter. Having repeatedly abused Starling's colleagueship and trust, and in this way having kindled the ire of Lecter—who respects and rather likes Starling notwithstanding the fact that she has devoted her career to catching him—Krendler is unmistakably a moral reprobate who deserves punishment. Lecter, nothing if not a moralist in his own right, intends to be his executioner. Having been displayed earlier in this and also in the previous two films of the series devoted to him—*Manhunter* (Michael Mann, 1986) and *The Silence of the Lambs*—as being capable of horrendous and savage acts of brutality (yet acts which fail to mobilize our moral indignation because they are committed against abysmally evil characters deserving of vengeance or because his exceptional charm and social grace, not to say his astounding erudition, make him something of an object of wonder for us), Hannibal the cannibal has pounced upon Krendler and drugged him. At this point, Lecter moves, as Garfinkel puts it, *out of the everyday*, and also embeds himself and his action in a type. That is, rather than being precisely and only the person he is, doing precisely and only what he is doing, Hannibal Lecter becomes—thanks to the objectivity of Scott's camera and the blithe calmness of Hopkins's performance—a dark epitome of whom we can justifiably say, "I call upon all men to bear witness that he is not as he appears but is otherwise and *in essence* of a lower species" (Garfinkel 251). He becomes *degraded*.

Krendler is restrained in a wheelchair in his own dining room, wearing an FBI baseball cap and an expression of smug boredom, while Lecter busies himself preparing an elegant repast at tableside, as though this is a fabulously expensive restaurant. Soon, however, we discover that Krendler is not bored, but deep in the throes of Lecter's drugging. In his attenuation of gaze and direction of focus Lecter begins to become, even more than biologically or medically minded, actually machinic, like a willful robot assigned the task of carrying out an autopsy. With the barely conscious Starling—standing in for us—as his raptly attentive audience, he pulls off Krendler's baseball cap to reveal that he has surgically incised the man's scalp all around, just beneath the hairline. Now, with mocking delicacy, he lifts off the skull cap revealing the pink brain resting beneath. Krendler, narcotized, is ignorant of what is happening. (Dramaturgically speaking, it is the perfectly stable supporting performance by Liotta that gives the emotional fill to Hopkins's brutality.) With a scalpel, Lecter slices off a section of the agent's cerebrum and drops it delicately into a chafing dish prepared with sizzling butter and garlic. He stands diligently cooking the brain, in the distanced and professional manner of a three-star chef. Krendler says, with an enthusiasm that is nauseatingly genuine, "That smells great!" Lecter amiably offers him a taste, and gently places a piece of the cooked meat in the agent's willing mouth. (Starling gags.)

A moment later, he removes Krendler from the scene by tossing a dish cloth on top of the man's face: the face is only a repulsive thing, and the dish cloth will make it go away. What all this amounts to, from a witness's point of view, is not mere ravenous cannibalism, nor mere killing, but utter and replete objectification of the human, the turning of Krendler into conscious meat (yet meat that is not conscious of *itself* as meat); the conversion of Krendler into a cannibal of the self; and all merely for Starling's—which is to say, our—momentary edification, nay, instruction. (It is a public execution.) Rather than being merely the man who is doing all this here, now, at this diegetic moment, Lecter has become the *sort* of man who does *a thing like this*: the act is typified as extravagant, conscienceless evil and its perpetrator as diabolical. If until now Lecter has been either crazy or eccentric in his peculiar tastes, fetishes, and observations, he is now not merely a person with some derangements but someone who is less than a person only masquerading as a person. This degradation accomplished in our sight, we are prepared to see him subjected to the most intensive and painful of punishments (still another public execution, even more brutal) but, of course, this film ends without offering that pleasure.

Noble Degradation

A concluding comment about the degradation of the villain: typically it is performed, or at least boldly attempted, by the film's heroic protagonist, who is established prior to this apotheosis as a symbol of all that is estimable and pure. The type of nobility shown in the hero, and his relationship with the villain he abolishes, depends on social structure. In societies formed around what Max Weber called "traditional" authority, the hero's strength derives from monarchy, which is to say, from divinity; and the villain's villainy springs from the netherworld or its earthly manifestations (296). Degradation of the villain means conversion or banishment to the realm of darkness, and can be accomplished with a swift stroke if emphasis is given to the triumphal redemption of the hero, who gains light by eliminating his foe. The increase in light can *be* the elimination of the foe: the hero's victory can stand in, onstage or onscreen, for the villain's demise. This is pretty much what happens at the end of *Star Wars*, when as the malevolent Darth Vader shuttles off to the black infinities of space, wiped from the screen, Luke Skywalker shines with his friends in triumphal glory. Luke's heroism derives from his love-link to Leia, and hers, being royal, is primally divine. That the chthonic Vader is not dead opens the door to the sequels we have all enjoyed (and then regretted), but that he vanishes into the black suffices to eradicate his sign as we are watching it.

A second possibility, Weber's "charismatic" authority, promotes our attachment to the hero purely on the basis of his charm: he is attractive to the crowd, and he is beloved. To mobilize him, the villain must be made not cosmologically or metaphysically negative but morally unattractive, unlovable. In Michael Curtiz and William Keighley's classic *The Adventures of Robin Hood* (1938), with both the serpentine Prince John (Claude Rains) and the wolfish Sir Guy of Gisbourne (Basil Rathbone), twin purveyors of violence and greed in merry olde England, what begins in the film as a kind of unctuous politeness and smarmy, cultivated superiority turns to abject greed and desperation in the conclusion. When they lose their posture they become unsalvageable, and Robin's (Errol Flynn's) smile seems to broaden and whiten at the same time. The cur grits his teeth before being rejected, this to enhance the shine of the hero even more in his adorer's eyes.

The age of postfeudal capitalism has led to "bureaucratic" authority and, as so many scholars have noted, the modern sensibility. With massive population increase and the development of urbanization and mechanized travel, a vast circulating population is continually subject to modes of systematization. The hero becomes a member of, or adjunct to, a police or intelligence operation, nowadays typically hooked into a diffuse international communications network that enables instantaneous point-to-point dialogue from anywhere, whether one is in motion or not. Villains likewise have fluid technical capacity and are joined to well-organized syndicates or nefarious invisible organizations. As with so much else in modernity, defining and punishing villainy are provisional, situational acts, subject to the prevailing winds of power. At the end of *North by Northwest*, then, it is a federal governmental agency, the Forest Service, not a lone hero, that uses sanctioned violence to terminate the villain's power.

At the end of Christopher Nolan's *The Dark Knight* (2008), Good and Evil come to the stalemate that is entirely predictable when technological and bureaucratic power fuse on both sides, the malevolent Joker (Heath Ledger) finally pronouncing upon his nemesis Batman (Christian Bale) an ultimate curse as he dangles at a height from the hero's outstretched lifeline: "You need me as much as I need you." Given that in modernity, identities are occupational, the villain, like any other character, has power to trade himself in at any point for someone less offensive, less problematic. He is only really bad *now*. History and the chain of misdeeds for which in more traditional narratives the villain must stand, evaporate in the blur of perpetual movement.

In this modern light, it is a chilling task to contemplate what, if he had not killed himself in 1945, even that epitome of negativity Adolf Hitler might have become in our globalized bureaucratic world, given the apparent abilities of threatening leaders to hide from those who seek them out, and the flattening, sanctimonious, nonpunitive eye of discursive critique (even such as this), and the apparently limitless capabilities of the spin doctors to relabel the murderous and antisocial among us as victims themselves, wounded brothers under the skin, potential heroes tragically warped in their youth.

Notes

1. It was not until the mid- to late nineteenth century that executions were withdrawn from public view; indeed, in Paris as of 1633 executions by torchlight at night were legally banned with the effect that they were always predictably brightly lit and easy to observe (Berthelot 930).

Works Cited

Ackroyd, Peter. *London: The Biography*. New York: Vintage, 2001. Print.
Agamben, Giorgio. *Infancy and History: On the Destruction of Experience*. Trans. Liz Heron. London: Verso, 1993. Print.

Berthelot, André, et al. *La Grande Encyclopédie Inventaire Raisonné des Sciences, des Lettres et des Arts.* Vol. 16. Paris: Socieeté Anonyme de la Grande Encyclopédie, 1886–1902. Print.

Dickens, Charles. Letter to *The Times*, 13 November 1849. Web. 16 May 2013. <http://charlesdickenspage.com/public_execution.html>

Duff, Charles. *A Handbook on Hanging.* 1928. New York: New York Review Books, 2001. Print.

Dumas, Alexandre. *The Count of Monte Cristo.* Trans. Robin Buss. London: Penguin, 2003 [1844–45]. Print.

———. *The Black Tulip.* Trans. Robin Buss. London: Penguin, 2003 [1865]. Print.

Foucault, Michel. *Discipline and Punish: The Birth of the Prison.* Trans. Alan Sheridan. New York: Pantheon, 1977. Print.

Foxe, J. *Actes and Monumentes of the Latter and Perillous Days Touching Matters of the Church.* London: J. Daye, 1563. Print.

Garfinkel, Harold. "Conditions of Successful Degradation Ceremonies." *American Journal of Sociology* 61 (March 1956): 420–24. Rpt. in *Toward a Sociology of Education.* Ed. John Beck, Chris Jenks, and Nellie Keddie. New York: Transaction, 1978. 250–57. Print.

Gunning, Tom. "Flickers: On Cinema's Power for Evil." *BAD: Infamy, Darkness, Evil, and Slime on Screen.* Ed. Murray Pomerance. Albany: State U of New York P, 2004. 21–37. Print.

Mandeville, B., M.D. *An Enquiry into the Causes of the Frequent Executions at Tyburn and a Proposal for Some Regulations Concerning Felons in Prison, and the Good Effects to Be Expected from Them.* London: J. Roberts, 1725. Print.

McGowen, Randall. "Civilizing Punishments: The End of the Public Execution in England." *Journal of British Studies* 33.3 (July 1994): 257–82. Print.

Ray, James. *A Compleat History of the Rebellion.* Bristol: S. and F. Farley, 1750. Print.

Sebald, W. G. *On the Natural History of Destruction.* Trans. Anthea Bell. Toronto: Vintage, 2004. Print.

Thackeray, William Makepeace. "Going to See a Man Hanged." *Fraser's Magazine for Town and Country* 22.128 (August 1840): 150–58. Print.

Weber, Max. *From Max Weber: Essays in Sociology.* Ed. and trans. Hans Gerth and C. Wright Mills. New York: Oxford UP, 1969. Print.

7

From Bad to Good and Back to Bad Again?

Cult Cinema and Its Unstable Trajectory

JAMIE SEXTON

In their introduction to *The Cult Film Reader*, Ernest Mathijs and Xavier Mendik itemize a number of characteristics that tend to be associated with cult films, including the condition of "badness":

> cult films are [often] considered bad, aesthetically or morally. Of particular interest are those films being valued for their 'ineptness' . . . often placing them in some kind of opposition to the 'norm' or mainstream. (2)

This chapter does not follow Mathijs and Mendik to investigate the cult status that (some) "bad" films achieve but more broadly seeks to track some of the ways in which the term "cult" itself has taken on particular connotations—both negative and positive—when used in the realm of film culture and, by doing so, to examine some of its contextually shifting uses. Nor is this chapter an exhaustive historical investigation of the applications and implications of "cult" within film culture (such a project has yet to be undertaken) but rather an analysis of the semantic shifts that "cult" has undergone, which can contribute to a fuller understanding of a term that has often proven to be somewhat bewildering.

In this chapter, I contend that the term "cult" has, on a very general level, undergone a shift from being a largely negative connotation ("bad") to a more positive or at least value-neutral one ("good") but has more recently become negative again in some quarters (back to "bad"). Throughout, I shall make some tentative speculations about why the term has undergone these changes, and also make some comments which point towards the difficulty of actually pinpointing "cultism" in relation to film culture (something returned to at the end of the chapter).

Bad Cults: The Negative Connotations of Religion

In *Fan Cultures*, Matt Hills explores discourses of cult in relation to media fandom and stresses that etymology, sociology, and history need to be considered in investigating how the term "cult" has spilled over into definitions of media patterns (119–27). Although Hills does trace some of the ways in which cult has been used within religious discourses, he omits the *historical* emergence of cult as a specific media term. In the interwar period the use of "cult" in relation to film culture was predominantly as a negative term. This was an era when a religious term was employed occasionally to refer to film matters. As the word was wielded by a number of intellectuals—including, Siegfried Kracauer, Walter Benjamin, and Harry Allan Potamkin—who perceived religion and mysticism as negative social forces, then it too became negatively encoded in relation to film.[1]

The first two of these writers—Kracauer and Benjamin—were associated with the Frankfurt School, which tended to see religion as a force that hindered social progress through mystification and which thus worked against people actually recognizing their "real" sociohistorical conditions. In this sense, religion was a form of dupery, a force that kept people in their place through consoling them with illusory rewards to be conferred outside of everyday existence. In a similar manner to the way religion was seen as functioning, the cinema was viewed as providing the predominantly working masses with pleasurable consolations in a sphere removed from everyday existence (through its unreality, its glamor, its illusory mechanisms), and which thus blunted their potential for recognizing the deeper roots of their social existence, and therefore contributing to the continuation of the status quo.

Kracauer used the term "cult" to describe how, in many of Berlin's picture palaces, the workers who made up the majority of the audience were distracted from critical thought through a combination of the films themselves and the ways that they were programmed. While he thought that films were potentially radical in offering a series of disconnected elements that mirrored the disorder of society—which could be used to allow working-class audiences to grasp the reality of social conditions—such disorder was masked by a veneer of organic coherence. This occurred within the films (an orderly narrative leading to a resolution) and in the way the films were part of a wider, seemingly coherent, program. Kracauer believed that this process aligned mass cinema with high art insofar as both cultural spheres separated art from everyday life and therefore constituted a sacred, self-contained space which blocked analysis of social conditions. Cult was thus employed by Kracauer to make comparisons between the reactionary processes of Berlin's picture palaces, high art, and religion. He wrote that the picture palace was directed towards "the lofty and the *sacred* as if designed to accommodate works of eternal significance—just one step short of burning votive candles" (327).

Benjamin's perspective on cult differed from Kracauer's in that, while Benjamin would again use cult as a generally negative term, he thought that the development of cinema as a commercial art form was moving away from cultic qualities. For Benjamin, an original work of art contained "auratic" qualities in that it was connected to the authenticity (and authority) of the work. With the introduction of mechanical reproduction, this notion of the aura was placed into doubt by "substituting a plurality of copies for a unique existence" (852). Benjamin saw the auratic status of the artwork as a negative quality, binding art to tradition, whereas the shattering of the aura could lead to art playing a more politically central role in the age of mechanical reproduction: "the instant the criterion of authenticity ceases to be applicable to artistic production, the total function of art is reversed. Instead of being based on ritual, it begins to be based on another practice—politics" (855). However, while Benjamin did largely praise cinema for moving away from cultist trappings, he also noted how residual cult values did persist within the medium, arguing that the industry's construction of the cult of the star tended to replace the spell of the aura with the "phoney spell of the commodity" (860).

Potamkin also used the word "cult" negatively in relation to film culture, but he did so relative to aspects of "minority," rather than mass culture. In particular, he took interest in sections of Parisian cinema culture, where minority film culture—in the form of ciné-clubs and film societies and associated small publications—flourished. For Potamkin, cult referred to a "faddist" mentality within this cultural sphere. He referred to *The Cabinet of Dr. Caligari* (Robert Wiene, 1920) as a cult film, but the majority of his discussion was devoted to the enthusiastic followings shown for Chaplin, Disney, and popular melodrama. While Potamkin castigated uncritical thinking, he also admonished those many viewers who sought "identity with popular taste," which he considered to be a "form of intellectual selling-out" (28).

In accusing cults of "never being self-critical" and thus "never objective," Potamkin used cult in a quasi-religious sense, but his discussion centered on a more unconventional minority of film culture (thus matching the growing connotations of cult with unorthodox forms of religious organization and behavior). Here, cult was again wielded in order to create a distance between the writer and a condemned group, but Potamkin wrote about a group whom he associated with: cineastes on the fringe of film culture. Thus, where the distance between Kracauer and his targets was obvious (the intellectual criticizing the masses) with Potamkin it was less so. He created *inner distinctions* by labeling cult viewers as the unthinking segments of a minority community, in contrast to people (like himself) who engaged more individually with films and were less swayed by fads and fashions.

Potamkin was a contributor to the influential film journal *Close Up*, and it may be no surprise that his position in some regards echoed an editorial published there two years before (in 1930) by Kenneth Macpherson. While Macpherson did not explicitly mention the word "cult," he referred to a similar phenomenon—faddism within sections of Parisian film culture—and he used the term "movieosophy" to describe the process. He wrote that "[exhibitors] simply won't show you anything but mediocre American films in the French specialist salles just now, just because they're *dans le movement*" (3). While "cult" is absent from his editorial, Macpherson did employ occasional religious metaphors to describe the trend, as in his contention that these audiences "want their ritual." And, like Potamkin, he accused such audiences of unthinkingly bowing to particular fads within minority film culture rather than actually making their own minds up about films. Once again, the cult crowd was seen as an other in the midst: a population who, in their desire to flout convention, merely constituted a different, but no less formulaic, cultural grouping.

Macpherson's omission of the word "cult" suggests that it was not used extensively in film culture at the time, and also points towards a difficulty involved in historically mapping cultism. Does one only pay attention to actual uses of the word, or does one consider attitudes, behaviors, and so on that seem to relate to conceptions of cult within cinema? If the latter is accepted, then we need to think about whether to provide a map of how cult was considered at the time or whether we *retrospectively* apply more modern conceptions of cult to past practices. The latter approach has, for example, been undertaken by Greg Taylor in his historical analysis of cultism and camp within postwar American film. If, however, we were to adopt cultism as outlined (explicitly) by Potamkin and (implicitly) by Macpherson, then the critics analyzed by Taylor would be considered the opposite of cultists: they would be considered too individualist and not "faddish" enough, thus alerting us to the instability of its connotations.

Perhaps because of the relative scarcity of the use of the actual term "cult" in film discourse during the interwar period, the era before World War II is often omitted from historical investigations of cultism. Yet this era may be identified with a number of practices (beyond those already documented) that demonstrate cultism *avant la lettre*, most notably the Surrealists, on account of their continual provocations and unusual viewing procedures. In addition, there is further evidence in *Close Up* of approaches that could be considered cultist from a more modern perspective. In particular, a column—entitled "Film Curiosities"—featured in the back pages of the journal (mostly in volume 4 from 1929) appears to neatly fit the cultist mold. Written by Oswell Blakeston, this column recounted (cultlike) audience experiences of:

1. Films that were so obscure that no other information about them was easy to come by,

2. Films that had suffered censorship problems and which the writer was viewing in an uncut form (tellingly, these were often in a Paris theater),

3. Films that were forgotten but which featured notable stars, and

4. Films that contained risqué content.

An interest in this type of film material—obscure, censored, forgotten, and morally "bad"—typifies an investment in cult cinema and the cultist's desire to discover material residing off the beaten track. It is also notable that Blakeston does not claim that these films are great works, but he does find interesting material within each example because of its novelty. In this approach Blakeston develops a somewhat idiosyncratic stance and style, searching films for scraps of pleasure and interest, even developing his own cultish attachments to obscure characters (e.g., he seems to develop a fondness for German actress Valeska Gert, particularly in relation to her "salacious" dances) and reporting on a midnight screening of *Thérèse Requin* (Jacques Feyder, 1928) at the Shaftsbury Avenue Pavilion in London.

Postwar Shifts

Mark Jancovich (among others) has argued that the postwar era is frequently identified as the period in which cult cinema emerges. This is also the period that has been identified by Taylor as when cultism emerged in film criticism (specifically within an American context). And Justin Smith, in a thesis on British cult cinema, has argued that the currency of "cult" as a critical term emerged in the 1960s, especially in relation to new American film criticism. Smith mentions that cult "almost certainly had earlier and wider usage across popular culture" (*Cult Films* 12), but it seems that the term began to be used in relation to film culture more frequently, if still only rather fitfully, during the postwar period.

Many uses of the word "cult" after World War II tend to follow the negative trends identified above in the 1920s and 1930s, although the religious connotations tend to be more implicit than before. The two main ways in which the term was used negatively were (1) in relation to those groups who championed marginal films, and (2) with respect to those who intellectually assessed and promoted populist films. The former referred to critics who advanced an appreciation of avant-garde films, as well as more "difficult" European art films. In 1954, Gerard Pratley dismissed such groups as a "small cult" of film society frequenters who championed obscure fare—such as the filmmakers Jean Cocteau, Maya Deren, and Hans Richter—in an elitist manner. Pratley wrote that many of these films were often baffling and even poor but that there was a "cult of unintelligibility" current among critics who praised such work and thus mistook unusualness and absurdity for profundity and progressivism. He proceeded to argue that:

> There is . . . a tendency on the part of some individuals to support such works simply because of the learned superiority which comes with proclaiming their enthusiasm for these bewildering puzzle pieces. This, in turn, is prompted by a fear that in disavowing these distortionist fallacies they will reveal their lack of profundity, be looked down upon with scorn, and ultimately be rejected from intellectual circles. (305)

Cultism once again refers to a kind of herd mentality, one which confers superiority—albeit of an anxious kind—and which hinders more individualistic reactions to a work.

The second mode of cultism identified by critics in the 1950s and 1960s also tended to be negative, but instead of situating cultism in small groups gathering around obscure films, it focused on individual thinkers taking popular/populist film entertainment in a serious manner, judging as art what was previously considered mere entertainment. Such a view is certainly evident in an essay by Eric Larrabee, who noted in critical writings of the day a "popular cult of pop culture" that encompassed film and other entertainment arts. Importantly, one of the books considered was Gilbert Seldes's *The Seven Lively Arts*, first published in 1924. Seldes's book was said by Larrabee to stand up well, and its author was singled out as a seminal figure in this cultist pursuit of finding serious value within popular culture.

The concept of auteurism was also associated with the "popular cult of pop culture," and (as it became increasingly influential among critics) was attacked by some for its cultist qualities. Among the many (and varied) critiques of auteurism was the accusation that it promoted a *cult of the director*, and thus echoed André Bazin's criticism of many of his *Cahiers du cinéma* colleagues for promoting "an aesthetic personality cult" (145). An accusation typifying such critiques was made by then *Film Quarterly* editor Ernest Callenbach:

> The cult of the director is like the weed-killers which began as plant-growth stimulators: too much of some benefits can prove fatal. The excesses of *auteur* criticism bring passably good directors into disrepute by unreasonably plugging their bad films. (17)

Cult once again was being used to refer to blind devotion of an individual, a type of approach that diluted the critical mind. Nevertheless, despite a number of critiques and countercritiques being penned by pro- and anti-auteurist critics, it is interesting to note that the cultist implications of auteurism were not always denied by its proponents. Rather, it was a term that could be worn as a badge of pride. Thus Andrew Sarris titled his 1970 collection of articles *Confessions of a Cultist*, which suggested guilt ("confessions"), but proceeded to explain the positives of such a (cultist) position, which he believed proved beneficial to the analysis and appreciation of the cinema.

While one needs to be cautious about oversimplifying the extremely complex terrain of discourses that employed the term "cult" in relation to film culture, the postwar period seems an era in which the values of cult begin to undergo a significant change. It is not that cult was never used positively before the late 1960s, or that it was only used positively thereafter, but its generalized employment does seem to edge from a predominantly negative use towards a more commonly positive uptake. In the 1970s cult was not merely used to describe elements of film culture: it became common to find references to cult movies and cult films. In this sense, a tentative argument can be made that the emergence of cult films was made possible by ironic tactics (such as those noted in relation to Sarris), which paved the way for a more positive conception of the term. In this sense, the cult film was born from irony.

A relatively early article musing on the phenomenon of a particular cult film, *Casablanca* (Michael Curtiz, 1942), was featured in *Films and Filming* in 1974 (figure 7.1). Written by Barry Day, it puts forward several reasons for *Casablanca*'s cult status, including its production history, textual material, and social relevance. *Casablanca* is first identified as cult because it has surpassed expectations to remain relevant over the years, with ongoing screenings at repertory cinemas and on college campuses. Among the reasons provided for *Casablanca*'s continued appeal (some of which are informed by viewer's comments) include:

1. Humphrey Bogart's star image which is given additional power through the way in which the film subtly plays with his persona (a hardened cynic in control, but here with an idealistic undertow).

2. The troubled production background of the film (screenwriter Howard Koch having to finish the script after the commencement of shooting) which sharply contrasts with the tidiness of the finished product, as though the film was touched by some kind of magic.

Figure 7.1. Cult favorites Rick (Humphrey Bogart) and Ilsa (Ingrid Bergman) in *Casablanca* (1942). Courtesy Warner Bros. / The Kobal Collection / Jack Woods.

3. The way in which some of the film's themes resonate with the contemporary social climate.

For Day, a postidealist era (in which the radical utopianism of the 1960s had faded into disillusionment) encouraged audiences to gain nostalgic solace from viewing the film; it offered an imaginary resolution to a vastly complex society. Rick Blaine (Bogart) is said to "synthesize a solution" and give "expression to idealism." Day concludes: "until we come up with some real alternative outlet, there is no reason why Sam shouldn't go on playing again and again as time goes by . . ." (24).

Nostalgia is perhaps the key theme feeding through Day's article, and it is important to think about the emergence of the cult film as a definable entity within a period when nostalgia for classical Hollywood filmmaking was on the rise. This could be contrasted to both the contemporary film industry and social reality as something distinctly other, a lost world that provided refuge from current troubles. Kracauer would have likely condemned this process as deflecting attention from social reality, but in Day's article such judgments are absent. Actually, there is a sense in which this other world of easy solutions feeds into the present; it can energize idealism through vicarious experience by showing audiences how cynicism can be overcome and action undertaken.

The increasing attention to the phenomenon of cult movies was not totally free of evaluative assessments, but these did tend to become less prominent, displaced by a concern to investigate the properties of such films, e.g., the exhibition and reception patterns that gave rise to a cult film and the reasons why particular films could be considered cult. A number of factors can be speculatively linked to the emergence of more positive attitudes towards film cultism, including: (1) the breakup of the studio system, (2) the general broadening of intellectual cultural inquiry beyond "high art," and (3) the significant social changes that were occurring.[2]

The first of these—the breakup of the studio system—led to the proliferation of niches in the sense of an increase in independent cinemas offering specialist fare, which could include reruns, art house, exploitation, and avant-garde/underground (even if these were not always easily demarcated). Affordable 16 mm projection equipment also led to increasing college and private film society screenings. The more specialized nature of audiences was, therefore, a crucial factor in the identification of cult viewing (Ray 137–43).

The late 1950s and 1960s saw an increased intellectual interest in popular culture, with film gaining greater respectability in light of the emergence of television as the new mass medium. Film was now being approached with greater regularity as an artistic medium, a disposition bolstered by the greater frequency of non-Hollywood productions available during this era. Allied to this broad development was a set of social changes that were crucial to the more positive embrace of cultism. These included the increased identification with, and stratification of, specific social groups—with the teenager and the counterculture being of particular importance to the recognition of niche audiences. Many such groups were labeled "deviant" in social and/or political terms, therefore imbuing them with subcultural status. The ways in which countercultural groups tended to incorporate stigmatized labels and twist their meanings, so that they became a positive badge of identity, relates to strategies of irony that lead to a change in the evaluative status of the term "cult." In addition, religion and mysticism became increasingly valued by some subcultural groups. This was particularly evident in the reaction to science and "progress" in some quarters and an embrace of religious and spiritual values, including a revival of interest in the occult (see Lachman).

Into the Present: The Return of Negative Cult?

The more positive approach to cultism that emerged in the postwar period and led to the establishment of the cult film paved the way for a large increase in writing on cult cinema from the 1980s onwards. In academic and journalistic articles cult cinema became both a topic of concentrated coverage and a frequently employed, generic term often used to refer to strange, offbeat, or quirky films. Articles analyzing the cult phenomenon of *The Rocky Horror Picture Show* (Jim Sharman, 1975) were published in the early 1980s (see Austin; Siegel), and the decade saw the publication of the first edition of Danny Peary's influential *Cult Movies*, a guide to one hundred films that further established cult cinema as a distinctive category. Other notable publications included Stuart Samuels's and J. Hoberman and Jonathan Rosenbaum's analyses of the midnight movie phenomenon. These works focused on audience reactions, as well as specific exhibition contexts characterized by (1) intense repeat viewing rituals (in the case of *The Rocky Horror Picture Show* accompanied by interactive audience performances) and (2) the screening of films in run-down areas, often at midnight.

While audience reactions and marginal distribution and/or exhibition patterns were key to the construction of cult, other approaches—such as Umberto Eco's study of *Casablanca* and cult cinema—attempted to explain *why* certain films gave rise to cultic appropriations. Eco argued that *intertextuality* was a particularly important aspect of the cult film, contending that *Casablanca* consisted of a large number of characters and situations that drew upon archetypal characters and situations from other films (208). The focus on intertextuality as an important component of cult texts would become particularly noted into the 1990s.

Two other important cult-related texts were also published in the 1980s that pointed to further generic connotations of cult cinema. These were Michael Wheldon's *The Psychotronic Encyclopedia of Film* and Vivian Vale and Andrea Juno's *Incredibly Strange Films*. Both books provided guides to films—largely exploitation productions—which often fell below the radar of mainstream film publications and were considered "bad," i.e., deviant, strange, or trashy. While these books only mention "cult" occasionally, their approaches and selection of films would become influential within cult cinema studies and culture. Their attempts to challenge taste and redeem films that had often been considered disreputable, for example, were addressed in Jeffrey Sconce's influential analysis of what he deemed "paracinema," which subsequently became an established subset of cult cinema studies (" 'Trashing' the Academy"). Exploitation and "trash" cinema, meanwhile, would increasingly become intertwined with the identity of cult cinema.

From the 1990s onwards cult cinema became even more widely referred to and studied. Important academic books (Telotte; Mendik and Harper; Jancovich et al.; Mathijs and Mendik; Smith) would continue to focus on cult cinema as a reception-based phenomenon and/or a textual/generic form of cinema. Previously mentioned concepts such as intertextuality, exploitation, irony, nostalgia, and intense audience attachment to films continued to be important, while other concepts were employed to make sense of cult films. For example, Barry Keith Grant wrote that "transgressive" textual markers were an important part of the appeal of cult movies and could be detected in a film's content, its attitude, or its style. This idea of transgression also linked to the reception of cult films as many such works were sought out by audiences looking for something different from the mainstream. As such, Jancovich has argued that cult films are taken up by audiences who discursively mobilize "subcultural ideologies" to distinguish themselves from "ordinary" filmgoers.

The increased attention paid towards cult cinema has led to it being recognized as a distinct area of film culture. There are now a number of courses on cult cinema taught at universities across the world and the term itself is used by an increasing number of people. Yet this does not always mean that it is easily understood or that there is a general agreement on its meanings. The imprecision of cult cinema is exacerbated by historical changes, in particular technological changes such as the growth of home-viewing platforms and the rise of the Internet. This has led to more people using the word "cult" and thus more films being labeled cult films. It has also allowed—through online sharing and shopping, as well as a growth of released titles on DVD and related formats—easier access to a range of films. Further, this has been recognized by film producers and marketers, who design or market films as cult in a self-conscious manner. Hills has commented on this process, arguing that "cult is 'in' the mainstream now, within its terms of reference even if the two labels haven't fully collapsed together" ("Cult Cinema").

The gradual mainstreaming of cult has led some commentators to return to more negative assessments, and to question its continued validity. Justin Smith, for example, has indicated that we now may have moved into a "post-cult" culture:

> It may be no stretch of the imagination to suggest that, by all accounts, we are now living in a post-cult world. The dark underbelly of genuine cult practice, with its midnight screenings, seedy grindhouse theatres, dodgy prints and subversive glamour, has been exposed by the twin beams of commercial niche marketing and literary criticism, from popular journalism to academic theory. (Rev. of *Donnie Darko*)

Elsewhere Smith claims that "subcultural distinction has been elided through hegemonic processes to the point that the cult is almost totally recuperated ideologically, and reproduced commercially to feed the personalised media culture" (*Withnail* 215).

For Smith, cult is now a historical signifier, pointing towards a period in film culture that doesn't exist anymore. Others have also broadly concurred with this argument, linking the continued "co-option" of cult by commercial agencies to its increasing irrelevance as a conceptual term. This is illustrated in the following two quotes, both of which come from a *Cineaste* special edition on cult cinema:

> Cult, like the now innocuous concept of "alternative" when affixed to a life style or a consumption choice, is simply a term for a product or activity that can be pitched by commercial agencies as existing outside the mainstream. (Stanfield 49)

> In its original form . . . "cultism" evoked an esoteric sense of social, cultural, and esthetic exile, a type of distinction difficult to maintain once every film became available to every viewer, and once domestic viewing replaced theatrical screenings as the privileged form of spectatorship. (Sconce, "Cult Cinema" 48)

Such responses seem problematic in that they privilege evaluative, unexamined assumptions over an investigation of how the term "cult" has operated across different contexts. Sconce's contention that hunting obscure movies is now a thing of the past, for example, relies on an exaggerated conception of cultural trends. It is certainly unarguable that it is easier to get ahold of obscure films than previously, but this is only the case for particular types of people (those who have knowledge of such "obscure" films, a knowledge which also depends on one's cultural capital). Sconce seems to generalize from his personal experience when it is surely the case that, while cult(ism) has proliferated, it has not been *totally* mainstreamed. A large number of film viewers are unaware of the growing number of independent and exploitation fare that is now readily available. Sconce privileges *access* as the litmus test of cultism, but equally important are issues such as knowledge, awareness, and expertise.

These quotations also point to a nostalgic harking back to a bygone era, contrasting a previous "authentic" era to a contemporary climate in which cult is merely an artificial construct. As a result, there is a yearning for a time when cult was more rarefied, when cult was less commercial, when cult *meant something*. As this chapter has indicated, however, there has never been an agreed-upon, fixed meaning of cult. Further, there has never really been a type of film/viewing experience that has been considered to be "genuinely" cult. The term has been used to refer to different types of films and different types of film viewing experiences throughout its historical adoption within film culture.

It is somewhat ironic that nostalgia, a crucial value leading to more positive approaches to cultism, has now returned to feed into its negative dismissal. Critics who hark back to a lost golden era of cult are, in a sense, attempting to freeze the concept in time. Yet cult persists: it continues to be wielded by a new generation of audiences, critics, and other actors who participate within the realm of film culture. Cult has retained much of its previous connotations, but it has also mutated across historical contexts. To argue that we are now living in a postcult culture is implicitly valuing the critic's own nostalgic perspective and devaluing the experiences of newer generations.

Rather than merely engaging in evaluative dismissals of cult and cultism based on nostalgically tinted assessments, it is important to take a more balanced approach to the subject. This should involve recognition of the instability of cult as a concept within film culture across contexts and awareness that, though its ambiguities may have increased, it has never been a straightforward term. As academics we should be allowed to engage in debates about the meanings—and problems—of the term, but we should also combine such a critical approach with a more observational awareness of its discursive "mobilization, and its varying interpretations by audiences" (Le Guern 4). In fact, I would argue that the study of cult cinema needs to be expanded. Hitherto, study of the subject has actually been relatively limited in terms of its contextual coverage, mainly focused on Anglo-American reception and weighted towards the younger male demographic. Study of cult outside of these contexts has been relatively rare, which in turn reinforces assumptions about cult cinema. In order to move beyond entrenched positions—both positive and negative, the good and the bad—there is still much work to do in this subject area.

Notes

1. In the interwar period, it should be noted, one of the most influential considerations of cult was written by Ernst Troeltsch, who described a it as a small, transient collective based around mystical and spiritual beliefs that did not constitute a religious organization in the conventional sense (Campbell 375–76).

2. I refer here primarily to the U.S. context, with some attention also paid to the United Kingdom. This is not, however, to privilege such regions: I am aware that there is more work to be done on cult cinema outside of these contexts.

Works Cited

Austin, Bruce. "Portrait of a Cult Film Audience: *The Rocky Horror Picture Show.*" *Journal of Popular Communication* 31 (Spring 1981): 43–54. Print.

Bazin, André. "La Politique Des Auteurs." *The French New Wave: Critical Landmarks*. Ed. Peter Graham and Ginnette Vincendeau. London: BFI, 2009. 130–48. Print.

Benjamin, Walter. "The Work of Art in the Age of Mechanical Reproduction." *Film Theory and Criticism: Introductory Readings*. Ed. Gerald Mast and Marshall Cohen. Oxford: Oxford UP, 1979. 848–70. Print.

Blakeston, Oswell. "Comment Review." *Close Up* 4.2 (1929): 72–74. Print.

———. "Comment Review." *Close Up* 4.3 (1929): 74–75. Print.

———. "Film Curiosities." *Close Up* 4.3 (1929): 91–94. Print.

———. "Film Curiosities." *Close Up* 4.5 (1929): 80–81. Print.

———. "Film Curiosities." *Close Up* 4.6 (1929): 80–83. Print.

Callenbach, Ernest. "The Auteur Policy." *Film Quarterly* 17.1 (Autumn 1963): 57. Print.

Campbell, Colin. "Clarifying the Cult." *British Journal of Sociology* 28.3 (September 1977): 375–88. Print.

Day, Barry. "The Cult Movies: *Casablanca.*" *Films & Filming* (August 1974): 20–24. Print.

Eco, Umberto. *Travels in Hyperreality*. London: Picador, 1986. Print.

Grant, Barry Keith. "Science-Fiction Double Feature: Ideology in the Cult Film." *The Cult Film Experience: Beyond All Reason*. Ed. J. P. Telotte. Austin: U of Texas P, 1991. 122–37. Print.

Hills, Matt. *Fan Cultures*. London: Routledge, 2002. Print.

———. "Cult Cinema: A Critical Symposium (Web Edition)." *Cineaste* 34.1 (Winter 2008). Web. 16 May 2013. <http://www.cineaste.com/articles/cult-film-a-critical-symposium>

Hoberman, J., and Jonathan Rosenbaum. *Midnight Movies*. New York: Da Capo, 1983. Print.

Jancovich, Mark. "Cult Fictions: Cult Movies, Subcultural Capital and the Production of Cultural Distinctions." *Cultural Studies* 16.2 (2002): 306–22. Print.

———, Antonio Lázaro Reboll, Julian Stringer, and Andy Willis, eds. *Defining Cult Movies: The Cultural Politics of Oppositional Taste*. Manchester: Manchester UP, 2003. Print.

Kracauer, Siegfried. "Cult of Distraction: On Berlin's Picture Palaces." Mathijs and Mendik, 382–85. Print.

Lachman, Gary. *Turn Off Your Mind: The Mystic Sixties and the Dark Side of the Age of Aquarius*. London: Sidgwick & Jackson, 2001. Print.

Larrabee, Eric. "The Popular Cult of Pop Culture." *American Quarterly* 10.3 (Autumn 1958): 372–74. Print.

Le Guern, Philippe. "Toward a Constructivist Approach to Media Cults." *Cult Television*. Ed. Sara Gwenllian-Jones and Roberta E. Pearson. Minneapolis: U of Minnesota P, 2004. 3–25. Print.

Macpherson, Kenneth. "As Is." *Close Up* 6.1 (1930): 1–6. Print.

Mathijs, Ernest, and Xavier Mendik. "Editorial Introduction: What Is Cult Film?" Mathijs and Mendik, 1–11. Print

———, eds. *The Cult Film Reader*. New York: Open UP, 2007. Print.

Mendik, Xavier, and Graeme Harper, eds. *Unruly Pleasures: The Cult Film and its Critics*. Godalming: FAB Press, 2000. Print.

Peary, Danny. *Cult Movies: The Classics, the Sleepers, the Weird and the Wonderful*. New York: Gramercy, 1981. Print.

Potamkin, Harry Allan. "Film Cults." Mathijs and Mendik 25–28. Print.

Pratley, Gerard. "The Cult of the Unintelligible." *The Quarterly of Film Radio and Television* 8.3 (Spring 1954): 302–06. Print.

Ray, Robert B. *A Certain Tendency of the Hollywood Cinema, 1930–1980*. Princeton: Princeton UP, 1985. Print.

Samuels, Stuart. *Midnight Movies*. New York: Macmillan, 1983. Print.

Sarris, Andrew. *Confessions of a Cultist: On the Cinema, 1955–1969*. New York: Simon and Schuster, 1970. Print.

Sconce, Jeffrey. "'Trashing' the Academy: Taste, Excess and an Emerging Politics of Cinematic Style." *Screen* 36.4 (1995): 371–93. Print.

———. "Cult Cinema: A Critical Symposium." *Cineaste* 34.1 (Winter 2008): 48–49. Print.

Siegel, Mark. "*The Rocky Horror Picture Show*: More than a Lip Service." *Science Fiction Studies* 7.3 (November 1980): 305–12. Print.

Smith, Justin. *Cult Films and Film Cults in British Cinema 1968–86*. PhD Thesis: U of Portsmouth, 2006. Print.

———. "Review of Geoff King's *Donnie Darko*." *Screening the Past* 23 (2008). Web. <http://www.latrobe.edu.au/screeningthepast/23/donnie-darko.html>

———. *Withnail and Us: Cult Films and Film Cults in British Cinema*. London: IB Tauris, 2010. Print.

Stanfield, Peter. "Cult Cinema: A Critical Symposium." *Cineaste* 34.1 (Winter 2008): 49–50. Print.

Taylor, Greg. *Artists in the Audience: Cults, Camp and American Film Criticism*. Princeton: Princeton UP, 1999. Print.

Telotte, J. P., ed. *The Cult Film Experience*. Austin: U of Texas P, 1991. Print.

Troeltsch, Ernst. *The Social Teaching of the Christian Churches*. London: George Allen and Unwin, 1931. Print.

Vale, Vivian, and Andrea Juno, eds. *Incredibly Strange Films*. San Francisco: V/Search, 1986. Print.

AUTHORSHIP

8

Coffee in Paradise

The Horn Blows at Midnight

Tom Conley

> INTERVIEWER: How did you become involved with Jack Benny in that crazy comedy *The Horn Blows at Midnight?*
>
> DIRECTOR RAOUL WALSH: He asked for me [laughs]. It's a terrible picture. I think he was in a band in heaven . . .
>
> —McGilligan and Weiner (40)

Maybe B for bad, A for auteur, and D for dumb. Scrambled, the letters can stand for bad dumb auteur. Or bad dumb director. In what follows "bad" cinema will be construed to mean films that a public enamored with great directors might have wished not to have had them made. These are the films that the adept of the auteur, however he or she might try, cannot explain away through ruse of theme and theory. A grounding axiom is that great directors, like great novelists, owe their stature to the fact that they are capable of realizing what are taken to be bad or dumb creations. Yet the attempt to redeem a film in the name of the auteur can become heuristic and lead to productive investigation in correlative areas of inquiry and, as a result, *make something other* from them. Insofar as the auteur is he or she who must have a body of work sizable enough to allow problematic themes to be iterated in different ways across a variety of genres and conventions, "good" films would be the jeweled expression of the contradictions comprising the traits of a director's signature, which can include all sorts of narrative configurations, locales and fields of tension in genres of modes that would otherwise be very foreign to one another.

In a more limited way the autograph would be discerned through a style of composing and editing; decisions that are visibly taken when a given space or sequence is framed; to an almost literal degree, the autograph a tracking shot traces as it frays its way through the space its movement seems to be inventing; or in a differential fashion, it would be manifest in the a visual and auditory arrangement of a sequence in which space and sounds *in* and *off* frame are correlated. All in all, the "good" film, seen as an iteration with others of the same director, would make manifest a persisting and compelling "vision of the world." Those which, attributed to the same director, fail to bring forward a world vision through the articulation of style and content, are generally deemed "bad" and, even if they are, belong to the ideology of the organic and singular artist who can make inferior films because the others of his or her canon are said to speak for themselves. Yet because a "good" deal of film theory is based on the principles of the auteur, its practice demands that a film attributed to a given director *must* be treated as a critical object and rarely as a work whose worth is determined by the degree of pleasure or disquiet it affords.

When appreciated for its negative virtue a "bad" film is symptomatic of issues that cause it to be qualified as such. These include, by way of hindsight, the vagaries—or prevarications—of "history" that critics summon to argue for or against the worth of a film lacking visual force; conflict, or circumstance said to mar the conception and production of a feature. A dubious "chemistry" is visible in the tensions of screenwriting: in the realm of classical cinema, actors who misplay the roles or botch their assignments, disruptive stylistic elements that call the storyline into question and also review and reception that typecasts a film according to quotients and quanta of entertainment-value.

These reflections are not aimed to show that for cinephiles a "bad" film is an impossibility, nor are they set forward to exonerate pantheon directors from what would be mistakes and miscues. Rather directors can be very much appreciated for what seems beneath or below the level of expectation associated with films under their names. We often breathe sighs of relief when we see that our genial directors can be as thoroughly uneven and mediocre as we are. In this respect Raoul Walsh was on the mark when, reflecting on a career that went from the beginnings of Hollywood to the decline of the studio system, from 1912 (*The Life of Pancho Villa*) to 1964 (*A Distant Trumpet*), he reputedly summed up his direction of 120 features and unattributed work on scores of others by noting that he had made a lot of "turkeys" along with a few good films too.[1]

One of his outstanding Christmas turkeys is *The Horn Blows at Midnight* (1945), the film that its lead actor, Jack Benny, proclaimed to have been the "worst film" in which he had ever played. Symptomatic of this is that it never affords mention in Walsh's autobiography, *Each Man in His Time*. Walsh makes mention of Benny in his "light comedy called *Artists and Models*" and praises the actor's mastery of "that elusive quality show people call timing," adding that he "was a fine comedian and a better serious actor than many of the older stars" (180). At the end of the memoir he relates that "the trumpet blew for Gary Cooper in 1961" (366), the year when he was sandwiched between Jane Russell and Marilyn Monroe at the occasion of Nikita Khrushchev's visit to Hollywood. Frank McCarthy, the organizer of the gala welcome, "was followed by Bob Hope and Jack Benny" (367).

Nonetheless the Cinémathèque française, the archive and beacon of the cinema of great auteurs, featured *The Horn Blows at Midnight* on March 29, 2001.[2] In his biography of *Raoul Walsh*, Pierre Giuliani notes:

> according to unanimous Anglo-Saxon criticism this film would be the worst that Walsh ever shot. Jack Benny was ridiculous, and the role he played contributed to his decline (he made only two films afterward). A vague reference to *Liliom* (Lang, 1933) does not even save its appearance. (112)

It can be said that by being so reputedly *bad* the film arouses suspicion about why and how it has acquired its dubious status. Suspicion often leads to fastidious inspection, which in turn forces reconsideration of the value judgments the historian and critic bring to the film.

∾

In the paragraphs to follow the argument advanced in favor of redeeming Walsh's "terrible" film is crafted upon the way its narrative uses an imaginary brand of coffee to allow it to bifurcate and follow two paths.

One, manifest, leads to an angelic world by virtue of what its trademark name—Paradise—prompts when an innocuous radio advertisement puts its listeners to sleep. In a stereotypical Freudian scenario a proper or place name leads to dreams about its field of reference. The latter is so clearly the trauma of World War II that in the context an elision of recent history amounts to its mention. The other, latent and of an equally stereotypical design, inspires an itinerary of inquiry about "coffee" as it had been used in comedies of similar facture. Along this line Walsh's film reaches back to Preston Sturges's caustic prewar comedy, *Christmas in July* (1940), a film whose "manifest" content is also shaped from the mention of a brand of coffee. In Walsh's feature the "paradise" that the stimulant brings is the setting for the classical (and even biblical) scenario of the battle of gods engaged with their botched creation. In the feature of 1946 it swings on the after-effects of screwball comedy, especially that of Sturges in his film of 1940.

Shot at the threshold of the world at war, *Christmas in July* shows that a horrendously unequal distribution of wealth is a major cause of collective misery: those who can eke out a living are crowded in tenements; most are immigrants who have little sense of how the rich lead their lives; many are Jewish and are seen, as if both by anticipation and retrospection, to be living in a kind of Eastern European ghetto displaced into New York City, under the firm control of an unremitting police force; those who are fortunate enough to be employed, living in fear of their foremen and superintendants, work in settings that betray the dehumanizing effects of Taylorism. Through tortuous turns of plot and occasional slapstick Sturges's film shows clearly that it can only temporarily palliate overweening social contradiction. It can be argued that in his film Walsh—and probably not in any conscious way, but unconsciously, through a field of reference and through the link of where anticipation gives way to amnesia—reaches back to Sturges. The film obtains its political and aesthetic force through an affiliation signaled by the marketing of coffee. In *Christmas in July* the slogan or sound bite that wins the day is "that if you don't sleep *it isn't the coffee it's the bunk.*" The bunk may indeed be the bed of nightmares present and past that the film avows it can only address by comic inversion. In *The Horn Blows at Midnight* the soporific counterpart is *Paradise Coffee is what makes you sleep*. In each feature the medium that conveys the message is called in question, and between them a more enduring relation with history and ideology is established.

The plot of *The Horn Blows at Midnight* would seem to be a symptom of the year in which in was made. A trumpet player (Benny) is in an orchestra hired to play background music for vocalists appearing on a late-evening radio show. During the break of an advertisement, hearing the soothing lilt of words selling Paradise Coffee, he gets drowsy. He begins to doze when the scene dissolves into paradise itself—a heavenly realm that has dominion over all the planets of the universe. At the outset of the dream-sequence, the godlike monarch (Guy Kibbee, who had been the studio director in the "manifest" realm of the picture), notes that the planet earth has gone awry and that for the sake of the heavenly machine it must be destroyed. But not so easily, since the heavenly beings are all too mortal: two envoys who had been sent downward to accomplish the task have erred. Another herald of apocalypse—Athanael (Jack Benny)—is needed to return to earth and, at a midnight hour of destiny, sound his horn and bring the world to its end.

Shy, gullible, unsure of himself, yet the object of the affections of a lovely an alluring angel (Alexis Smith, the orchestra's harpist), Athanael descends to the sublunar world by way of an elevator that brings him to the lobby of an elegant hotel (figure 8.1). There follows his adventures that lead him to meet the pair of deviant angels (John Alexander and Allyn Joslin—the first and second trumpeters of the orchestra in the diurnal-nocturnal "real-life" sequence), who have now accustomed themselves to earthly pleasure and take note of the exterminating angel's mission. They are so successful in foiling his plans that the overseer of the empyrean calls upon the affectionately bumbling angel to help him realize his mission. A comedy of errors ensues. The renegade angels collude with a jewel thief to retrieve the trumpet, but as fate would have it, Athanael saves Fran Blackstone (Dolores Moran, who is the orchestra's violinist) from suicide. The hero is obliged to pawn his instrument when, because the gods had failed to furnish him with an expense account, he is unable to pay for a meal he has taken at a restaurant. In hot pursuit of the furtive object, the angels follow the hero to an amusement park where, having befriended a boy from the *Our Gang* series (1922–44), aptly named Junior Pulpinsky (Robert Blake), Athanael is fired from a gun in the mode of a V-2 Rocket or the missile that Barbenfouillis had launched in Méliès's *A Trip to the Moon* (1902).

Just before the eleventh hour comes to a close, everyone converges upon the upper reaches of a skyscraper near Radio City Music Hall, where Athanael will sound the trumpet of doom. The instrument

Figure 8.1. Elizabeth (Alexis Smith), the orchestra's harpist in *The Horn Blows at Midnight* (1945). Courtesy Warner Bros. / The Kobal Collection.

changes hands in the midst of a tussle on the upper terrace high over the city. Athanael goes over the edge and is miraculously held from falling to the street. In classic slapstick that recalls *Safety Last* (Fred C. Newmeyer and Sam Taylor, 1923), the five players dangle and then swing from the upper reach of the building. Midway beneath them, we discover, is a gigantic mechanism (whose miniature model had been seen in the studio at the beginning of the film) set on display to sell Paradise Coffee. At short intervals a gigantic pot pours a torrential draft of coffee into a cup (of the shape and size of a small swimming pool) before a spoon drops sugar into the brew and stirs the murky liquid. Athanael, more of an apoplectic than apocalyptic Gabriel overcome by timidity, cannot hold on to the feet of the fourth link of the human pendulum. He falls into the pool where, saved from striking the asphalt below, he is doused with coffee then cream and sugar and stirred by the spoon. Catching the lip of the mechanical utensil that stirs the brew, he again hangs on for dear life before falling once and for all, whereupon the scene dissolves back to the orchestra where, dozing off, he has fallen off his chair and is assisted by neighboring musicians who happen to be those who were involved in the imbroglio that has just ended. The world has not yet come to its term. The reluctant angel of death is a hapless trumpeter who had been lulled by the drift of the words and sounds of the Paradise Coffee radio spot. Wresting himself from the arms of Morpheus while his companions in the orchestra soften his fall from his chair, he is delighted to be alive and amid his fellow musicians.

The scenario is so patent and topical that mention of sources would risk regress to every cliché of dreamwork. It recalls the famous falls of literature, indeed the accidents or *events* in by which writers engage the problem "that to philosophize is to learn to die." By creative means, be they meditation or narration, they soften the edges of death by miming its onslaught or set themselves in its midst. They die in our fiction of a mystical voyage in order to return to the terrestrial world in which they live and know they will eventually die.³ In the same vein the film might be a parody of the mystical voyage, a narrative of travel to a realm beyond our own, that an individual takes and returns in order to tell of his or her transformation (see Certeau). The voyage can belong to what anthropologists call "the quest for power": a member of a society leaves his or her familiar world and later returns from other realms with a new and self-assuring agency that allows the person to gain power and prestige (see Lévi-Strauss).

The allure of *The Horn Blows at Midnight*, if an allure there is, belongs to that of the comic strip appended to the end of *The Interpretation of Dreams*, where the founder of psychoanalysis reprints the six cartoons of a wet-nurse's dream of her charge's micturition while aboard an ocean liner. Hearing a boy wailing when asleep in the cabin, she dreams that he begins to urinate in the street so amply that it becomes a canal in Venice on whose waters a gondolier guides his vessel. In the next panel the flooding turns into the sea on which the liner itself is sailing. In the last frame she awakens in time enough to respond to the child's cries (367–68). The dream, synchronous with the wailing, is of the same temporality as Walsh's film. In view of the practitioners of mystical voyages the feature would be a patent piece of wish-fulfillment, a *prayer*, indeed an escape from the world of 1945. The narrative would flesh out the kinds of fantasies that advertisers of coffee or any stimulant would seek to inspire in their viewers or readers. What is shown being dreamt in the space of a second or two becomes the subject of over seventy minutes of time spent in dissolution and disbelief. A zany variant on Fritz Lang's much bleaker *Woman in the Window* of the year before (and indeed a panel of a diptych that includes *Scarlet Street*, 1945) would also have some relation with Michael Powell's strongly meditative *Stairway to Heaven* (also 1945).

Seen amid features of the war years that are taken to task for wafting spectators away from the condition of the world in which they are made, *The Horn Blows at Midnight* would be doubly bad for being existentially irresponsible. In light of Jean-Luc Godard's reflections on the state of the image in the wake of the Holocaust, the film would be avowing, on the one hand, that its plot to destroy the world is built upon recognition of such baneful depravity that it "prefers not to" bring forward reflection on the human condition while on the other, it is symptom of Hollywood's utter failure to address a general state of ruin that owes to what it has partially wrought. The film and its director-auteur can thus be target for admonishment or else a historian's topic, much as would be *The Wizard of Oz* (Victor Fleming, 1939) for the relation of fantasy to the world at large.

Or are they? Walsh would soon direct *Objective, Burma* (1946), a film that brings the spectator in such proximity to the gruesome character of war that it self-consciously refuses to display the horror it shows its soldiers witnessing. The "good" faith of this film might have a counterpart in the "bad" faith of *The Horn Blows at Midnight*. Appreciation of the nonsensical narrative accrues when its initial sequence can be seen referring to cinema at the threshold of the war five years earlier. At the risk of alienating the reader, close inspection of the initial shots of *The Horn Blows at Midnight*—taken up in the next four paragraphs—reveals why the film appears to be the dexter panel of a diptych of which *Christmas in July* is quite possibly its sinister counterpart.

The beginning of *The Horn Blows at Midnight* seems to be dissolution *into* a dream built from the images of cinemas made prior to the traumas of World War II. The title and the credits end where the director's name is displayed over a horn aiming at a bell tower on which the hands of a clock hands are set at midnight. The image and the name of the director fade into black before the narrative begins with a view of the outside of the Federated Recording Studio located on a busy street of a city that could be Manhattan. A cut to the second shot that dollies in on the sign announcing "Paradise Coffee Program" shows that the broadcast is in rehearsal and not yet on the air. The camera glides through the adjacent room to the door of Studio C (in deco Italic), behind which, in the fourth shot, an orchestra of about twenty musicians plays behind a portly female vocalist, seen immediately and obviously as the person of Margaret Dumont. She turns about and smiles by the microphone before, much as she had in her aria at the end of *Duck Soup* (Leo McCarey, 1933), her gestures and gaze gave blessing to the liberation of the land of Fredonia. Here a dolly-in cuts to the figure of a discerning pianist and conductor (Reginald Gardner) who takes her cue and plays. Cut to Dumont, waving a peacock feather in her right hand who begins a screeching aria (something like "a handle and a hummingbird, oh ho, ah ha") before the third of the three trumpets (Benny) botches the movement and causes the conductor to stop and tap his wand. "Boys, boys, watch what you're doing," he says, just as the shot cuts to the six musicians, one of whom is an attractive woman playing a harp. Medium shots and countershots follow: the conductor reminds them that "that's a C-minor chord" and that the brass had better get its act together. Once again the third trumpet goes off key. "Oh, ho! This is absurd! Are you musicians or butchers? Who is playing these repulsive notes? Would you mind playing my composition as I wrote it?"

The sequence sets in place the musicians who will figure in the dream. The conductor's invectives aimed at the third trumpet causes the studio director, a bald man (Kibbee) seen behind a glass partition that gives onto the orchestra pit) to settle down and get to work. Next to him Sloan (Franklin Pangborn), the radio engineer, is clearly a very familiar figure who sits at the controls. In a cameo role much like Dumont's, he twists and turns excruciatingly when the director insists that the orchestra is playing for a very "eccentric sponsor, you know. He likes everybody in the orchestra to play the same song." A countershot records the antsy Sloan (who is less a character than Pangborn playing Pangborn) looking at the director in keen agreement before the narrative gives way to dialogue between Athanael and the harpist, Elizabeth (Smith). Athanael decries his lot in life while she reminds him that he nonetheless is working and living fairly well (to which he responds in caricature of himself as he had been known in other roles). Like Pangborn, Benny plays Benny, but in strong likelihood, for reason of the presence of the World War II, the other roles to which he refers could not fail to include his rendition of Joseph Tura, a hammy and clearly Jewish actor in Ernst Lubitsch's hilarious but bleak comedy of three years before, *To Be or Not to Be* (1942). Benny/Athanael feels he is nonetheless "a great artist" whom fate has unfortunately relegated to the rank of third trumpet. "It's an ungrateful world, Elizabeth. If I had my way," he adds sarcastically, "a lot of things would be different."

The history of things between *To Be and Not to Be* and this film can only be inferred: cut to the scene of the orchestra through the director's studio and the moment when everyone is "on the air." A shot records a radio broadcaster (Truman Bradley) crossing the stage in front of the automated advertisement, shown in miniature as if it were in anticipation of a television commercial, that stands in the foreground of the recording room. He arrives at the microphone. "Gentle people," utters the broadcaster in a suave baritone, it's fifteen minutes before midnight" (now in a cut to a medium close-up), "and Paradise Coffee, the coffee that is heavenly [his eyes turn skyward to register what he thinks about the corny prose he is reading verbatim from a piece of paper] brings you *sleeeepy* time music. . . . And why? Paradise Coffee is what makes you sleep."

The film cuts to a close-up of Benny who now begins to fall under the spell of the broadcaster's words. "The sleep you miss so much. Sleep, blessed sleep" (cut back to the broadcaster in close-up, who now reads the words tongue-in-cheek) "the sleep you always miss so much when you are awake. Because you aren't sleepy." Cut to a close-up of the advertisement that is clearly out of place because the scene of the mechanized pot, creamer, and spoon that pour their contents into the cup below would belong to visual publicity and not to a radio broadcast. The sound of trickling liquid accompanies the shot recording the spot as it unfolds in front of a signboard that heralds: "Paradise Coffee. It's Heavenly!" The announcer continues, voice-off, as the camera dollies in on the mechanical advertisement. "First you pour Paradise Coffee gently into that waiting cup . . . then perhaps a dash of cream to lend that pearly, glittering tint. Then add sugar to taste . . ." The film now shows Benny falling asleep as the voice-off continues, but more directly, as if both to Benny and the spectator who would also be close to slumber: "Not too much now . . . and then sip . . . our Paradise Coffee." A close-up of the mechanism is accompanied by the words "and indeed, Paradise Coffee is heavenly." The adverb cues the film to cut back to Benny, eyes closed, who is finally sleeping.

The voice-off continues unctuously, "now sleep, peacefully, contentedly, as if in the arms of angels." Benny begins to snore, eliciting disgruntlement from the announcer, who continues (now *in*), "you sleep on a billowy cloud, drifting through the majestic nothingness of infinity, listening to a celestial symphony . . ." [cut to Benny who now snores very loudly] that lulls your earthly cares away. It's paradise [Benny is now in a watery dissolve] . . . it's *heavenly*." The film dissolves into a view of a cloudy sky on which is written, in Hallmark cursive, "Heaven 1945–46." Thus begins a flashback—or forward—to a "heavenly symphony" in which thousands of musicians play violins or sing silent hosannas below the threshold of a great dictator in paradise. Benny and Smith count among thousands of souls seen as if either through a fly's eye or from an upper terrace of the Vatican.

Because, much like a *mise en abîme* in which the greater structure of the film is duplicated, the opening sequence requires at least two viewings. The heavenly imbroglio that leads the characters to fight among themselves on the precipice of the skyscraper is fashioned from the players who, except for the radio announcer, were shown at war or in slumber in the studio. The shift from the recording loge, the site in which the film had been shown "developing," begs the viewer to account for what will become a redistribution of the dramatis personae. The first and second trumpeters are, naturally, the fallen angels with whom Benny (whose unlikely name, Athanael, is fitting for the empyrean realm) is at war because they had chided and insulted him for his miscues. And the loving Elizabeth, of the same name on earth as in heaven, keeps caring for the trumpeter who could (variously) be her child, a misbegotten lover, or a gay companion who poses no erotic threat to any female at all. The director of the studio becomes the godlike patron of the clouds, while the bass player (Mike Mazurki) becomes a thug whose black machinations relate him to the noir films in whose backgrounds he figures. And so on, except for what Dumont and Pangborn bring forward in the opening shots. Dumont (Madame Traviata) clearly alludes to the world of the Marx Brothers, both *Duck Soup* and, more tellingly, *A Night at the Opera* (Sam Wood, 1945), for reason of the musical context and the memory of a film made in the last of the prewar years.

When Pangborn is seen in the setting of the radio studio whose sponsor is Paradise Coffee a direct and startling reference is made to the opening sequence of Sturges's *Christmas in July*, the feature whose acerbic narrative is built on an advertisement for coffee. In that film a coffee company of the corporate order of General Foods holds a contest to obtain a slogan that will make its brand become a lasting memory-image for the American public. Sitting at nighttime atop a tenement in view of a cityscape, an impoverished and desperate couple listens to a radio set adjacent to where they are sitting. They await news of the winner. The young but slightly aging fiancé (Dick Powell) has submitted an aphorism that he believes will carry the day. Yet because the award committee is bogged down and awash with thousands of submissions, the news of the winning words is yet to arrive. How they are chosen, how they are victims of a colossal misattribution, and how they eventually arrive at an unlikely destination assuring a happy ending constitute a story built upon an unyielding structure of depression, uneven distribution of wealth, social inequity, and police brutality.

The immobility of the Depression is marked in the opening shots. Following the credits that place the writer-director's name against a view of Manhattan's skyscrapers illuminating the night, the camera pans down to become a long two-shot of the couple, sitting atop a tenement behind which the city is visible, who imagine what it might be to live in a four-room apartment. The fiancée (Ellen Drew) explains how the walls can be maneuvered to engineer the illusion of a multiplication of rooms, which her spouse rejects as idle dreams. A soothing musical background, seemingly emanating from the radio whose dials he manipulates with his left hand, is in counterpoint with the accruing acrimony of the couple's debate (registered in two close-up shots/countershots of the husband and wife as they speak). A second two-shot restages the scene (she utters, "Nothing's too good for you except a palace on Fifth Avenue") while he, his elbow on the radio (after she has knocked her fist on its wooden frame as if in hope that what the words it soon speaks will bear truth), tells her to be quiet and listen.

"I give you coffee, ladies and gentlemen, the end of the perfect dinner, the beginning of the perfect day" [her fist taps on the radio as we hear "perfect day"]. A crescendo of music accompanies a dolly-in and a lap-dissolve to a skyscraper on which is mounted an illuminated advertisement for "Maxford House Coffee." A neon-silhouette of a person lifting and drinking a cup of coffee is adjacent to the slogan that reads, "good to the last gulp." The dolly-in to the building gives way to an establishing shot of the studio in which the announcer, Don Hartman (Franklin Pangborn), stands by a microphone with his assistant. The shot cuts to a medium close-up of the elegantly dressed announcer (Hartman wears a carnation on the lapel of his tuxedo), at once smug and nervous, who reads his script: "And now, ladies and gentlemen, the moment we have all been waiting for: we are about to give you the result of the $50,000 Maxford House New Slogan Contest."[4] The announcer continues to enumerate the order of the six prizes that are accompanied by as many shots of groups or individuals across the social spectrum who listen eagerly or distractedly to their radios.[5] Soon the plot reveals that Jimmy's slogan reads, in answer to the words he imagines inaugurating the spot, "if you don't sleep at night," *it isn't the coffee it's the bunk* (Henderson 222).

"Bunk," what seems to be the floating signifier that can refer to coffee and to cinema (including *Christmas in July*), might also be a watchword for *The Horn Blows at Midnight*. Like *Christmas in July*, the film makes clear that it is just that, and that its bunk is of the order of a dream that the features of 1940 and 1945 have crafted. Both films "distanciate" themselves from their content, and both use the cue of "coffee," a universal stimulant of cinema, to engage contradiction and amnesia. When seen adjacent to each other both films address the question that Pangborn, the harried announcer of *Christmas in July* had posed in the early version of the screenplay, prior to its elision in the completed film:

> The friend of the poor man AND the rich man, the solace of the unhappy and the ally of the merrymaker. To what do we turn in times of stress and national extremity? What is called for first in any disaster, be it a flood, a blizzard, a war, or any other human crisis? To what do we turn as naturally and instinctively as we turn to prayer . . . and sometimes, with more immediate results . . . Ladies and gentlemen? I GIVE YOU COFFEE. (Henderson 212)

Pangborn's unspoken words in the elided portion of the script could serve as a model for *A Horn Blows at Midnight*. The casual reference to a war anticipates the war that Walsh's film had elided but made present in the fantasy of heaven. The obvious erasure is elegantly undone through the allusion to the caffeine of the prewar film. By these means, it can be stated retrospectively, the seemingly "bad" film becomes something quite other than what its reception might have made it to be. The similarity of the sequences brings into coincidence two directors of very different formation and vision, and it serves as an emblem for the presence of the war in anticipation and in an uncanny, almost future amnesia of retrospection (because the film premiered on April 28, 1945, less than two weeks before the end of the war in the European theatre of operations). Further, it serves as a measure of the critical view that both films appear to take of their own content, their moment and of the industrial machinery that crafts them.

In guise of a short conclusion it can be said that the principle of the auteur encourages transverse analysis of the films that compose an oeuvre. The very agency that comes with transversal reading takes value judgments as a means of turn viewing into a critical operation. An auteur's film cannot be bad simply because those who have been or remain worthy of the name cannot fail to make what seem to be bad movies. In a greater matrix the criterion of quality gives way to what critics long ago called *le travail du film*: that is, to the way that films open themselves to the labor of analysis, a process that reaches issues that are far from the settling and settled effects of categorization or value judgments based on reception (see Kuntzel; Bellour 330–38).

Yet a nagging question remains. In his own estimation Walsh observed that his film was not merely bad but indeed *terrible*. Terrible what? Terrible how? A director-auteur who grows into the industry, who makes one feature after the next and who accumulates a mass that qualifies as an oeuvre acquires a signature on the basis of work both good and triumphantly "bad." What adepts of reception or the pleasure of entertainment call inferior works tend not to recognize their ideological wealth, in other words, the ways that they produce (and do not reflect) our "imaginary relation with real modes of production." When these films, like the novels of relentlessly creative writers of the ilk of Balzac or Dickens are seen at once circulating in the greater currents of their industry and drawing on their own relations with their coequals what qualifies as "bad" can only remain between ironic quotation marks. For what concerns analysis of Walsh's unlikely and terrible film, for all of its bunk, its coffee is a heavenly catalyst of investigation.

Notes

1. See interviews in *Cinéastes de notre temps* and *The Man Who Made Movies*. In his interviews and autobiography Walsh speaks unabashedly about his bad films. In his exchange with Walsh, McGilligan recalled that *Under Pressure* (1935), a film he had never seen, took place in a tunnel. To this, Walsh replied: "Yes, we never got out of the tunnel. Terrible, terrible picture" (24). A propos *The Revolt of Mamie Stover* (1956), Walsh felt that the script, having eviscerated the book's principal subject, prostitution in Hawaii at the time of the attack on Pearl Harbor, was the cause for a bad picture: "They wrote a script and we put it on. And it was nothing" (48). And in recalling *The King and Four Queens* (1956), he said: "No good, no good" (48).

2. See the program for the Palais de Chaillot (March/April 2001), 42.

3. It suffices to recall that in "De l'exercitation" (Of practice) Michel de Montaigne puts his new invention (the essay) to the test when he writes

of the traumatic fall from his horse that left him paralyzed and taken for dead before he left a beatific coma and painfully regained consciousness. His tale becomes the cause and reason for self-study, indeed for the very enterprise of the personal essay and the self-portrait.

4. A facsimile of the original script, titled *The New Yorkers* is found in Brian Henderson's *Five Screenplays by Preston Sturges* (211). Henderson's careful treatment of its origin as a play and transformation into a film addresses its ambiance: "It is the late depression, and everyone seems ground down by years of struggling; those who have jobs cling to them. No one in this film would find the 1933 song 'We're in the Money' amusing. The bravado of the early depression is over" (193).

5. The last in the sequences sets Sturges himself, in a straw hat, listening with two African Americans, one of whom is Fred "Snowflake" Toones, the bartender in *The Palm Beach Story* (Sturges, 1942).

Works Cited

Bellour, Raymond. *Le corps du cinéma: Hypnoses, émotions, animalités.* Paris: POL, 2009. Print.

Certeau, Michel de. "The Madness of Vision." Trans. Michael Smith. *Enclitic* 7.1 (Spring 1983): 24–31. Print.

Cinéastes de notre temps: Raoul Walsh ou le bon vieux temps. Dir. Hubert Knapp with assistance of Patriok Brion and Axel Masden. ORTF, 1966. Film.

Freud, Sigmund. *The Interpretation of Dreams.* Ed. James Strachey. London: Hogarth, 1978. Print.

Giuliani, Pierre. *Raoul Walsh.* Paris: Edilig, 1986. Print.

Henderson. Brian. *Five Screenplays by Preston Sturges.* Berkeley: U of California P, 1984. Print.

Kuntzel, Thierry. "Le travail du film [1 and 2]." *Communications* 19 (1972): 25–39 and 23 (1975): 136–89. Print.

Lévi-Strauss, Claude. "La quête du pouvoir." *Tristes tropiques.* Paris: Plon, 1955. 37–45. Print.

The Man Who Made Movies: Raoul Walsh. Dir. Richard Schickel. 3DD Entertainment, 1973. Film.

McGilligan, Patrick, and Debra Weiner. "Can You Ride a Horse: Interview with Raoul Walsh." *Film Crazy: Interviews with Hollywood Legends.* Ed. Patrick McGilligan. New York: Saint Martin's Griffin, 2000. Print.

Montaigne, Michel de. *Essais. Oeuvres complètes.* Ed. Maurice Rat and Albert Thibaudet. Paris: Gallimard/Pléiade, 1962. Print.

Walsh, Raoul. *Each Man in His Time: The Life Story of a Director.* New York: Farrar, Straus and Giroux, 1974. Print.

9

The Risible

On Jean-Claude Brisseau

ADRIAN MARTIN

Into the Whirlpool . . .

Bad cinema has something to do with childhood. More exactly, the beginning of calling certain films, or certain parts and elements of them, bad has to do with a loss of innocence, being driven from the Garden of Eden. This Eden is, quite simply, the blessed time, long ago, when you or I could watch anything, anything at all—without judgment, without barriers. We could watch the most fantastic fantasies, the most tearjerking melodramas, the most breakneck adventures, the spookiest horror films without drawing any kind of line. Without separating the good from the bad, the wheat from the chaff, the exception from the rule. Anything went, back then. We had a lot to learn—far too much. What comes after the Fall, is discernment, refinement, cultivation, sophistication, taste—everything that brings us together in any forum devoted to cinema studies today and everything we are struggling to escape, to smash, in the name of bad cinema.

Bad cinema, in my view, cannot and should not be corralled down to one kind, type, or genre of film. The general orientation in such discussions towards B cinema, exploitation cinema, paracinema, underground or outlaw cinema, porno and gorno and all the rest of it, has only one radical point as far as I am concerned: it provides the beachhead, the wedge that is meant to free you (viewer-spectator) of your inbred cultural attachment to all those normative, almost unconscious values of what constitutes good cinema, the professional film, the well-made film: a solidly crafted script, plausible narrative, three-dimensional characterization, subtle acting, an appropriate musical score, telling dialogue, and so on. We all think we are beyond these horrifyingly middlebrow, petit bourgeois cultural values, but they rise up in us in the least conscious, most casual, reflex, everyday moments of critical opinion.

When I was about six years old, I saw a film. Like every film I had seen up to that point, it was the greatest film I had ever seen, the greatest film ever made. Only much later, in the years of learning, did I also come to discover that it was created by an important auteur, Otto Preminger, that is regularly related to something called film noir, and that it has prominent fans. The film is from 1949 and is called *Whirlpool*. Go and watch the absolute greatest scene from this movie: a man, in post-op, suffering serious pain, hypnotizes himself in a little mirror and simply walks out the hospital in perfect, blissful health (next up, he even drives a car).

When I look at this scene today, I think of it as poetry, surrealist poetry. But when I was six, I regarded it not as magic, not as fairy tale, but as pure science. The spectacle of the self-hypnosis of "the mysterious Doctor Korvo" (the film's French title) riveted my tiny, unformed self with its instant revelation of every kind of mystery: the mysteries of medicine, of pain and endurance, of body and mind. Today, I can also see that the scene perfectly condenses at least fifty-three different theories of psychoanalysis, including the psychoanalysis of cinema itself. In order to hypnotize himself as he hypnotizes others—with a mere look, a mere word, a click of his fingers—Korvo (José Ferrer) must turn himself, project himself, into an other. So he gazes into the looking glass, and he really does becomes someone else, someone who looks back and gives the silent command to arise and walk out, issuing from those grim, Mabusean eyes.

There are some people—there have always been and always will be such people—who find this climactic scene in *Whirlpool* beyond the pale. Unbelievable. Ridiculous. Silly. Risible. There are some people who reject the film in toto for such reasons; and there are those who praise the film for exactly the same reasons: because it is stupid fun, crazy stuff.

As for me, I am trying to forge a path that is not *between* those two responses—the risible is either the unacceptable ridiculous or the acceptable ridiculous—but *beyond* them, outside this binary choice altogether. It takes a lifetime of work to get back to the film critic you were at the age of six, and to do this honestly, without delusions of an impossible return to innocence, but also without (as much as possible) the entire culture of defenses, rationalizations and tastes that you have been assiduously schooled in down all the years. "Criticism is always that," Serge Daney once remarked, "an eternal return to a fundamental pleasure." But this eternal return is not just involuntary, unconscious, or symptomatic. It can also be the basis for a willed adventure.

Notes from the Underground

I wish to evoke for you a still frame: contemplate it well in your mind's eye. There are about ten bad things going on at once in this image. There is a guy who has descended into a hellish criminal underworld on the outskirts of town, an underworld that runs, in its entirety, down the length of one slim corridor. There are people off screen who are laid-out flat on the cement floor, stoned on hard drugs. There is a watcher at the foot of the stairs who greets every visitor with a rifle to their stomach. There is a gang leader, a particularly mean and tough woman, who is sitting at a table counting ill-gotten gains. And there are at least five distinct—or rather, indistinct—people lost in various states of undress and several forms of sexual rapture: two couples, and a lonely figure in her bra who briefly implores the visitor to get with her.

This film is from the year 2000. It is called *Les savates de bon dieu*, literally translated as *Workers for the Good Lord* but I would render it as *God's Little Minions*. It is written, directed, and produced by the French filmmaker Jean-Claude Brisseau. Around the world, it is among the least screened and least seen of his dozen feature films. In fact, it was described to me by one film festival–travelling pundit as Brisseau's "most insane" film, and that is what compelled me to seek it out.

I started with a still because this is how the film itself starts, with flashes of a story already almost over, already tipping into romantic catastrophe. Note that the domestic dispute that triggers the film is all about a baby, a little child, and this dramatically significant person, constantly referred to, is someone we *never see*, or even hear, in this scene or any other of the film. The strange authority, the compelling weirdness of Brisseau's storytelling style, is captured in this very particular left-out detail. A great many details that storytelling filmmakers—not to mention their audiences—would regard as crucially important are breezily skipped in Brisseau's movies.

Here are several preludes to the oeuvre of Brisseau. I hasten to add that I am not going to bother to argue that we should perceive Brisseau as an auteur because any one who sees even just two of his films can instantly tell that we are in the company of someone whose concerns, obsessions, tastes, and distastes, whose very unconscious, are sprayed all over the surface of the screen at every moment, just like many revered bad cinema auteurs from Edgar G. Ulmer and Joseph H. Lewis to Samuel Fuller onwards (Martin).

From film to film by Brisseau, we can immediately see the figures of the Dark Angel and the Redemptive Angel; we see the bestiary of flying creatures, from a tiny yellow canary to a soaring eagle; we hear the favorite musical tunes and motifs literally replayed from one soundtrack to the next, with composer Jean Musy's permission; we see the incredible attention to the intensity of light, and the classical symmetry of the pictorial compositions; we see the fires and the explosions, the skies and the fields; we see the banal office jobs, the classrooms—because Brisseau was a teacher for twenty years before being discovered as a filmmaker by Rohmer and Pialat—and the suburban vistas; we see the violent, shouting outbursts by frustrated men against the prison of their daily world, and we see all the statuesque, naked women that have earned Brisseau the tag—long before he turned sixty—of dirty old Frenchman . . . and before he was successfully taken to court by four women on sexual harassment charges arising from his extremely unprofessional audition process, a very public case which Brisseau promptly dramatized—in full self-pitying victim mode—in *Les anges exterminateurs / The Exterminating Angels* (2006) (see De Baecque; Quéré). I will not defend Brisseau's actions in that matter or his various justifications for those actions in interviews and on film, but I do think it is necessary to separate that scandal from most of the work he has made to date.

Consider two indelible movement-images from across the span of Brisseau's career: first, a shouting man from his second feature, his first professional production on 16 mm for television, called *La vie comme ça / Life the Way It Is / Life's Like That* (1978); and second, a naked masturbating woman (Coralie Revel) from the opening moments of what is to date is his best-known and most seen film, *Choses secrètes / Secret Things* (2002). Violent male hysteria on the one hand and female orgasm on the other (the latter element frequently projected into *Eyes Wide Shut*–type tales of errant wandering and self-discovery in a mythic underworld, however earthly, even corny, a form that underworld might take). Such are the extreme poles of Brisseau's poetics, his universe. I want to take that universe, not in this instance as an object of study in itself (although it certainly stands up to scrutiny on that level), but as a case study in bad cinema culture.

In 2009, at the Las Palmas Film Festival in Spain, I had a chance to re-see, on a big screen, the film that introduced me to this director, twenty years before: *De bruit et de fureur / Sound and Fury* (1988). It is always instructive to confront one's memories, the constructed mental picture of a film from the past, with the real thing. I remembered *De bruit et de fureur*—a movie about tough suburban life and delinquent teenagers at school—as a much smoother, more fluidly developed, more conventionally coherent film than it actually is. My memory had completely rearranged its jagged, lurching, elliptical progression of events into a classic three-act structure (shame on me!). My memory had also beefed up the production values of the film: it is sparse, quite austere, with very few locations, precisely a B film. In fact, as Brisseau points out in interviews, he has always made films on very tight budgets, a kind of art house or exploitation cinema, as indeed many art filmmakers, from Jean-Luc Godard to Rainer Werner Fassbinder and beyond, have frequently done.

But one true impression of *De bruit et de fureur* had stuck very faithfully to me, and now I was able to gauge precisely how Brisseau had built it up. The film begins abruptly—after a weighty passage from Shakespeare's *Macbeth* printed on screen—with a small teenage boy showing up at the apartment of his mother in an unglamorous Paris suburb. This mother is a character whom we will never, ever see in the whole course of the film. Her daily and nightly absence is marked by the Post-It notes she leaves her son, like "Remember to eat" and "Do your homework." Again, that very characteristic Brisseau elision is very antirealistic. The boy arrives with a bird in a cage; in it is the small yellow canary, already mentioned, which for a split second, a few frames, transforms into a raging, caged eagle. To whom that image, that projection belongs, exactly, to boy or bird or Brisseau, we will never know. So there is this sweet little kid, the least thuggish male in the entire story. Instantly, standing alone in the apartment, he is beckoned by an apparition—a transparently veiled, naked adult woman with a live eagle perched on her arm (rather like the figure appearing and disappearing in *Choses secrètes*), who gets him into the bedroom. Every night, some kind of strange sex goes on in this room between boy and phantom, most of which we do not see, but we do sometimes notice the marks it leaves on the boy's body, like the scratch from the eagle's claw on his face. Absolute perversity, absolute decadence, right alongside absolute sweetness, light and innocence, and with no real way to tell them apart or separate them—this is the Brisseau formula so disconcerting to so many spectators. And this little boy is, in a way, exactly the child—the doubled, polymorphous child, passively acted upon by the world and also acting upon it, violently—that Brisseau, through his art, seeks to be, to become once more. A child of cinema.

Brisseau's *Noce blanche / White Wedding* (1989), made in the aftermath to the mild sensation stirred by *De bruit et de fureur*, has an indelible opening. A middle-aged, heavy-set teacher stands before his classroom of fifteen-year-old teenagers, and asks: "What is the unconscious?" I shall never forget or forgive, at the Melbourne preview for newspaper and magazine reviewers of this film, the howls of derisive laughter that greeted this line. (For a quite opposite and respectful reaction, see Masson.). This demonstrated that the reviewers (1) did not know much about the French education system, and (2) were enslaved by the heavy, oppressive chains of what they deemed to be dramatically risible. *Noce blanche* is about the transgressive relationship between a middle-aged teacher and one of his teenage students, played by pop star Vanessa Paradis (figure 9.1). And this is where the dirty-old-man charge got going, with a head full of steam, in Brisseau's career.

Figure 9.1. François Négret and Vanessa Paradis in *Noce Blanche* (1989). Courtesy Films du Losange / The Kobal Collection.

I was led to fix on Brisseau by way of a stark duality: on the one hand, the many fierce, unkind, dismissive things said about his work by so many critics, usually always about how silly and risible his work is, and on the other, an army of dedicated supporters who often do not get to say much more than they love the films because they find them mad, crazy, delirious, wild, strange, weird, insane, and excessive. Already, I have needed recourse to a few of these words to describe the form and effect of Brisseau's films, just as Bordwell does when he writes (affectionately):

> Tsui Hark is the mad genius of Hong Kong cinema. The problem comes with assigning proportions. 10% mad, 90% genius? 50–50? 99% mad, 1% genius? [. . .] A Tsui film will contain something brilliant, something banal, something silly, and something just weird.

But this ceaseless talk of madness and the like can too often return us, inexorably, to a kind of tacit or implicit judgment according to, imprisoned in reference to, the norm. That is the problem with all arguments that go the path of the transgressive and excessive: they are only a heartbeat away from locking us back into the normalized State of Things, the Middle of the World. These contrasting positions (of the risible and the crazy) create a kind of deadlock that I want to try to break.

It is instructive to examine the bad press that Brisseau has received. I take my examples from the reviews of Brisseau's most recent film, which is called—with some bravery considering the court case and media exposure he underwent beforehand—*À l'aventure* (2009), which could be translated as *On with the Adventure!* Chris Bourne, in an online review, calls it "his silliest film yet" with "ridiculous dialogue . . . delivered woodenly," and "an awkward mix of soft-core sex tableaux and long stretches of pseudo-philosophy." Brisseau gets this kind of slam frequently. The Bourne Cinema Conspiracy (the name of the website) goes on: "Brisseau, based on this film and his previous work, *The Exterminating Angels*, would be well-advised to go into full-blown pornography—that at least would be a little more honest in its aims than the false profundity he indulges in here." But the most revealing quip from Bourne is this: "Nothing here bears the slightest resemblance to recognizable human behaviour or logical sense." This gives us, via reversal, a handy motto generated out of a normative value judgment; the triumph of bad cinema would be precisely when nothing bears the slightest resemblance to recognizable human behavior or logical sense.

Case two: a piece by Richard Porton in the progressive Canadian magazine *Cinema Scope*, a review of the Rotterdam Film Festival subtitled "Ghosts, Girls, Guns" (actually, not a bad title for a study of Brisseau). With admirable honesty, Porton tells us he attended this film in search of a salacious thrill from the person he tags "a reliably randy auteur" (54), and places on a par with Catherine Breillat. Alas, he finds *À l'aventure* "considerably more interested in mystical mumbo jumbo" than hard-core sex, and a series of sadomasochistic tableaux that are "more reminiscent of a Rosicrucian correspondence course than the unexpurgated *Justine*" (54–55). Like Bourne, Porton cannot resist offering a comical synopsis—every Brisseau film can easily be made to sound ridiculous by retelling the plot with the literary equivalent of raised eyebrows—which tends to replace discussion of the film in any other terms. The final blow comes as a twist on the usual anti-Brisseau putdowns: the film is risible, yes, but not risibly over-the-top; Porton finds it, instead, "risibly tame" (54). Brisseau is risible when he overperforms and risible when he underperforms—this guy just cannot win.

Brisseau's antirealism is a barrier to many critics, viewers, and reviewers. Realism is another of those old-fashioned things we think we are all past—that we do not require or demand anymore—but the truth of our responses frequently tells a different story. Criticism leans upon the old adage of the willing suspension of disbelief, but actually such suspension is, in practice, rarely willing or able. One index of this is Brisseau's very functional, direct way with characterization and the depiction of character drives, which is akin to the B-movie mode of Ulmer or Joseph Lewis. People are introduced with one trait that overrides all else—like desire or revenge or compassion—and little or no backstory arrives to fill out or explain the basis for such motivation: this is just the way they are, eternally, or until they somehow radically change. Situation, incident, and strong plot moves (often considered by his detractors and fans alike as "outrageous") take precedence over what we have come to expect as three-dimensional psychology. It is little wonder that when Brisseau expresses (as he often has) his great love for Alfred Hitchcock's *Psycho* (1960), he describes it in these terms: "the situation [that is, the shower murder] is so powerful that the audience is no longer interested in the characters who then appear" (33). So spectacle takes precedence over character, but Brisseau's own films compel us to think about spectacle in a more intimate way.

Here is what I mean. When I remember that *Les savates de bon dieu* was described to me as Brisseau's most insane film, I have a strong feeling that the following scene was the one they had in mind. It involves the cops finally catching up with the lovers on the run, as well as their companion in crime and teacher of life lessons, an exiled African prince named Maguette (played by Emile Abossolo M'bo), a rather fantastical (and often richly comical) character whose tools include palm reading skills (to decipher the past), a bank of computers (to predict the future), and some mystical tribal sticks and stones (to call upon divine intervention, if needed). And such intervention is definitely needed in this scene that rests upon a breathtaking elision of something possibly going on off screen. It is a tense stand-off: our renegade heroes are surrounded by the police. Suddenly, things—heavy things, things that start fires—begin *falling from the sky*, inexplicably. No one in the movie discusses this miraculous event; it just happens.

Take It or Leave It

Another way of putting all this is to suggest that in Brisseau's work there is a very uninhibited relation to melodrama, a form that, interestingly, he says he did not like much when he was in his late teens and twenties, when he became a *Cahiers*-reading, Cinémathèque-attending cinephile ("I rejected the vast majority of them"), but only came to really appreciate them in his forties (Strauss). Melodrama is one of those forms that you and I, critics and teachers, fans and historians, think we are pretty cool with these days, after the rediscovery and re-evaluation of Douglas Sirk and Vincente Minnelli, after Pedro Almodóvar and Todd Haynes. But melodrama in certain forms—raw, naive, hyper-direct—still inflames a wall of modern resistances (Routt). It is something we need to surround and inoculate with irony, with camp, with sophistication, in order to take the required dose. Intriguingly, in the fallout from the release of his epic *Australia* (2009), Baz Luhrmann complained on television that the reason so many critics did not like it is because they are unfamiliar with or phobic in the presence of melodrama. And he may actually have a point there.

Brisseau often uses melodrama, and this recourse to the genre often makes his audiences uneasy. His film noir in color, *L'ange noir* (1994), which is particularly inspired by the William Wyler–Bette Davis melodrama *The Letter* (1940), begins straight in: a man leaves a wealthy middle-aged woman's room, shaking his head as if to say, *Well, that's that; it's over.* The woman, in the same frame, instantly raises a pistol and proceeds to shoot him five times, the last time right in the head. A maid appears. Without a word of explanation, this maid throws her mistress down on a bed, tears her clothes off, slaps her around brutally, and trashes the furniture. And throughout, in a typical Brisseau touch, deep light suffuses the rich colors of walls, décor, clothes, and the thick blonde hair of the lady of the manor, played by the French pop star Sylvie Vartan. It takes us a little while to figure out that the women are staging signs of a rape, to lay the legal defense of murder. There is then a police investigation of the crime scene; for this entire sequence, the corpse of the guy with his brains blown out lies pristinely at the bottom of the ornate Sirkian stairs. This amounts to the first fifteen minutes of the film; we have not even yet discovered that the dead brute is in fact France's "Public Enemy Number One," a daring crook who is in fact a modern Robin Hood who gives away all his criminal gains to the poor, and preaches social anarchy in nationwide television interviews (furthermore, the part is taken by the now largely forgotten mainstream-anarchist filmmaker of the 1970s, Claude Faraldo). It will be a great day indeed when Brisseau turns his attention to Reality TV as a pretext or backdrop for one of his lurid tales.

There is a lot of humor in Brisseau—black humor, subversive humor, sometimes simply low humor worthy of the Farrelly Brothers—but when it comes to the melodrama aspect, he is earnest, serious as a heart attack. No irony of a distant, distancing, contextualizing sort; no frames around the material that allow that kind of reading. If we find self-mocking or other-mocking quotational irony in Brisseau's work, we are forcing that frame upon it; we are erecting that defensive wall between us and the film. Brisseau may indeed be virtually alone among those we label cinephile filmmakers (from Godard to François Ozon) in that his movies, so full of loving immersion in cinema history, never generate from that immersion a second degree or postmodern layer of self-consciousness. When Brisseau makes a melodrama, an adventure film, a film noir, or a chronicle of erotic libertinage, he really makes one—all-out, seriously, uninhibitedly.

The earnestness of Brisseau's work is what wins it its badness—earnestness and naiveté. Just as we can never forget that Brisseau is someone who made his first feature with friends on Super-8 (*La croisée des chemins*, 1975), someone who never received formal filmmaking training, we can never forget that Brisseau is an autodidact from the working classes, very proud of all the learning and aesthetic experience he has accumulated. Much spectator revulsion to Brisseau involves a snobbish reaction to this self-made culture that his films so enthusiastically exhibit. This patchwork of culture seems, in the eyes of these others, naive, incoherent, thrown together, an unpardonable mixing of the high and the low—Shakespeare with porn, Bach with ghosts, Vermeer with violence, Weil with UFOs. This is one of the reasons that Brisseau is not always included in high-flown academic discussion of the contemporary French cinema of the body (alongside, say, Claire Denis, Gaspar Noé, or Philippe Grandrieux), although he logically could belong there, as if he counts as a bit of an embarrassment in such intellectual art-cinema company. Brisseau's films flaunt his philosophical interests (Masson), but it is not the kind of reading list that accompanies current courses on film and philosophy.

Take, for example, *Céline* (1992), which struck some on its release as the ultimate New Age pamphlet. It is about a young woman (played by Brisseau's longtime partner-collaborator Lisa Hérédia) grieving after her father's death. It starts out as a kind of exploration, or even advertisement, for the healing powers of yoga and meditation, and it brings to these New Age subjects the intensity of a Carl Dreyer or Terrence Malick film. But as usual, Brisseau takes this premise, eventually, to another level altogether. Céline starts having visions of primal deserts, and then she starts levitating, and finally she becomes a kind of saint, performing miracle cures for the local god-fearing rural population. There is even an exalted place for the modern myth of the Chariots of the Gods in this movie. But it is absolutely nothing like the episode "The Miracle" in Roberto Rossellini's *L'amore* (1948), Paul Schrader's *Touch* (1996), or Pier Paolo Pasolini's *Teorema* (1968). There is no other side to this spectacle of faith or belief, no taint of a scam or a delusion, no shade of a perfectly rational, deflating explanation for it all. As always, Brisseau's film offers itself to you with a single, implicit rider, which is quite simply *take it or leave it*—enter right into the movie, or just walk away. To take it you have to take it all, engage with it all, not cherry-pick the acceptable elements from the unacceptable ones, which is what the act of criticism (consciously or not) does all the time. And if you leave it, it is your problem and not the film's. Bad cinema can teach us this ethical lesson: we are forever projecting our own resolved badnesses (personal and social) onto the films we cannot accept.

Death to the Social Worker

It is always the mix of things that disturbs critics of Brisseau. In *Choses secrètes*, the Sadean tale of erotic becoming rubs shoulders with metaphysics and mysticism and then with deliberately mundane intrigues of office politics borrowed from some forgotten, decidedly noncanonical 1950s Hollywood melodrama about climbing the corporate ladder, while the sisterhood vibe between the main characters evokes all the *Sex and the City* episodes to come. In *De bruit et de fureur*, the social issue/problem/concern of the film, which is so palpable—it offers an incredible portrait of the social and familial conditions that brutalize kids—suddenly comes up against a moment of outrageous spectacle that made the audience I recently saw it with explode with liberating laughter. A prim, bespectacled school councilor decides to visit the apartment of her problem student in the projects, unaware that the father she seeks to have a rational discussion with, stalks the passageways of this tiny space with his favorite shotgun in hand. When she finds the front door open, she walks in; instantly, the dad grabs her brutally from behind, puts the firearm to her head, and focuses her attention on the words writ large all over the facing wall, which reads, "Death to the Social Worker." And how often we have all dreamed this scene: the vulgar, vibrant antisocial revenge against the social functionary do-gooder.

This scene offers another way to sum up Brisseau's intriguing view of the world, especially as it relates to the privileged, decisive figure of the school, the classroom. If it is a place where, in a one-to-one relation, somebody can learn culture and ideas and raise themselves up from the lumpenproletariat mire (just as Brisseau considers himself to have done), it is also an intolerable, utterly boring, and crushing prison, the space of miserable, deathly social control. In Brisseau, there is a force—a "life force" (*élan vital*) but also a violent, antisocial, anarchistic, gleefully destructive force, often depicted as the two-faced Janus or "mad love" (*amour fou*)—which lies everywhere and at all times, just waiting to be ignited—hence, the astounding proliferation of fires, Molotov cocktails, bombs, and explosions of every kind in his films.

The mix of things in a Brisseau film is scandalous, even when not every ingredient in that mix is obviously or conventionally scandalous, when some of those ingredients are, in fact, as ordinary as they come. *Les savates de bon dieu* stews up so many things at once, or in rapid turnabout succession. It's the story of a failed marriage and the birth of a new love, a criminal-lovers-on-the-run adventure, a fantastical African character straight out of the tales of *A Thousand and One Nights*, an urban gangster exposé, a Robin Hood fantasy of class retribution and wealth redistribution, an ennobling lesson in teaching and learning, a mundane low comedy of grannies and the sudden upward mobility of the poor, intimations (as always in Brisseau) of the supernatural or the divine, and the usual erotica. A montage sequence in the film, among the most remarkable passages in any Brisseau movie, exists precisely to mix and mess many of these ingredients up, to somehow blend them into an impossible, higher, sublime unity. It takes in robbery, redistribution of wealth, nudity, landscape, and a poem by Jacques Prévert.

...And on with the Adventure

What is it about hypnosis and film? I began this reflection on Bad cinema with the self-hypnosis scene in *Whirlpool*, quite innocently, months before I finally got to see Brisseau's *À l'aventure*, the unfolding plot of which I had avoided reading about beforehand. How awesome it was to discover that hypnosis is the principal subject of this film: hypnosis (individual then group) as the path to (1) "violent sexual orgasm" and (2) divine mystical ecstasy (levitation included, as in *Céline*). This is among Brisseau's most elegant and beguiling films, as well as, indeed, his most risible, in its relentless, unstoppable quest to dramatize the maxim (pronounced by a wise old man on a park bench) that "God loves those who dare." Once again, Brisseau's typical off-screen ellipsis tells all: a psychoanalyst leaves his fabulous new lover for the older woman he has hypnotized into levitation, but we learn in an offhand aside during the final dialogue that this latter adventurer has subsequently left him to become a nun. More than ever, Brisseau's characters turn in a veritable whirlpool of self-discovered and other-prompted transformations, and who better than a handsome hypnotist to stand for the other?

I end with an eternal return to a fundamental pleasure, namely, Otto Preminger. Not *Whirlpool* this time, but something written about his most famous film, *Laura* (1944). Every cinephile will know that this film hinges upon a woman (Laura, incarnated by Gene Tierney) thought dead, immortalized in a portrait on a wall, who—at a completely unforeseen and surprising moment—just walks back into the room and into the plot, alive. Whatever purpose this moment serves within the system of the film itself (and this aspect has been much studied, for instance, by Kristin Thompson), the very audacity of it points forward to so much bad cinema, including that of Brisseau. Sudden moves that scramble the realist premises of a plot, that take the film to some more intense, more hallucinatory level, that treat characters, stories, locations, and themes as the immaterial, endlessly transformable figures that they all fundamentally are.

Way back when *Laura* was first released in postwar Paris, the critic-filmmaker Jacques Doniol-Valcroze took the delirious, inspiring measure of this magnificent screen moment, writing: "When Laura pushes the door and enters, in flesh and blood . . . we exclaim to ourselves: *the cinema, truly, is a beautiful invention*" (qtd. in Legrand 294). A beautiful invention—the line makes me recall the title of the 1986 book by a true apostle of bad cinema, the underground critic Jairo Ferreira, *The Cinema of Invention*, and also the conclusion of an essay by Philip Brophy, who wrapped up a 1988 article on "The Body Horrible" by declaring that "my writing is impelled by the belief that some of the films mentioned here—for good or for bad—will in the hopeful future be more widely recognised as illustrative of a sublime cinematic invention" (67).

Why does the cinema, good or bad, need to invent, not just in a craftsman-like, generic way, but in startling, unexpected ways? To invent is to push past, push beyond what is merely given, what is immediately thinkable, imaginable, acceptable, in life as in art. Henceforth, nothing will bear the slightest resemblance to recognizable human behavior or logical sense. To reach the sublime or the ecstatic (including the sublimely or ecstatically abject), we need to throw away all the bases—however perfectly and lovingly we may lay them out at first—and ignite all the charges. We shall need to go through the reasonable and the rational, the recognizable and the logical, and then also through the risible and the mad, through them and beyond them . . . And then go on with the adventure.

Works Cited

Bordwell, David. "Happy Birthday, Film Workshop." *Observations on Film Art*, 11 Apr. 2009. Web. <http://www.davidbordwell.net/blog/?p=4210>

Bourne, Chris. "*Film Comment* Selects 2009 Review Round-up." *The Bourne Cinema Conspiracy*, 26 Feb. 2009. Web. <http://chrisbourne.blogspot.com/2009/02/film-comment-selects-2009-review-round.html>

Brisseau, Jean-Claude. "*Psycho.*" *Projections 4 and a Half*. Ed. John Boorman and Walter Donohue. London: Faber and Faber, 1995. Print.

Brophy, Philip. "The Body Horrible: Some Notions, Some Points, Some Examples." *Intervention* 21/22 (1988): 58–67. Print.

Daney, Serge. "*Les Cahiers du cinéma 1968–1977.*" Web. <http://home.earthlink.net/%7Esteevee/Daney_1977.html>

De Baecque, Antoine. *L'ange exterminateur*. Paris: Grasset, 2006. Print.

Ferreira, Jairo. *Cinema de Invenção*. São Paulo: Embrafilme/Max Limonad, 1986. Print.

Legrand, Gérard. *Cinémanie*. Paris: Stock, 1979. Print.
Martin, Adrian. "The World Ten Times Over: Ongoing Adventures in Pulp Poetry." *La Furia Umana* 4 (Spring 2010). Web. <http://www.lafuriaumana.it/index.php?option=com_content&view=article&id=142:world-ten-times-over&catid=34:locchio-che-uccide&Itemid=53>
Masson, Alain. "L'irréductible." *Positif* 345 (November 1989): 19–20. Print.
Porton, Richard. "Ghosts, Girls, Guns." *Cinema Scope* 38 (Spring 2009): 53–55. Print.
Quéré, Julie. "L'aurore de l'ange, de la lumière au cinéma." *Feuille*, 13 Jan. 2008. Web.
Routt, William D. "On the Expression of Colonialism in Early Australian Film: Charles Chauvel and Naïve Cinema." *An Australian Film Reader*. Ed. Albert Moran and Tom O'Regan. Paddington: Currency Press, 1985. 55–66. Print.
Strauss, Frédéric. "Jean-Claude Brisseau. Une cinémathèque imaginaire." *Bibliothèque du film*, 2000. Web. <http://www.bifi.fr/public/ap/article.php?id=64>
Thompson, Kristin. *Breaking the Glass Armor: Neoformalist Film Analysis*. Princeton: Princeton UP, 1988. Print.

10

The Evil Dead DVD Commentaries

Amateurishness and Bad Film Discourse

KATE EGAN

In July 1999, Elite Entertainment released a special edition of Sam Raimi's debut feature film, *The Evil Dead* (1981). Included on this special edition were two commentary tracks—the first from director Raimi and producer Robert Tapert, and the second from Bruce Campbell, the film's principal actor and (along with Raimi and Tapert) one of the film's executive producers and founders of their production company, Renaissance Pictures. Subsequent to the release of Elite's special edition, these commentary tracks were included as special features on five further DVD releases of the film by Anchor Bay Entertainment between 2001 and 2007.

Since the appearance of the Elite special edition, *The Evil Dead* commentaries have been consistently singled out for praise in mainstream press reviews of the various DVD editions of the film, in fan reviews (for instance, on imdb.com), and on specialist online sites devoted to reviewing DVD releases (including *DVD Times*, dvdreview.com, and the specialist DVD commentary review site, ratethatcommentary.com). Without question, one of the key attractions of the commentaries, for these fans and critics, is the way in which they recount, in both an entertaining and informative fashion, *The Evil Dead*'s particularly grueling, event-filled production story. As an extremely low-budget film produced by three novice filmmakers from Michigan with no studio support, *The Evil Dead* has now become well known, in fan circles and beyond, for the memorable anecdotes, experiences, and events associated with its production—including, a number of 24-hour shooting stints, reports of injuries sustained by actors and crew, the use of stand-ins to cover for absent principal actors, and the creation of homemade camera rigs and primitive special effects (see Warren; Campbell; Egan).

In an insightful essay, Catherine Grant has illustrated how many DVD commentaries function less as vehicles that attempt to determine the ways in which the film text itself (and its narrative) should be interpreted and understood, and more as direct, moment-by-moment retellings of "the drama of a movie's source," which convey stories about that film's production in relation to particular relevant moments in the film (104). Furthermore, and related to this, several academics have illustrated how DVD extras (and, in particular, DVD commentaries) can have an educational function, turning DVDs into "film school[s] in a box" and serving as "master classes," which teach aspiring filmmakers the basics of film production in a number of different ways, including specialist production procedures relating to special effects and aspects of the production schedule, such as pickups and foley work (see Klinger, "DVD Cinephile" 26; Badley 55; Grant 110; Gray 247).

The focus on amateur filmmakers and production-related stories in *The Evil Dead* commentaries seems to ably illustrate and support these arguments. However, the purpose of this chapter is to focus on one aspect of *The Evil Dead* commentaries that seems to distinguish them from the examples taken up in much previous academic work, namely, the degree to which these commentaries actively *foreground* the film's "bad" features, including its narrative implausibilities and plot holes, the poor quality of the film's acting and special effects, and its other mistakes and continuity errors. As I will go on to argue, *The Evil Dead* is not a straightforward example of bad cinema or, by any means, the only example of a low-budget film whose meanings have been informed by extra-texts designed to foreground "bad" or low-quality aspects of the production. However, what the case study of *The Evil Dead* commentaries highlights is a number of bad film–related framing strategies that support the notion (put forward by Catherine Grant) that DVD commentaries can work to present a film to its audiences as an artifact produced in a particular context and to therefore allow filmmakers to use the medium of the DVD commentary to reflect on that context. In the case of *The Evil Dead*, this relates to the particular ways in which the film has come to be appreciated as a cult film.

As I have argued elsewhere, the film's status as cult has clearly been informed by the fact that it was made for a drive-in and theatrical audience but that it has achieved its most sustained success on video and DVD (mediums that allow viewers to recognize production flaws in a way that wasn't anticipated by the filmmakers when the film was originally conceived). Furthermore, this also relates, in the case of *The Evil Dead*, to the ways in which a focus on "bad" qualities can allow a now well-known, established filmmaker like Raimi to reflect on his low-budget rookie filmmaking past in relation to the subsequent development of his filmmaking skills and career. As a consequence, this chapter will consider how these discourses and perspectives intertwine and connect with the "bad" readings of *The Evil Dead*'s production put forward in these commentaries, and therefore illustrate one of the ways in which a focus on the "bad" in a DVD commentary can be employed as a vehicle of reflection (on a range of previous production and reception contexts) for particular filmmakers.

The Text as "Bad" Object in DVD Commentaries

Both before and during the course of *The Evil Dead*'s multiple releases on DVD, many of the stories and anecdotes associated with the production

Figure 10.1. Amateur horrors in *The Evil Dead* (1982). Courtesy Renaissance Pictures / The Kobal Collection.

had circulated via a number of sites and contexts. These included magazine and television interviews conducted with the filmmakers at the time of the release of *The Evil Dead* and on the release of the film's sequels: *Evil Dead II* (1987) and *Army of Darkness* (1992); Campbell's innumerable appearances at fan conventions in both the United States and elsewhere; online fan sites devoted to *The Evil Dead* films; and Bill Warren's 2000 book *The Evil Dead Companion*. As a consequence, the focus on the key events of the film's "making of" story in Elite's DVD commentaries enabled these production tales and experiences to, as one *DVD Times* review notes, be "collected in one place" ("Evil Dead Trilogy") and (as they continued to circulate on subsequent DVD releases) allowed these commentaries to play a key role in the wider dissemination of *The Evil Dead*'s "making of" story. Indeed, in the booklet "Bringing the Dead Home for Dinner" (included in Anchor Bay's 2002 Book of the Dead DVD edition release), the "well-documented" nature of *The Evil Dead*'s production experiences and anecdotes is explicitly acknowledged, and DVD users who have yet to hear such anecdotes are encouraged to "pop in the DVD" to "discover true and tall tales that will both entertain and truly de-mystify the 'glories' of independent filmmaking" (Felsher 6).

In 2008, as part of my research on *The Evil Dead*'s cult reputation and status, I surveyed 406 user reviews of the film on imdb.com (stretching from 1999 to 2008) in order to gain a further sense of the reasons why fans of *The Evil Dead* found it to be unique, distinctive, or special. Across these reviews, the sense that access to the film's "making of" story (particularly via Elite's DVD commentaries) had enhanced fan appreciation for Raimi's debut feature is consistently evident, and this appreciation is made manifest in two key ways. First, the film's production story informs fan respect for the Renaissance partners' status as amateur filmmakers, working on an extremely low budget and having to overcome innumerable obstacles and difficulties in order to get their film made. As one reviewer notes, "after listening to the commentary on the special edition DVD, I appreciate the film even more" ([n.e.o], 30 May 1999); while another remarks that: "you can't really appreciate what they had to go through to make this film till you hear these excellent [commentary] tracks" (Raistlin, 14 Jan. 2000). Second, and connecting with the above focus on DVD commentaries as "master classes," access to this production background also seems to inform *The Evil Dead*'s status as a motivational film, particularly to aspiring filmmakers. As one reviewer notes, "watching a movie like this inspires me, especially since I've always wanted to make a horror movie" (mattymatt4ever, 7 Jan.

2003). For another, the film is not only "entertaining" but "also educational in the sense of filmmaking" (ryang film, 5 Feb. 2007), and for a third, the film "is a great example of how to, or [the] measures you go to, [to] get into the film industry" (Richard Pullen, 19 July 2002).

As a consequence, *The Evil Dead*'s "making of" story (whether recounted in print or DVD commentary form) has served, for these fan reviewers, to enrich their appreciation of the film, and to function as a kind of how-to manual for prospective amateur filmmakers. These appeals, which have been enhanced and heightened via the circulation of this story on *The Evil Dead* DVD commentaries, do clearly connect, then, with the above-cited arguments and discussions about the functions of DVD extras as promotional and discursive tools that work to inform viewer reception and appreciation, and "construct . . . the text as meaningful object" (Gray 242). For Gray, as well as Grant and Klinger, however, the recounting of production stories and the educational function of such stories in DVD extras are ultimately seen to function to enhance the aesthetic, artistic, industrial, or cultural value of the film itself. For Grant, the production stories recounted in director Mike Figgis's commentary for *Timecode* (2000) work primarily to foreground Figgis's authorial vision for the film and the achievement of this vision in the film itself. For Gray, the commentaries and other extras on *The Lord of the Rings* DVDs celebrate the hard work and skill of the filmmakers and thus function to "cloak" the production and the films "in an aura of artistry and excellence" (251). Finally, for Klinger, while the information about production processes on DVD commentaries and other extras can have an educational function (allowing viewers to feel that they are being given access to the secrets of filmmaking), the primary function of this information is to encourage viewers to appreciate and celebrate the "effective illusionism" of filmmaking and the "talented film professionals" who create "movie magic" ("Contemporary Cinephile" 140).

In contrast to this, Raimi, Tapert, and Campbell focus frequently, in their commentaries, on *The Evil Dead*'s flawed or ineffective aspects and on the gaffes and mistakes which are visible in particular scenes. For example, during the course of the two commentary tracks, the following comments are made at particular moments in the film:

> RAIMI: How can that board completely trap him? (laughs). That's the most absurd image I've ever seen. . . . Bad wig, now she's got black hair all of a sudden. We've got a wig, it'll match the light not the colour . . .

TAPERT: Yes, you go to a cabin in the woods for a weekend, you chop up your friend. Of course you bury them before you call the police . . .

CAMPBELL: That's a little cheesy matte shot up in the right hand corner there. Uh, if you look closely you'll see the actual square round the moon. I hate it when that happens . . .

CAMPBELL: There's a nice cheesy scar there, basically a rectangular scar with no blending whatsoever. But this was not a sophisticated motion picture, folks. At the time we thought it looked great. We just figured, put enough blood on there and it'll be fine.

Grant does note that director's commentaries can potentially focus not just on a director's "achievement" of his or her vision but also on their "failure or inability to achieve [it]" (112). However, if DVD commentaries are primarily vehicles of promotion, the question of why *The Evil Dead* commentaries (and indeed other commentaries) might focus as much on failure or ineffectiveness as on success and achievement remains underexplored. As the above extracts from the commentaries indicate, Raimi, Tapert, and Campbell's foregrounding of narrative implausibilities, continuity errors and unconvincing visual and makeup effects (as well as the frequent comments Campbell makes throughout his commentary about his poor acting) seem to suggest that the commentaries are informed by what Jeffrey Sconce has termed a "paracinematic" discourse or approach: that is, one which involves the identification and celebration of just these kind of low-quality or flawed aspects of a film. Indeed, like the films that Sconce focuses on, *The Evil Dead* was a film made within impoverished production conditions, with a lack of time and money leading to "restrictions on rehearsal time, set-ups, retakes and other elements directly impacting the . . . filmmaker's ability to 'polish' a film" (Sconce, "Esper" 18).

Despite this, *The Evil Dead* is not a clear-cut example of a paracinematic film, at least in relation to two of the key factors discussed by Sconce. First, Sconce argues that paracinematic culture focuses on the celebration and appreciation of "forms of cinematic 'trash,' whether such films have been either explicitly rejected or simply ignored by legitimate film culture" ("'Trashing' the Academy" 372). *The Evil Dead* is a low-budget horror film that was released in U.S. cinemas without an MPAA rating and removed from legitimate circulation in the United Kingdom for a long period in the 1980s because of its association with the "video nasty" scandal. However, despite this initial association with illegitimacy and rejection, it should be remembered that the film received positive critical notices (for its groundbreaking visual style and formal creativity) from the moment it first appeared on the film festival circuit in 1982. It went on to become a huge commercial success when first released to video in 1983, and has subsequently been celebrated and acknowledged, by critics, fans, academics, and filmmakers alike as a landmark American independent horror film and as the debut of a talented, and now high-profile, film director in Raimi.

Second, Sconce notes that paracinematic films "rarely exhibit . . . pronounced stylistic virtuosity as the result of a 'conscious' artistic agenda" ("'Trashing' the Academy" 385). However, as Raimi has acknowledged on innumerable occasions, while the Renaissance partners' decision to make their debut feature film a horror picture was largely strategic (in that many successful or influential horror films made during the 1960s and 1970s had been made on a low budget), the widely regarded stylistic flair of *The Evil Dead* was very much informed by Raimi's desire to create effective horror and suspense sequences through experimentation with camera work, editing, and sound design (Warren 37).

This is not to suggest that the low-quality aspects of *The Evil Dead* haven't been acknowledged in press and online reviews. However, many reviews have also urged audiences to "look past the [film's] less-than-stellar acting, the dubious dialog and the thin character writing, [to] see one of the greatest horror films ever created" (Grann-Bach, 14 Jan. 2006). By contrast, Campbell's DVD commentary consistently emphasizes the "bad," encouraging listeners to look for and focus on a range of flaws and gaffes in the film. Throughout the voice track, Campbell draws attention to the film's mistakes sometimes before they even appear on screen, readying the viewer to "notice there's a lot of editing here, to take out various lame things that didn't work," or to "look closely" in order to examine the square around the matte of the moon in a number of the film's external location shots. Furthermore, while Campbell does acknowledge the effectiveness and skill of Raimi's formal and stylistic approach at a number of points in his commentary, Raimi says very little about his intentions in relation to the stylistic or narrative meaning of the film, and the critical praise that the film has received over the years is barely acknowledged in either commentary.

The question that arises is exactly what function this focus on low quality elements, errors and implausibilities has in these commentaries, and how this relates to the conveyance of the film's entertaining and informative "making of" story. For me, this consistent attention to the "bad" aspects of the film and its production seems to have a number of functions in the DVD commentaries, all of which relate to aspects of *The Evil Dead* that have fed into the film's status and appeal as a cult film (see Egan). These aspects include:

1. The historical and industrial context within which the film was made and which informed its production,
2. The filmmakers' interest, when planning and making their film, in evoking particular kinds of reaction and response from audiences,
3. The distinctive personalities of Raimi, Tapert, and Campbell, and
4. The potential for aspiring filmmakers to relate to the film because of its low-budget and amateur origins.

Historical Context

As I have argued elsewhere, *The Evil Dead*—made between 1979 and 1980—emerged at a transitional stage in the historical development of key exhibition sites for low-budget horror films. While the film achieved its greatest success on video, it was conceived just prior to the establishment of home video as a key distribution and exhibition platform for low-budget horror and had thus been made with the U.S. drive-in audience in mind. During the course of Tapert and Raimi's commentary, this historical context comes sharply into focus as they view and comment on a sequence where, as a female demon is shot in the face, a tube pumping fake blood attached to the actress is clearly visible. As the demon is shot and the tube is revealed, the following comments are made:

RAIMI: Boy, talk about seeing that tube!

TAPERT: Yeah, well digital clean-up (as a demon appears from the bottom of the frame) Jump cut!

RAIMI: Jump cut, right?

TAPERT: Yeah.

RAIMI: These things can all be seen now. This is before video existed that we made this picture. We just thought the audience would see it once on the big screen, and wouldn't be around to study [it].

In this example, a focus on error-spotting is related to the film's status as an artifact from a past era of film production and consumption. Raimi's identification of the jump cut and the nondiegetic tube (and his subsequent comment that "these things can all be seen now") draws attention to the film's failure to live up to the standards of what Klinger has called a "digital aesthetic" form of film appreciation. As Klinger argues, particular kinds of films (most prominently high-budget studio blockbusters) "transfer particularly well" from theatrical exhibition to DVD because digital technologies tend to replicate, or even enhance, the sound and image qualities of these films ("DVD Cinephile" 30). By contrast, while for many reviewers *The Evil Dead* DVDs' digitization has enhanced the film's innovative sound design and camerawork, the "digital clean up" process has also, as Raimi and Tapert's comments illustrate, exposed the rudimentary and low-budget nature of some of the film's editing tricks and special effects. By pointing to the film's initial exhibition context—as a low-budget drive-in picture that was expected to be viewed only once—Raimi and Tapert draw attention not to the "happy marriage" between "feature films and post-theatrical formats" (30), but to a yawning gap between the two. Furthermore, Raimi's explanation for the jump cut also draws attention to the distance between the initial audience for, and the audience now viewing, the film, and listening to the commentary, multiple times.

References to *The Evil Dead*'s (early) theatrical audiences occur throughout both commentaries and emerge in two key ways. First, mention is made of certain moments where audience members (presumably during the film's initial theatrical run) laughed at or commented on an implausible aspect of the film's story. For instance, as Campbell's character Ash is shown attempting to pour water into his dying friend's mouth, Tapert notes: "I just remember this sequence being in theatres and people just thinking he's just the ultimate idiot. . . . They really howled at him dumping water down a dead man's throat." Second, the filmmakers (and particularly Campbell) often take on the role of an incredulous audience member, shouting back at the screen or commenting on implausible aspects of the unfolding action during the course of their commentaries. For example, in an early scene in the film where the character Scotty suggests to the others that they get in the car and take the bridge out of the woods, Campbell calls out "No, you can't take the bridge 'cause there is no bridge, you knuckle head. You know that." And at a later point in the film, he responds to Ash's anguished question—"why are you torturing me like this?"—with the answer: "because you're so stupid."

Audience Reactions

The filmmakers' adoption of these registers—either talking about past audience responses or taking up the position of a critical audience member—seem to be informed by the fact that the filmmakers (and Raimi in particular) were centrally concerned with eliciting strong responses and reactions from the audience and (as they note in their commentaries) they attended many initial screenings of the film in order to gauge these reactions. The filmmakers' experiences with initial audiences seem to feed into the ways in which they engage with *The Evil Dead* during their commentaries.

On the one hand, the references to past audience reactions allow them to illustrate how the film's initial reception has now become part of its "making of" story. If a "paracinematic" attention to aesthetic aberrance within a film "seeks to push the viewer beyond the formal boundaries of the text," to focus on factors relating to the film's "impoverished" production context (Sconce, "'Trashing' the Academy" 387), then the attention to flaws and errors in *The Evil Dead* commentaries encourages viewers to go even further beyond the text to consider its reception: the reactions of past audiences to the film. On the other hand, the filmmakers' familiarity with typical audience responses to implausible moments in the film also enables them to distance themselves from the film, to take up the position of an incredulous audience member and to look at the film as an artifact made many years before in a different kind of exhibition context.

Distinctive Personalities

The entertaining way in which Campbell adopts the role of a critical audience member also feeds into another function of the commentaries, namely, how they serve, purely and simply, as a vehicle for the distinctive personalities of these three filmmakers. In an article that discusses cult film critic, Joe Bob Briggs's DVD commentary for Elite's *I Spit on Your Grave* (Meir Zarchi, 1978), Tristan Fidler acknowledges the ways in which Briggs's voice track can be appreciated "as an entertainment in itself," with Briggs throughout paying "equal attention to his roles as film critic, B-movie historian and cult personality." Like Campbell's commentary for *The Evil Dead*, Briggs's voice track features a number of sarcastic, tongue-in-cheek wisecracks about the film's plot holes and other imperfections. Moreover, since the initial release of *The Evil Dead*, Campbell has, like Briggs, built up a substantial fan following as a cult personality, which (informed by his appearances at fan conventions and his performances in *The Evil Dead* sequels) has centered on his talents as a slapstick comedian, his hapless but likeable everyman persona, and his wisecracking, sarcastic comedic delivery. On ratethatcommentary.com, Campbell's "delightful sense of humour" (pat00139, 27 March 2007) is seen as a key attraction of commentaries he has recorded for all three of the *Evil Dead* films. In this sense, the potential to showcase his particular brand of comedy (and his much-loved personality) through a focus on *The Evil Dead*'s flawed aspects is clearly and gleefully exploited by Campbell throughout the DVD.

Campbell utilizes the much-discussed immediacy of the DVD commentary—that is, the ability for commentators to engage with a film on a moment-by-moment basis (Parker and Parker)—for comedic purposes throughout his commentary. In one early passage, Campbell readies the viewer for a gaffe, noting that—at the end of the dialogue sequence playing out on the screen—he can be seen struggling to get his jacket on, compelling Raimi to cut before the end of the sequence to hide the gaffe. As the onscreen Campbell is seen fumbling with his jacket, we hear him act out his younger self's thought processes, exclaiming: "let me just put my jacket on here I, oh, oh, ohhh. I hate it when that happens." Furthermore, Campbell also frequently uses the film's low cultural status as a horror (or exploitation) film unconcerned with narrative depth or nuanced characterization for comedy mileage, noting at one point that "this was high drama this scene, I want you to know, method acting." Indeed, this approach seems to draw attention to the fact that the film's most important drama is not in the narrative but in the "making of" story that the commentaries primarily recount (see Grant).

On a wider level, the focus on the film's errors throughout both commentaries has been seen (by fans and critics alike) to be informed by three other key characteristics of Raimi, Tapert, and Campbell's personalities—their modesty and self-deprecation, their fun and unpretentious attitude to filmmaking, and (as the magazine *Fangoria* noted at the time of the release of *Evil Dead II*) the "sustaining camaraderie which sets them apart from other, more desperately competitive filmmakers" (O'Malley 38). The error-spotting and affectionate ridicule that occurs throughout both commentaries thus serves as an effective vehicle for these oft-identified and valued characteristics of Raimi and company. Among imdb.com reviewers, these characteristic personas clearly feed into an admiration for *The Evil Dead* as a production based on "humble aspirations" and made by a group of friends who were prepared to take a chance, and tell "a zombie story as best as they [knew] how" (Bogmeister, 25 September 2005; Thomas, 28 May 2003).

Amateur Aspirations

While the commentaries showcase Campbell and Raimi's comedic skills and thus foreground some of the distinctive characteristics that have made them successful media personalities, the focus throughout both commentaries on their experiences while making the film also draws attention to the filmmakers' past status as amateurs. This focus on the nonprofessional as a distinct aspect of *The Evil Dead* and its production story works in a number of ways, all of which can be seen to enhance the appeal of Raimi, Tapert, and Campbell to aspiring filmmakers. As I have argued elsewhere, this focus on amateurishness allows Raimi and the others to present themselves as very ordinary human beings rather than skilled filmmakers or artists. Raimi and Tapert, in particular, often reminisce about silly antics that occurred off screen around particular moments in the film, including cutting each others' hair and poking Campbell with sticks so that he had a limp in particular scenes. In other instances, they point out that props had come from their family homes, including a T-shirt from Raimi's summer camp and a tape recorder borrowed from Campbell's father. Consequently, at these points, the filmmakers seem to approach the film as if it were a home movie of their past youthful experiences, placing emphasis on their status as three old friends and the film's significance as a record of the fun they had during the formative years of their friendship.

Crucially, the commentaries allow the filmmakers to reflect not only on their personal life histories but also on their professional filmmaking careers through their focus on the film's errors and flaws. Indeed, many commentators and critics (including Campbell himself) have discussed the significance of *The Evil Dead* as an initial, flawed experiment in feature filmmaking and an attempt to develop the filmmaking skills that were honed and improved upon as the *Evil Dead* series went on.

Rebecca and Sam Umland, for instance, have discussed the first film's status as an "immature" work when compared to its sequel (36), and Campbell in a press interview to advertise one of *The Evil Dead* DVD releases noted that the series documented the "slow build" of Raimi et al. "becoming more sophisticated filmmakers" (qtd. in Kirkland 19). In this respect, if the focus on flaws in the film's commentaries seems to suggest that the filmmakers are approaching the film as a "paracinematic" text, then the key factors being drawn upon to do so are not just its "impoverished" production conditions or "technical ineptitude" (Sconce, "'Trashing' the Academy" 385) but also professional filmmaking *inexperience* (a word that is frequently mentioned in the commentaries).

In his commentary, Raimi often looks at the film from the perspective of an experienced filmmaker musing on his past and reflecting on what he might do differently if he could go back and make *The Evil Dead* again. On some occasions, this reflection takes the form of amusement or embarrassment at the implausible aspects of the film's narrative, with Raimi audibly cringing at the ridiculousness of Campbell's character being trapped under some shelves for a lengthy period of time or commenting on the inexplicable placement of bones in the cabin as an homage to *The Texas Chainsaw Massacre* (Tobe Hooper, 1974). "In a slaughterhouse picture you understand why there are hanging bones. In our picture, I'm not sure I get it yet. [I'm] still working on . . . the answer to that." On other occasions, Raimi (although clearly amused by the ineffective aspects of the film) almost seems to be scolding himself for not staging a sequence more persuasively. For example, of an early scare sequence in the film in which a trap door suddenly rattles and moves up and down, Raimi says: "I always keep thinking that we should have been so much more subtle on that. Why was the damn thing moving so much? A little goes a long way."

Conclusion: Theories of Paracinema, Theories of the DVD

This focus on errors in order to reflect on a director's past inexperience (and implicitly, the subsequent development of skills) seems to have a number of functions in *The Evil Dead* DVD commentaries. On the one hand, it illustrates how a focus on the "bad"—unsuccessful or ineffective—aspects of *The Evil Dead* serve to present the film as an artifact of Raimi's (and Tapert and Campbell's) rookie filmmaking past. It is notable that Grant's arguments about director's commentaries and Sconce's about "paracinematic" film appreciation both shed light on this tendency in these commentary tracks. Grant argues that the documentation of a film's "making of" story on the director's DVD commentary places emphasis on a film's status as a "created product . . . issuing from a particular authorial context" (111). Sconce argues that a paracinematic focus on plot holes, poor acting, and continuity errors in "bad" films from the past allows the viewer to recognize the artificial, constructed nature of that film's narrative and thus opens "a passageway into engaging a larger field of contextual issues surrounding the film as a socially and historically specific document" ("'Trashing' the Academy," 392–93). By reflecting on *The Evil Dead*'s ineffectiveness or low-quality aspects from the perspective of a commentary track recorded over nineteen years after the film was made, Raimi, Tapert, and Campbell are able to illustrate how the film's construction and production was informed by a range of contexts—not only the kind of low-budget production context discussed by Sconce but also, and in line with Grant's argument, by the more particular context of their filmmaking careers. As a consequence, this focus on imperfections and errors underscores the status of the film as a "historical document" in two ways: first, as a document of the impact of the production and exhibition contexts associated with low-budget filmmaking in the late 1970s and early 1980s, and second, as a record of the development of Raimi, Tapert, and Campbell's filmmaking career.

This reflective focus on inexperience and amateurishness can account for *The Evil Dead*'s appeal to fans (a film that can be admired) and also to aspiring filmmakers (a film that is inspirational and educational). Raimi, Tapert, and Campbell's retrospective identification of moments that worked or didn't work in *The Evil Dead* potentially functions as a low-budget filmmaking "master class" that focuses not only on what to do if you are an inexperienced filmmaker working on a low budget (for instance, how to create inexpensive camera rigs or special effects or, in the case of Campbell's gaffe with his jacket, how to cut away if an actor fluffs his performance) but also what not to do when making your first feature film. Sconce has argued that the flaws and mistakes in low-budget paracinematic films can work as effective teaching tools for film studies students, in that identifying these errors can shed light on formal conventions and strategies that are invisible or harder to identify in "more apparently 'seamless' productions" ("Esper" 30). In this sense, *The Evil Dead* commentaries also seem to work as effective teaching tools for aspiring filmmakers, enabling such viewers to not only relate to the filmmakers but also benefit from and learn from the mistakes these amateurs made during their initial filmmaking adventures.

This kind of appeal can also have a wider promotional usefulness, in the sense that DVD special editions can serve to imbue particular film titles with legitimacy and authenticity (see Klinger "Contemporary Cinephile"; Guins). The focus in *The Evil Dead* commentaries on the scrappy, ineffective, or flawed aspects of the film and its production can work to maintain and perpetuate the film's appealing and relatable status as an authentically amateur (and thus nonmainstream and non-Hollywood) production. Indeed, the commentaries frequently couch their production stories about gaffes and mistakes in terms that clearly distinguish the film from the discourses of "movie magic" that Klinger argues are prominent in many of the extras accompanying bigger budget Hollywood titles onto DVD. However, what this effectively illustrates is the range of functions and roles—from personality vehicle, to reflective cinema history lesson to filmmaking "master class" to authentication strategy—that a focus on the "bad" and failed aspects of a film can have when they are foregrounded, discussed, and capitalized upon in a DVD commentary.

Works Cited

Badley, Linda. "Bringing It All Back Home: Horror Cinema and Video Culture." *Horror Zone: The Cultural Experience of Contemporary Horror Cinema.* Ed. Ian Conrich. London: I. B. Tauris, 2010. 45–63. Print.

Campbell, Bruce. *If Chins Could Kill: Confessions of a B Movie Actor.* Los Angeles: LA Weekly Books, 2002. Print.

Egan, Kate. *The Evil Dead.* London: Wallflower, 2011. Print.

The Evil Dead: Full Uncut Version. Dir. Sam Raimi. Anchor Bay Entertainment UK, 2002. DVD.

"The Evil Dead Trilogy." *DVD Times,* 22 Aug. 2003. Web. 9 July 2007. <http://www.dvdtimes.co.uk/content.php?contentid=5502>

Felsher, Michael. "Booklet: Bringing the Dead Home for Dinner." *The Evil Dead: The Book of The Dead Full Uncut Special Edition DVD.* Anchor Bay Entertainment, 2002. Print.

Fidler, Tristan. "'They Don't Call 'em Exploitation Movies for Nothing!': Joe Bob Briggs and the Critical Commentary on *I Spit on Your Grave.*" *Colloquy,* 18 Dec. 2009. Web. 8 July 2010. <http://www.colloquy.monash.edu.au/issue018/index.html>

Grant, Catherine. "Auteur Machines? Auteurism and the DVD." *Film and Television After DVD.* Ed. James Bennett and Tom Brown. London: Routledge, 2008. 101–15. Print.

Gray, Jonathan. "Bonus Materials: The DVD Layering of *The Lord of the Rings.*" *The Lord of the Rings: Popular Culture in Global Context.* Ed. Ernest Mathijs. London: Wallflower, 2006. 238–53. Print.

Guins, Raiford. "Blood and Black Gloves on Shiny Discs: New Media, Old Tastes, and the Remediation of Italian Horror Films in the United States." *Horror International*. Ed. Steven Jay Schneider and Tony Williams. Detroit: Wayne State UP, 2005. 1532. Print.

Kirkland, Bruce. "*Evil Dead* a Scream!: Splendid New Three-disc Set Brings Campy Cult Classic Back to Life." *Ottawa Sun* (29 December 2007): 19. Print.

Klinger, Barbara. "The Contemporary Cinephile: Film Collecting in the Post-Video Era." *Hollywood Spectatorship: Changing Perceptions of Cinema Audiences*. Ed. Melvyn Stokes and Richard Maltby. London: British Film Institute, 2001. 132–51. Print.

———. "The DVD Cinephile: Viewing Heritages and Home Film Cultures." *Film and Television After DVD*. Ed. James Bennett and Tom Brown. London: Routledge, 2008. 1944. Print.

O'Malley, David. "*Evil Dead II*: To Bleed or Not to Bleed?" *Fangoria* 63 (May 1987): 34–38. Print.

Parker, Deborah, and Mark Parker. "Directors and DVD Commentary: The Specifics of Intention." *Journal of Aesthetics and Art Criticism* 62.1 (2004): 13–21. Print.

Sconce, Jeffrey. "'Trashing' the Academy: Taste, Excess, and an Emerging Politics of Cinematic Style." *Screen* 36.4 (1995): 371–93. Print.

———. "Esper, the Renunciator: Teaching 'Bad' Movies to Good Students." *Defining Cult Movies: The Cultural Politics of Oppositional Taste*. Ed. Mark Jancovich, Antonio Lazaro Reboll, Julian Stringer and Andy Willis. Manchester: Manchester UP, 2003. 14–34. Print.

Umland, Rebecca and Sam Umland. "The Epic Horror of the *Evil Dead* Trilogy: From the Backwoods of Tennessee to Lord Arthur's Court." *Video Watchdog* 46 (1998): 32–51. Print.

Warren, Bill. *The Evil Dead Companion*. London: Titan, 2000. Print.

11

Liking *The Magus*

I. Q. Hunter

> I have to break off for a fortnight to go down to Majorca, where they're filming *The Magus*. . . . Most of the time I feel like a skeleton at the feast: this isn't what I had imagined, either in the book or in the script.
>
> —Fowles (*Wormholes* 20)

The only way to kick off this chapter is to quote the one thing you might have heard about its subject: Woody Allen's quip that if he lived his life over again he'd do everything exactly the same, with the exception of watching *The Magus*.

The Magus (Guy Green, 1968) was a disaster, a comprehensive "BADaptation"[1] of John Fowles's best-selling cult novel, first published in 1966 (a revised version came out in 1977). Leonard Maltin's description of it as "pretentious, hopelessly confusing . . . tiresome" accurately sums up the critical consensus (858). Even Michael Caine said it was the worst film he had been in (quite an admission) because no one knew what it was all about (*The Magus*).[2] It is true that the film wasn't a high-profile catastrophe that brought down a studio, as *Heaven's Gate* (Michael Cimino, 1980) did, or bury a reputation for good, as *Lady in the Water* (2006) and *The Happening* (2008) buried M. Night Shyamalan's. But universally execrated, it acquired a reputation as one of British cinema's most embarrassing misfires.

Michael Caine plays Nicholas Urfe (his name echoes both Earth and Orpheus), a callow English teacher with literary pretensions ("I have everything a poet needs except poems"), who comes to the Greek island of Phraxos after his predecessor at the school committed suicide. Nicholas is taken up by Conchis (Anthony Quinn)—the magus, or magician, of the title—who poses variously as a Greek millionaire, a psychiatrist, a dead person (his grave in the local cemetery marks his "death of convenience," as he puts it, in 1944), a wartime collaborator, a film producer, a theater director, a fraud, and God. Conchis leads Nicholas through a series of psychodramas designed to shake him out of narcissism and into a state of bemused enlightenment. Nicholas, with "all the symptoms of contemporary genius," is burdened with representing the over-rational and disbelieving twentieth century and its self-absorbed decadence in the 1960s. Additionally, Nicholas is torn between two women: a French airline hostess Anne (Anna Karina), who seemingly killed herself because of his indifference, and Lily (Candice Bergen), who claims by turns to be Conchis's mistress from 1915 who still thinks it is World War I, a psychiatric patient (called Julie Holmes) whom Conchis is treating, and a screen or theater actress under Conchis's direction, though she may also be the embodiment of a Greek goddess.

The film centers on two melodramatic set pieces that dramatize moral choices and Nicholas's emergence as an enlightened hero. The first consists of powerful but unreliable flashbacks to Conchis's time as mayor of the island under Nazi occupation, when the Germans, led by Captain Wimmer (Corin Redgrave), force him to choose between allowing the execution of eighty villagers and killing three partisans by battering them to death with a machine gun butt. The second, less accomplished sequence is an hallucinatory trial in which a drugged Nicholas endures a computer's scathing summary of his character, a silent film of Lily making love to another man, and Conchis's inviting him to judge and flog her and symbolically rid himself of her influence. Nicholas awakens in a hotel room in Athens that transpires to be a mock up on Phraxos and sees Anne still alive in a distant boat—she apparently agreed to connive in Conchis's "godgame" (the film's working title, according to some sources)—and the film ends with an enigmatic shot of a smiling sculpted head and a quotation, spoken in voiceover by Conchis and then Nicholas, from T. S. Eliot's *Four Quartets*: "We shall not cease from exploration, and the end of all our exploring will be to arrive where we started and know the place for the first time." Caine's subsequent "toothy, getting-of-wisdom laugh," one of Caine's biographers wrote, "is among the most misjudged moments of his entire career" (Bray 112).

Given its unfortunate reputation, *The Magus* vies with Roland Joffé's *The Scarlet Letter* (1995) and Terry Gilliam's *Fear and Loathing in Las Vegas* (1998) as an object lesson in how not to adapt a classic or cult book (though conventionally, of course, all adaptations of "good" books are regarded as failures of accurate reproduction). Although Fowles had written the screenplay, he thought the film had "no poetry, no mystery" (Warburton 303), and he (and his biographer Eileen Warburton) blamed its failure on Guy Green whose "talent," according to Warburton, "lay in the gritty, understated, down-to-earth, and proletarian" style of his earlier films such as *The Angry Silence* (1960) and who "hated ambiguity, symbolism, and literary references, the very stuff of *The Magus*" (296). *The Magus* in short comes down to us as a definitive "badfilm," to use a later term in cult film studies: a film whose badness, floating free of historical context and the idiosyncrasies of personal taste, seems almost indisputable and for all time.

Until 2007, when *The Magus* came out on DVD, its badness was hard to verify. The film was rarely revived except for occasional cable television screenings or critically reappraised (the website rottentomatoes.com boasts just one review of it, in Spanish). Few recent accounts of the film exist, so far as I can tell, aside from Tim Lucas's insightful *Sight and Sound* review of the DVD release of "one of the few forgotten films of a decade . . . fecund with invention and brilliance," which praises its ambition: "a film of some intelligence and pretension (not in a bad sense) to art, more interested in amplifying the viewer's mind with questions than in answering them" (81). While some reviewers on the Internet Movie Data Base (imdb.com) admire it passionately, the site's users—who frequently quote Woody Allen—more often suggest merely that it is not quite as bad as they feared. Unlike the book, *The Magus* has not (*pace* its Wikipedia entry) acquired a revisionist cult following or at any rate one contactable by an Internet search. Nor has the film's toxic reputation inspired its ironic revival as an object of pitying or enthusiastic scorn, even as an example of Michael Caine's unswerving commitment to starring in as much dross as possible.

This chapter has the modest aim of briefly telling you why I like *The Magus*, in spite of its secure niche in British cinema's Hall of Shame. I shall touch on why it reputedly fails as an adaptation, but instead of exhaustively listing its treacherous deviations from Fowles's novel (inevitably, all literary adaptations betray their source in some way), I will explain why viewing it through the prism of adaptation studies is liable to blind us to its merits as a film. *The Magus* is perfectly redeemable from "badness" and may even rise to the heady heights of "actually quite good" when viewed not as a failed adaptation but rather as a compromised experiment in British art cinema, intertextually torn between the different possibilities of film in the late 1960s and struggling to negotiate them productively.

∾

There are many kinds of films labeled bad, that is, bad as an intrinsic and almost generic quality. Bad films range from hapless exploitation movies, such as *Manos: The Hands of Fate* (Hal Warren, 1966), which had no reason to be good by conventional standards, to *The Postman* (1997), Kevin Costner's lumbering vanity project and Tommy Wiseau's jaw-dropping *The Room* (2003), whose perfect storm of awfulness rebukes lazy aesthetic relativism. Michael Adams's book *Showgirls, Teen Wolves and Astro Zombies* is a spirited romp through an evolving canon of failure, which mostly consists of ultra low-budget efforts lacking craft, realism, taste, and the fundamentals of film style. Of course, tastelessness, refusal to adhere to communal standards of craftsmanship, and even flagrant idiocy can be redescribed as the bold subversions by a warped auteur of the reigning codes of a dull and compromised industry.[3] For as Adams says, "what's regarded as classy, sophisticated, or important filmmaking is sometimes less honest, authentic, and passionate than the clumsy efforts of spirited amateurs" (318).

The dumb refusal of exploitation films—and insanely pretentious art films like *The Last Movie* (Dennis Hopper, 1971) or *The Brown Bunny* (Vincent Gallo, 2004)—to acknowledge classical restraints can—as Jeffrey Sconce argued of *Maniac* (Dwain Esper, 1934)—jolt sympathetic viewers into clarifying and questioning dominant stylistic and aesthetic conventions, which become more obvious and seem ever more arbitrary when they are flagrantly and unsystematically deranged. Some of the most derided films ever made contain pleasures unimaginable in mainstream successes. Liking bad films, especially bad (which is to say almost all) exploitation films, offers cineastes an irresistible refuge from dominant tastes: "the romanticisation of low-budget auteurs as frustrated and demented geniuses (à la Ed Wood) or courageous problem-solvers (à la [Roger] Corman) has been a central project of the bad cinema cult over the last twenty years or so" (Sconce 20).

That said, the cult of bad films has sometimes been a front for crass middlebrow standards. Take for example the Medved Brothers' ludicrous inclusion of *Last Year at Marienbad* (Alain Resnais, 1961) and *Zabriskie*

Point (Michelangelo Antonioni, 1970) in *The Fifty Worst Movies of All Time* (1978). The brothers' reactionary cult of badness, which rarely questions its smug criteria of condemnation, is single-mindedly normative and directed as much against experimental or nonmainstream styles of film as against breaches of classical Hollywood style. Fortunately one of the recent achievements of cultism is that, contra the Medveds and in the spirit of Manny Farber's celebration of "termite art," it has taught us to see the alleged badness of *films maudits* as a style of *film brut*, as well as a distinctive mode of film production, a symptom of economic restraint, and a resource for creative exploration. Think, for instance, of how exploitation films inspired John Waters, Tim Burton, and Quentin Tarantino, and the flamboyant art film *Boom!* (Joseph Losey, 1968). Even *The Room* at times seems to be doing something different from and more interesting than simply comprehensively failing.

In the taxonomy of bad films, *The Magus* is altogether more restrained. Its badness, if that is what it is, is not the kind that forces itself on the viewer so that he or she appears to have entered the realm of the aesthetically unwell. *The Magus* is an example of failed mainstream art cinema, or as Lucas puts it, "a not entirely phony Hollywood stab at the Art Film" (81), and precisely the kind of aspirational head film that one imagines would infuriate the Medveds (though, as it happens, it appears in none of their books).

Kitsch perhaps but not mind-bendingly camp, *The Magus* is hard to pin down to one generic location, a feature of numerous films in the late 1960s as the mainstream struggled to capture increasingly mercurial and countercultural audiences. *The Magus* is a thriller, a kind of war film, a travel brochure, a star vehicle, and a mystical fantasy as well as a film-of-the-book, that abiding stand-by of respectable British cinema. At once (and let's be frank) mildly pretentious, weakly symbolic, intellectually and often stylistically flat, *The Magus* is essentially middlebrow, which in itself makes it a derided cultural object. One feels it might have got a better reception if it had had subtitles. In fact, the film has many of the same qualities that some critics hold, rather snobbishly, against Fowles's novel: a popular, nonintellectual's idea of an intellectual workout, barely a notch or two up from something by Colin Wilson and, worse still, most likely sharing a fanbase with *The Lord of the Rings*, another long, complex, hermetic, world-building, best-selling hippie favorite concerning a quest for the meaning of life.

It may be disappointing therefore to point out that *The Magus* is perfectly well made. There are none of the continuity errors (visible booms, chainsaw editing, flimsy sets) or radical deviations from Hollywood style that make semi-amateur productions like *The Room*, *Ben & Arthur* (Sam Mraovich, 2002), and *Plan Nine from Outer Space* (Edward D. Wood Jr., 1959) such guiltless and guileless pleasures. Nor do we find the camp over-the-topness of *Boom!* or the drug-fueled vim and political savvy of *The Last Movie* (films which, inviting cult re-evaluation of their aesthetic crimes, open onto alternative universes of excitingly calamitous deviations from agreed norms). Billy Williams's location shooting in Majorca (standing in for Greece after the political situation made filming there impossible) is detailed and seductive. The mise-en-scène and costumes, working variations on Aegean blues and whites, is meticulously controlled. And the clash of acting styles—Bergen (astonishingly beautiful but inexperienced) is wan and awkward, Quinn hammily macho, and Caine characteristically curt and impassive—suits the theatrical unreality of the enterprise (see figure 11.1).

Figure 11.1. Lily (Candice Bergen) in *The Magus* (1968). Courtesy 20th Century Fox / The Kobal Collection.

Existentialist themes (inspired by the novel) come through very strongly and it would take an exceptionally *distrait* viewer to miss the film's heartfelt, if commonplace, message: the necessity, in the face of cosmic indifference, of making the radical choice for love, freedom, and the value of everyday life. (Of course, if mystery is considered a key component of this material, then the obviousness of the message counts severely against it.) Whereas the German Captain Wimmer extols the Nazis' project of bringing "order into the chaos of Europe," Conchis teaches acceptance of chaos and—in the enigmatic, possibly unintelligible, final line—the inevitability of becoming a traitor: "We are all cast as a traitor. For one simple reason. We have all failed to love."

On one level the film of *The Magus* is an intellectualized male variation on E. M. Forster's *Room with a View* or *Shirley Valentine* (Lewis Gilbert, 1989): that is, a stereotypically touristic evocation of a shallow, aimless Englishman gaining self-discovery along with sex and a suntan. Conchis liberates Nicholas rather as Zorba liberates Alan Bates's uptight, overly rational Basil in *Zorba the Greek* (Michael Cacoyannis, 1964). In both films Anthony Quinn embodies an irresistible continental life force, of the sort absent in the disenchanted Britain of the permissive 1960s.[4] On another, more ambitious level, *The Magus* is a modernist existential puzzle film, like (at a stretch) *L'avventura* (Michelangelo Antonioni, 1960), with which it shares an island setting, convoluted story line, themes of bourgeois deracination and enlightenment, and the conclusion that life is a game of chance with unknowable rules. And indeed *The Magus* represents a significant attempt in British cinema, by a British director adapting British source material, to register some of the advances of the art cinema of the 1960s.

With its foreign location, eroticism (a couple of mild sex scenes with a topless Anna Karina, recruited to evoke the French New Wave), tricksy plot, and philosophical bent, *The Magus* self-consciously follows the lead of *The Birds* (Alfred Hitchcock, 1963), which essayed an Antonioni-esque open ending, *The Graduate* (Mike Nichols, 1967), and *Bonnie and Clyde* (Arthur Penn, 1967) in drawing on the experimentalism of French and Italian directors. Lucas compares *The Magus*, for example, with Jean-Luc Godard's *Le mépris* (1963) set in Capri (81). Nicholas's "nowhere man," fending off life's meaninglessness behind dark glasses like Marcello (Marcello Mastroianni) in *La dolce vita* (Federico Fellini, 1960), is close relation to Thomas (David Hemmings) in *Blow-up* (Michelangelo Antonioni, 1966), another vacuous product of swinging London who learns the value of chaos and ambiguity.

Guy Green commented on the freeing up of film style and theme in the mid-1960s and its influence on *The Magus*:

> During the last ten years or so the cinemagoing public has been "educated" in using their imaginations. There was a time when the exhibitors would say: "Don't have many flashback sequences . . . that's death at the box office. The audience will never understand it." Now it is completely accepted. They have been educated out of the conventional dissolve. They are no longer upset by the sudden cut, and this saves time and makes pictures get on with it. I have been made freer to make this particular film by what has been presented in recent years from France and England. I can make my points far more quickly with this freer kind of editing. I am not going overboard in that direction but I am using that part of the new cinema language that the audience accepts. (60)

Green is referring here to the hard Resnais-style cuts with which he introduces flashbacks in *The Magus*, as when past and present sex scenes between Nicholas and Anne are intercut to confuse time frames (again very Resnais-like) and suggest their psychic simultaneity. Green employs flash-cuts to the past to link Nicholas's experiences with Conchis's: for example, when Nicholas is poised to flog Lily in the trial scene, a flash-cut to Conchis about to strike one of the partisans economically asserts the similarity of their moral choices: between lashing out under orders and taking responsibility for their own actions. Green makes impressively vivid and thematically apt use of associative flash that were entering the grammar of mainstream British films in the late 1960s—for example, *Performance* (Donald Cammell and Nicholas Roeg, released 1970 but filmed in 1968)—and even exploitation films—such as *Permissive* (Lindsey Shonteff, 1970).

Equally striking is that flashbacks in *The Magus* are often untrustworthy. The ones to Conchis in 1915 are believable only if one accepts that Lily really was alive during the Great War; while the flashback dramatizing a priest's account of partisans ambushing German soldiers is suspect not only because the priest is revealed in the trial scene to be one of Conchis's co-conspirators, but also because the machine-gunning of the Germans is curiously (even laughably) bloodless, like a clip from an old-fashioned war film. The realism of events is in fact questionable throughout. The flashbacks to an Athens hotel room are rendered unreal when after the trial Nicholas discovers himself in an identical room that is actually (like Conchis's villa) a standing set on Phraxos. The climactic trial scene can be read equally as an acid trip, a nightmare, or the narrative wrap-up it purports to be. Its status is wholly unfathomable. That all the villagers are there implies either that Conchis conscripted them into his "meta-theatre" or that the village is a stage set and the villagers are actors. Neither solution is realistic or satisfactory.

It is certainly arguable that *The Magus* domesticates these fashionable art film tropes—playing with time, fracturing the diegesis, sabotaging the credibility of the plot—instead of putting them to work in a genuinely cutting-edge narrative. The decision to focus on events in 1944 gives the film a solid dramatic core but also means importing (or pastiching) the clichés of the World War II movie, such as superciliously sneering Nazis. Even so, the film's attempt to combine a mainstream star vehicle and existentialist art cinema at a time when "the Hollywood industry was struggling—sometimes in quite bizarre ways—to remain au courant" (Benshoff 93) comes across as admirable and progressive, even if it does not really work.

Warburton quotes David Tringham, the film's first assistant director, admitting that:

> *The Magus* required "boldness, imagination, risk-taking," and a "broad brush" while Green's strength lay in quasi-documentary, realistic work. Fowles, in writing the script had been "manoeuvred" by the director and producers into oversimplifying his rich, complex book, stripping away the mystery and ambiguity that were its essence. (298)

This point alludes to a frequent criticism of British cinema as limited by its traditions of documentary and kitchen-sink realism, as well as a more damaging charge against cinema itself as (in Fowles's words) a "too realistic medium" (296). But *The Magus* is compromised too by its subordinate relationship to the novel and the obligation somehow to adapt and reproduce the novel's style and themes.

Adaptation studies have been haunted until recently by the assumption that the film version of a literary novel will never be as good as the book. Although, in truth, it is often unhelpful to compare films evaluatively with their source novels, comparison between novel and film of *The Magus* is unavoidable given the book's literary and cult status. Adaptation scholars will grumble and snipe, but critics and audiences generally want to know whether the film of a well-regarded novel matches up to the book, which invariably means calibrating the degree to which the adaptation is "faithful" to the controlling master text. Even viewers who have not read the novel may feel perturbed or cheated to discover that the film "betrays" its source by deviating from its letter or spirit.[5]

The problem with tethering a film to a single originary novel in even the most sophisticated analysis of a film's intertextual relationships is that it risks:

1. Overlooking what the film is doing in addition to imitating just one other text,

2. Judging the film by standards insensitive to the medium's specific industrial, economic and aesthetic determinants, and

3. Crassly underestimating the range, depth, and subtlety of cinema's expressive resources.

Adaptation, no less than sequels and remakes, will necessarily seem a diminished category of cinema if adaptations are compared to and judged solely by their adequacy to pre-existing literary novels. The original novels will *always already*—as deconstructionists might say—be regarded as superior to their adaptations for two fundamental reasons: the novels came first and they are verbal rather than "visual." Fowles puts the (rigged) case against cinema very bluntly:

> One has in fact only to do a film script to realize how inalienably in possession of a still vast domain the novel is; how countless the forms of human experience only to be described in and by it. There is too an essential difference in the quality of image evoked by the two media. The cinematic visual image is virtually the same for all who see it; it stamps out personal imagination, the response from individual *visual* memory. A sentence or paragraph in a novel will evoke a different image in each reader. The necessary cooperation between writer and reader—the one to suggest, the other to make concrete—is a privilege of *verbal* form; and the cinema can never usurp it. (*Wormholes* 21)

Although being "like" or "true to" another text is unquestionably some kind of aesthetic achievement, the "failure" of adaptations to reproduce the "literariness" of literary novels has frequently been invoked to argue for the essential inferiority, or "badness," of all cinema to literature, not only for conveying interiority and complex ideas, but even (as Fowles argues) visual images.

The Magus makes innumerable changes to Fowles's novel. Some of the key ones are as follows (inevitably this will read like a charge sheet). The plot is simplified and the backstory and most of the symbolism are excised. The long opening and final sections set in England are cut, and the past is invoked strictly through flashbacks. Direct literary references extend no further than the quotation from "Little Gidding" and a brief shot of Nicholas's copies of a volume of W. H. Auden and of William Empson's *Seven Types of Ambiguity*. Anne, who is called Alison in the novel, is no longer Australian but French. Nicholas Urfe's character undergoes a considerable transformation; instead of being a middle-class public school type, he now conforms to Caine's hardening screen persona—an ornament of the "new elite," as he is introduced in a party scene, the "classless and rootless" son of a bus driver. One of the film's more audacious touches is that its lead character is relentlessly dislikeable, a "bastard," as Nicholas describes himself, an aloof, nostril-flaring, arrogant product of swinging London's fashionable ennui ("I find life . . . long," Nicholas remarks to Conchis), whose self-centeredness apparently drives Anne, the most sympathetic character in the film, to suicide.

Given the length, range of reference, and unrelieved literariness of Fowles's novel it might seem easier to place it into the lazy category of the "unfilmable novel," a loaded term usually condescendingly referring to the intrinsic limits of cinema rather than ungainly or failed qualities in any particular novel. But in fact there is nothing especially "uncinematic" about Fowles's novel with its theatricality, emphasis on landscape, flashback structure, and romantic interest. Green, contradicting Fowles entirely, regarded the story as wholly cinematic:

> It isn't a routine straightforward plot, but one that is built out of impressions; in fact the kind of story that only the cinema can tell. On the surface it is a love story, an emotional triangle that everyone can understand. Underlying this is the theme of the dissatisfaction of the human being, of his continuous searching, and of that moment when he so often finds that what he has been looking for is right there on his own doorstep. There is also an existential theme, one of personal

responsibility, where people are free to do exactly what they wish only provided that they will accept the responsibility for their actions. It is in exploring these themes that I have really been able to employ "the language of cinema." (59–60)

Here, Green seems to be right, even if his enthusiasm is self-interested and, given the film's reception, somewhat overly optimistic. The novel's playful Chinese box structure, some of which is carried over into the film, anticipates contemporary "mindfuck" or puzzle films like *The Sixth Sense* (M. Night Shyamalan, 1999), *Shutter Island* (Martin Scorsese, 2010), and David Fincher's very *Magus*-like *The Game* (1997). The novel's Jungian existentialism and focus on its hero's journey to individuation (Presley) is cut from the same cloth as the archetypal narratives almost all Hollywood films strive to reproduce nowadays. (This suggests that *The Magus* may be due for a sympathetic remake, or—if fidelity is an issue—then perhaps as a very long television serial.)

The Magus builds on the novel's cinematic elements so that the film tries to work *as a film* rather than an abridgement or set of pass notes; the resources of cinema are used to seed its elaborate plot with coherent themes. Structural and thematic repetitions, especially doublings, are carefully emphasized, for example:

- Nicholas replaces a dead teacher; Conchis and Anne both fake their deaths.
- Lily is also Julie.
- The eighty deaths on Conchis's conscience (the word his name alludes to) are repeated in miniature by the one (Anne's) on Nicholas's conscience.
- There are two love scenes, both associated with water.

There are also some quite subtle visual rhymes, for example, between a shot of the outstretched arm of a statue of Poseidon and one of Lily extending her hand towards Nicholas. Objects, shown in close up throughout the narrative, visually concretize symbolic meanings explicated by the characters: Anne's flower paperweight, bought after her abortion, represents for her "the core of things—purity" and "something not spoilt"; the smiling sculpture is an emblem of the universe as a cosmic joke—"the ultimate reality," Conchis says, "the smile."

The *Magus* is intertextually related—has criminal conversations with, to pick up on the language of infidelity—to a number of other texts than Fowles's novel. For attentive viewers these texts—films (adaptations in fact) rather than books—interpose themselves suggestively between the novel and the film. Bray, for instance, suggests that *The Magus* plays as a retread of one of Caine's signature roles: it is "a kind of post kitchen sink/prototype hippie retread of *Alfie* (Lewis Gilbert, 1966) [with] Caine playing the feckless young gadabout sowing his seed whenever he fancies until a beautiful girl and a sage old man teach him the meaning of true love" (111). Equally crucial is *Zorba the Greek*, which proved the defining role of Quinn's career and the crucial moment in his developing screen persona, which from the strongman in *La strada* (Federico Fellini, 1954) to Gaugin in *Lust for Life* (Vincente Minnelli, 1956) and yet another Conchis-like Greek millionaire in *The Greek Tycoon* (J. Lee Thompson, 1978), ensured his type-casting as an earthy, hypermasculine phallocrat. Indeed, *The Magus* invites interpretation as a disguised remake of *Zorba*. Although Conchis educates Nicholas through art, sculpture, and philosophy, and Zorba inspires Basil with his peasant independence, gusto, and "madness," both characters succeed in invigorating their English protégés by their intimacy with ancient wisdom. (Albert Finney later reworked Nicholas/Basil, as one half of a San Franciscan couple in *The Picasso Summer* [Serge Bourguignon, 1969]).

Conchis, being an intellectual Zorba, can further be read as a portrait of Quinn himself: Conchis combines the womanizing Zorba-like Quinn of public legend with the aesthete, poet, and talented artist of his private life (with a nod, it seems, to Picasso, to whom Conchis is compared in the novel). Conchis's confusingly international, rootless identity matches Quinn's as well. Although Mexican-American Quinn achieved stardom in Italian films and played a bewildering range of foreign characters in Hollywood: Irish-Mexicans, Latinos of all descriptions, and an Arab in *Lawrence of Arabia* (David Lean, 1962). In *The Guns of Navarone* (J. Lee Thompson, 1961), Quinn played a Greek partisan, a characterization that inflects his role in *The Magus*. The film's intertextuality might be taken as a weakness, since it makes its significance parasitic on allusions to and memories of earlier films. But it also underscores, like the casting, the film's hybridization of competing modes of 1960s cinema: British film (Caine), continental art cinema (Karina), and Hollywood prestige project (Quinn).

Furthermore, *The Magus* is a highly self-reflexive piece of filmmaking, a film about the making of what might now be called a reality film, produced and directed by Conchis himself, at the climax of which Nicholas slashes a whip through a cinema screen. Nicholas likes to think he is "still living [in] a big existentialist novel," presumably rather like Fowles's. Lily, upholding his fantasy as it is her purpose to do, agrees that life on Phraxos is "like being half way through some fantastic book," but Anne, the voice of realism, tells him that "this is life, not an existentialist novel." Nicholas is in fact not the hero of a great literary novel but an unwitting actor in Conchis's unscripted experiment in filmed meta-theater. (Nicholas prefigures here the lead character of *The Truman Show* [Peter Weir, 1998].) He is not alone.

All of the characters, including Conchis, are performers with no core reality, going through their changing allotted roles (for Nicholas: clown, traitor, prisoner, judge) in the film within a film. There is no clear distinction between the levels of representation. Even Bergen's flat performance is functional because it underscores, with a hint of Sirkian distanciation, that she is just acting—acting an actor acting, as it were, rather than simulating a real person's inner life. Similarly, Quinn and Caine, whose roles play off their established screen personae, offer performances that seem deliberately to parody the mannerisms of their usual acting style: Quinn is expansive and over-emphatic, while Caine alternates between impassivity and staccato barks of anger.

The characters, in other words, are not so much representations of believable characters as approximations to shifting archetypes. Conchis often appears godlike but sees himself as Pilate, the ultimate collaborationist and traitor; his very last line is "What is truth?" Nicholas is merely an animated stereotype, as the computer in the trial scene cuttingly explains: "a familiar type of male parasite . . . a machine for self-gratification. He is shallow, he is vain, he is egocentric." Conchis tells Nicholas, to general laughter, that there is no hope for him, except as an actor (as Caine, of whose screen persona Nicholas is a summary and condensation, obviously is). Lily is a blonde Jungian anima (like H. Rider Haggard's *She*), but also a nymph from Greek mythology, and when she sends Nicholas an apple, Eve. Anne, by contrast, is the sexy and accessible "foreign" woman of popular British fantasy. "Do you know how many men I have slept with this year?" she asks Nicholas, describing herself ruefully as a "human boomerang."

In cherry-picking a few of the film's symbols, themes, cinematic allusions, and self-reflexive tics, this chapter hasn't attempted to establish whether they derive or deviate from the meanings of the novel. Relating *The Magus* to *L'avventura*, the New Wave, *Alfie*, or *Zorba the Greek* rather than Fowles is not (or not merely) cinephile perversity but rather a small intertextual reorientation that overlays the novel's points of reference—Sade, *The Tempest*, *Le Grand Meaulnes*—with cinematic precedents, allusions, and other interpretative possibilities. *The Magus* is no less coherent—and certainly more coherently and intricately organized than its reputation suggests—if it is analyzed as a meaningful textual object with its own thematic concerns; it is inspired and structured by the novel, perhaps, but exhibits its own integrity, significance and (alas) style of relative failure.

In the end, having watched *The Magus* a number of times, I like it a good deal. By my last viewing I had finally learned to enjoy it as a film rather than continuously reverting mentally to comparing it with the novel, by now a much loved but largely misremembered blur. *The Magus* is a genuinely fascinating meditation on the artifice of cinema, whose ambiguities this chapter has been able only superficially to explore. The film's take on the meaning of life and its criticism of the arrogant cool of the 1960s new masculine elite are somewhat gauche, but they are not unpersuasive. In short, *The Magus* is an unusually ambitious art film to emerge from British cinema in the late 1960s, even if it is hamstrung by its framing as a conventional literary adaptation (not something that Godard's *Pierrot le fou* [1965] or *Le mépris* had to contend with). Some of its pleasures for the contemporary viewer are perhaps incidental—the excellent photography, Candice Bergen's *photogénie*, Caine's always compelling screen presence, John Dankworth's evocative easy listening score—while others are more retrospective and extratextual, such as its status as an artifact of aspirational 1960 middlebrow chic.

Some of its appeal may certainly involve cinephiliac special pleading. Clear-headed, objective discussion of *The Magus* intertwines confusingly with the private significance of the film and very specific and personal emotional memories of the novel, which I first read while holidaying on a Greek island (as I suspect did many of its fans). Michael Adams notes that cultists sometimes invest too much in their passionate re-evaluations of bad films and their attempts to convince themselves that "a Z-grade 1960s biker flick [is] the ne plus ultra of undiluted rebel cinema or that a 1990s straight-to-video slasher [is] actually a cunning social critique" (4). The same may be true of dodgy art films like *The Magus*, which, interpellating me now as *Showgirls* once did ten years ago, may have led me only to reveal yet again my incorrigible lack of taste. I confess both a weakness for defending bad films that speak to my obsessions and erotic fantasies and an abiding uneasiness with luxuriating in the failures of an art form I both love and measure out my life with.

Even so, and with my cultist's hat still firmly on, I rather wish *The Magus* had been, under less restrained (English?) direction, a thoroughly "loathsome film" of the kind analyzed by Harry Benshoff: more camp, queer, blatantly experimental, and at the sharpest cutting edge of the 1960s counterculture. I wish in fact that it was not so obviously a literary adaptation, condemned eternally to be categorized as the "film of a book," a smudged and indistinct copy of a pristine original.

But loathsome films are rare in British cinema and anathema to its tradition of faithful literary adaptation, with the exception of a few mavericks like Ken Russell, whose *Women in Love* (1969) was also photographed by Billy Williams. A wilder, madder film of *The Magus* might have not only creatively and substantially distanced itself still more from the novel but also engaged the same countercultural (cult) audience as *El topo* (Alejandro Jodorowsky, 1970). Perhaps, by a fine irony, it might even have proved more faithful to the magical excesses of Fowles's cult novel. (Lucas suggests that Nicolas Roeg would have made more of the material [81].) But to do that it would have had to be a different kind of film, an impossible film probably for the British cinema of the period, and—like a perfect "faithful" adaptation—one we must project for ourselves in the private screening room of our imaginations.

—For Elaine

Notes

1. Constantine Verevis coined this term for his paper, "BADaptation," at B for Bad Cinema: Aesthetics, Politics and Cultural Value conference at Monash University, Melbourne, 16 April 2009. See Verevis's chapter in this volume.

2. It is not academically respectable to quote Wikipedia, but in this instance the entry is a fair summary of received opinion about the film.

3. See Hunter, "Beaver Las Vegas!" for an effort to reclaim *Showgirls* (Paul Verhoeven, 1997) along these lines.

4. I have argued that this theme also energizes a number of Hammer's films of the period, such as *The Gorgon* (Terence Fisher, 1964), *She* (Don

Chaffey, 1964) and *One Million Years BC* (Don Chaffey, 1966). See Hunter, "The Gorgon."

5. The tired "fidelity" debate in adaptation studies, which for many scholars in the field has been decisively settled in favour of "intertextuality," is addressed by Stam and Leitch.

Works Cited

Adams, Michael. *Showgirls, Teen Wolves, and Astro Zombies: A Film Critic's Year-Long Quest to Find the Worst Movie Ever Made*. New York: It Books, 2010. Print.
Benshoff, Harry. "Beyond the Valley of the Classical Hollywood Cinema: Rethinking the 'Loathsome Film' of 1970." *The Shifting Definitions of Genre: Essays on Labeling Films, Television Shows and Media*. Ed. Lincoln Geraghty and Mark Jancovich. Jefferson, NC: McFarland, 2008. Print.
Bray, Christopher. *Michael Caine: A Class Act*. London: Faber and Faber, 2006. Print.
Farber, Manny. "White Elephant Art vs. Termite Art." *Film Criticism* 27 (1962–63): 9–13. Print.
Fowles, John. *The Magus*. London: Jonathan Cape, 1966. Print.
———. *Wormholes: Essays and Occasional Writings*. Ed. Jan Relf. London: Jonathan Cape, 1998. Print.
Green, Guy. "Guy Green Talks About The Magus." *Films and Filming* (January 1969): 59–61. Print.
Hunter, I. Q. "Beaver Las Vegas!: A fan-boy's Defence of Showgirls." *Unruly Pleasures: The Cult Film and Its Critics*. Eds. Xavier Mendik and Graeme Harper. Guildford: FAB Press (2000): 187–201. Print.
———. "The Gorgon: Adapting Classical Myth as Gothic Romance." *Monstrous Adaptations: Generic and Thematic Mutations in Horror Film*. Eds. Richard J. Hand and Jay McRoy. Manchester: Manchester UP, 2007. 12739. Print.
Leitch, Thomas. "Twelve Fallacies in Contemporary Adaptation Theory." *Criticism* 45. 2 (Spring 2003): 149–71. Print.
Lucas, Tim. "Road to Enlightenment [review of *The Magus* DVD release]." *Sight and Sound* (February 2007): 81. Print.
The Magus (film). Wikipedia. Web. 22 May 1013. <http://en.wikipedia.org/wiki/The_Magus_%28novel%29>
Maltin, Leonard, ed. *Leonard Maltin's Movie Guide 2009 Edition*. London: Plume, 2008. Print.
Medved, Harry, and Michael Medved. *The Golden Turkey Awards: The Worst Achievements in Hollywood History*. London: Angus & Robertson, 1980. Print.
———, with Randy Dreyfuss. *The Fifty Worst Movies of All Time (And How They Got That Way)*. London: Angus & Robertson, 1978. Print.

Presley, Delma E. "The Quest of the Bourgeois Hero: An Approach to Fowles's *The Magus*." *Journal of Popular Culture* 6.2 (Fall 1972): 394–98. Print.

Sconce, Jeffrey. "Esper the Renuniator: Teaching 'Bad' Movies to Good Students." *Defining Cult Movies: The Cultural Politics of Oppositional Taste*. Ed. Mark Jancovich, Antonio Lázaro Reboll, Julian Stringer, and Andy Willis. Manchester: Manchester UP, 2003. 14–34. Print.

Stam, Robert. "Beyond Fidelity: The Dialogics of Adaptation." *Film Adaptation*. Ed. James Naremore. New Jersey: Rutgers UP, 2000. 54–76. Print.

Warburton, Eileen. *John Fowles: A Life in Two Worlds*. New York: Penguin Books, 2004. Print.

12

BADaptation

Is *Candy* Faithful?

CONSTANTINE VEREVIS

In the not so distant past, adaptation studies typically focused on the translation of books, especially classic and canonized literary novels, into films. As Thomas Leitch points out in "Twelve Fallacies of Adaptation," this approach has meant that fidelity to a literary source is often taken as the most appropriate method for analyzing adaptations. Associated with this method are several misleading notions: first, the understanding that source texts are more original than adaptations; second, that adaptations only ever adapt exactly one text apiece; and third (an assumption underpinning the first and second), that adaptations are intertexts whereas their sources are singular texts (Leitch 161–66). Although the question of fidelity continues to dominate popular reviews of film adaptations, Leitch's essay (and other recent scholarship on adaptation[1]) now routinely works with a much broader definition of adaptation, whereby it is no longer taken to mean simply novel-into-film (with the further assumption that the novel is "better") but also engages with films derived from such nonliterary sources as comic books, electronic games, and theme park rides. Emphasizing intertextuality over fidelity, such work locates adaptation within a range of long established industry practices that recycle and serialize narratives in the form of remakes, sequels, television series, novelizations, videogames, and the like.

Recently, I. Q. Hunter has taken up the idea that "adaptation is a rational commercial strategy for commodifying textual material by disseminating it across numerous media" in order to consider the seemingly marginal phenomenon of the exploitation film as a mode of adaptation. This final approach overlaps with the notion of "BADaptation," a concept employed to engage with and challenge those approaches to adaptation and remaking that routinely employ a rhetoric of betrayal and degradation, of "infidelity" to some idealized original. The case study for this inquiry is Christian Marquand's 1968 version of *Candy*, the lavish French-Italian film production adapted (in at least some way) from Terry Southern and Mason Hoffenberg's 1958 satiric novel *Candy*,[2] which itself adapts (in at least some way) Voltaire's 1759 picaresque *Candide, or Optimism*.[3] Upon its theatrical release, the *Candy* film was accompanied by a radio and print advertising campaign that read: "Is Candy faithful? . . . Only to the book!" The disingenuous question angered Southern who saw the film as a misadaptation, or BADaptation, of his best-selling novel.

This chapter seeks to understand the perceived mistranslation of *Candy* by taking up Francesco Casetti's suggestion that what matters in an account of adaptation (and misadaptation) is not the greater or lesser fidelity to a source, but the reformulation, or repurposing, of the text within a new discursive field (82–83). Key questions for an assessment of BADaptation include:

- Is a film adaptation intrinsically BAD?
- Are all film adaptations BADaptations of some more authentic artifact?
- What happens when one adapts a "bad object"—in the case of *Candy*, a faux pornographic novel?
- And does its repurposing result in a BADaptation or a GLADaptation?

Candy, or Libertinism

Elle ne savait pas combien elle était vertueuse dans le crime qu'elle se reprochait.[4]

The story of *Candy* develops out of New York's Greenwich Village in the mid-1950s when Terry Southern wrote an unpublished short story about an American girl—with a sweet "jelly-box"—named Candy Christian. Southern recalls:

> I wrote a short story called "Candy Christian," about a fabulous, blue eyed, pink-nippled, pert-derriered darling who was compassion incarnate, living in the West Village, so filled with universal love that she gave herself—fully, joyfully—to [anyone . . . including] a demented hunchback. (*Flashing on Gid* 230)

According to Southern, everyone he showed the story to "loved the girl—all the guys wanted to *fuck* her, and the girls wanted to *be* her—and they all said: 'Yea, Candy! Let her have more adventures!'" (Interview with Lee Server 1, emphasis in original). Among those who read the piece was writer Alexander Trocchi, founder of *Merlin* literary magazine and a friend of Southern's from his early expatriate days in Paris over the period 1948–53. In a *Grand Street* interview, Southern recalled:

> I showed the story to [Alex] Trocchi. He wanted to publish it in *Merlin*—for nil recompense. I told him no thanks. . . . "Well, in any case," said Trocchi, "this spunky heroine of yours should have more adventures! I would like very much . . . to see her involved with the Roman Catholic Church." I asked him if he would like to write such an episode himself . . . [and] he might have done so, had not another great friend of mine, Mason Hoffenberg, poet and hemp-maven extraordinaire, surfaced at almost the same moment and been doubly keen for the opportunity. (*Flashing on Gid* 230)

In 1953, Trocchi and his co-publisher at *Merlin*, Richard Seaver, had assisted literary bootlegger Maurice "Gid" Girodias in his launch of a new publishing house, Olympia Press. Initially, Olympia sought to "place before the general public complete and integral texts of banned masters" (Campbell 128), but within a year Girodias expanded the operation to include "modern fiction"—essentially, a series of pornographic books—written by commissioned authors and published in English (131). Wanting to reserve the Olympia brand for a more discerning readership, Girodias catalogued the new works under a different imprint—the Atlantic Library—publishing ten titles between January and June 1954, four of which were written by none other than Trocchi, under the pseudonym "Frances Lengel" (132–34). The commercial success of the Atlantic

Library, prompted Girodias to repeat the strategy, creating "The Traveller's Companion," a series of pocket-sized books, with olive-green paper covers, a green border on the title page, and distinctive black lettering for the name of the book and the author (136).

With the new series from Olympia came a need for additional writers, and Trocchi suggested that Southern contribute a commissioned work for a cash advance and monthly retainer. Southern—hoping to establish himself as a "legitimate" writer—was initially hesitant (see *Flashing on Gid* 231), but with no contract yet in sight for his recently completed book manuscript, *Flash and Filigree*, he contacted Girodias in December 1956 proposing that he write a novella titled *Candy*, under the pseudonym Maxwell Kenton, for the Traveller's Companion series. In the letter, Southern emphasized the episodic and open-ended nature of the book, stating:

> The story I have in mind is in the tradition of *Candide*, with a contemporary setting, the protagonist an attractive American girl, Candy, an only child of a father of whose love she was never quite sure, a sensitive progressive-school humanist who comes from Wisconsin to New York's lower-east side to be an art student, social worker, etc. [. . .] Candy has an especially romantic notion about "Minorities," and, of course, gets raped by Negros, robbed by Jews, knocked-up by Puerto Ricans, etc.—though her feeling of "being needed" sustains her for quite a while, through a devouring gauntlet of freaks, faggots, psychiatrists, and aesthetic cults—until, wearied and misunderstood she joins a religious order . . . [and then] moves another step towards the mystical to the Far East to become a Buddhist [. . .] As her spiritual self rises nearer nirvana [she comes to] the ultimate realization that the Buddha too, *needs her!* (qtd. in Southern, *Candy Men* 53–54)

Girodias replied positively the following day, and Southern, at this time based in Geneva (1956–58), undertook to extend and develop Candy's erotic adventures. However, circumstances rapidly changed when, in March 1957, Andre Deutsch of London began preparation to publish *Flash and Filigree*, and accepted Southern's proposal for a new novel, *The Magic Christian*.[5] Increasingly absorbed with the latter, Southern secured an extended deadline from Girodias and invited his friend, Mason Hoffenberg—who had already written *Until She Screams* (1955), under the pseudonym Faustino Perez, for the Traveller's Companion series—to help him finish *Candy*. After an extended period of exchange and revision, the completed manuscript was submitted to Girodias in May 1958, and—with the late inclusion of a prefatory quote from Voltaire—*Candy* by Maxwell Kenton,[6] was published in Paris in October, as No. 64 of the Traveller's Companion Series, with an initial print run of 5,000 copies (Southern, *Candy Men* 130). The book quickly became highly sought after contraband, and Girodias undertook to work around the problem of export prohibitions by reissuing the novel in December 1958 with a different cover and front pages, under the title *Lollipop* (see Southern, *Candy Men* 131–32). The book—*Candy / Lollipop*—became a solid earner for Olympia Press, but Girodias's failure to remit royalties to the authors—along with ongoing ambiguity over international copyright—led to a decade-long period of litigation (1958–68). In 1963, having failed to negotiate a satisfactory settlement, Southern's representatives began preparing a contract for Putnam to publish a hardback edition of *Candy* for sale in the United States and its territories (186).

In New York, Putnam immediately began an aggressive marketing campaign promoting the work, and by the time *Candy* was released in May 1964 advance reviews—emphasizing the book's "hip, Beat, and banned Parisian origins"—were coming out for one of the year's most anticipated books, one that *Newsweek* would describe as: "the first genuinely comic pornographic novel" (qtd. in Southern, *Candy Men* 238). In addition, the release of *Candy* coincided with the U.S. premiere of *Dr. Strangelove, or How I Learned to Stop Worrying and Love the Bomb* (Stanley Kubrick, 1964). The film was based on a screenplay that Stanley Kubrick had commissioned Southern to transform "from heavy-handed melodrama to 'a Kafkaesque nightmare comedy'" (Southern, *Candy Men* 189). At this time, Southern was labeled the idea man behind both the *Candy* novel and the *Dr. Strangelove* script, with *Newsweek* writing: "Terry Southern has assaulted mankind for its perverse use of the two most dynamic forces in the modern world: sexual energy and nuclear power" (245).

Southern became something of a media celebrity: he was profiled in *Playboy* magazine (August 1964), traveled with Bob Dylan on his 1965 European tour, and later appeared—the only person in shades—on the iconic sleeve for The Beatles' *Sgt. Pepper's Lonely Hearts Club Band* (1967). Southern's visibility, along with advance controversy and debate over *Candy*'s "decency," saw the book rapidly become a massive best seller, with ten thousand cloth copies sold in its first two days of release (see Southern, *Candy Men* 235–47).

The irony of *Candy*'s massive popularity was not missed by writer Nelson Algren who, in a cover story for the *Nation*, observed that all of Southern's novels, including *Candy*, had initially been turned down by American publishers. Algren noted that Southern's work, which had hitherto been avoided by U.S. critics who found it "too obsequious to damn and too chinchy to praise," and who themselves were either "too dull to catch [Southern's] mockery or too timorous to catch the anger beneath it" found it necessary for Southern to "get banned in all the right places" in order to bring "the whole bicycling throng of cocktail party taste-makers pedalling like mad" (511). Against those who would decry *Candy* for its "sick sex," Algren's rejoinder was: "but sex in this country has been sick for so long, has been a wasting affliction instead of joyous fulfilment for so long, that by restoring the comedy of it, Southern has done something that we should be grateful for" (511).

At the beginning of 1965, negotiations began for a Dell paperback edition of *Candy*, but ambiguity in the book's international copyright led to several bootleggers typesetting their own imprints (Southern, *Candy Men* 257–60). With *Candy* now redeemed (critically and commercially) as a number one, national best seller, but with prospects of receiving royalties from the paperback editions becoming increasingly remote, Southern and others turned their attention to setting up a movie deal. *Candy*'s sexual politics had marked it out as a controversial ("bad") object, but this very controversy had made it a massive commercial success and ideal (that is, "good") property for adaptation. Southern was told that, if he could settle the copyright issue with Girodias, United Artists would pay $130,000 to acquire the film adaptation rights (269).

Producer-director Frank Perry went further, contracting Southern—who, with completed screenplays for *Dr. Strangelove*, *The Loved One* (Tony Richardson, 1965), and *The Cincinnati Kid* (Norman Jewison, 1965), was by this time a much sought after Hollywood writer—to prepare a script for *Candy*. In the meantime, Girodias initiated his own European deal for a film of *Candy*, to be directed by actor Christian Marquand and starring Marquand's close friend, Marlon Brando. Marquand, who had appeared with Brigitte Bardot in Roger Vadim's *And God Created Woman* (1956) and would go on to act in films such as *Ciao Manhattan* (John Palmer and David Weisman, 1972), *The Other Side of Midnight* (Charles Jarrott, 1977), and *Emmanuelle IV* (Francis Leroi and Iris Letans, 1984), was well connected in the French film scene and enjoyed a high-profile marriage with teenage sexpot, Tina Aumont (see *Ciné-revue*, 1966).

At the beginning of 1967, with French and American rights for *Candy* finally clarified but with a lapsed deal at United Artists, Southern's agents issued a press release, ostensibly quoting Southern:

> Within the last couple of weeks [the *Candy* case] was decided in our favor, in a French court. He [Girodias] was going to appeal, so we made a settlement [. . .]. Earlier, United Artists had taken an option on *Candy*. . . . Now it's available again. [. . .] A certain amount of advance legwork has been undertaken by the French actor Christian Marquand, who, I gather, would like to be in it. A crony of Marlon Brando, Marquand has obtained a commitment from Brando—and also from Richard Burton and Peter Sellers[7] [. . .] for "cameo" appearances in the film, if and when. (qtd. in Southern, *Candy Men* 304)

Commenting on the type of picture that might result, Southern added: "I think maybe [the film] should go the underground route and achieve its success like the book. [. . .] I'd like them to try to make it an interesting, low-budget movie" (304).

It soon became evident to all that Marquand was not only planning to be in *Candy* but also to direct it, and—unbeknown to Southern's agents—Girodias had already sold the option to Marquand who now controlled the film rights (Southern, *Candy Men* 305). Marquand, in turn, brought on board Italian-American producer Robert Haggiag, who set about securing a theatrical distribution deal with Selmur Productions, a subsidiary of ABC television. Filming was to commence at the beginning of 1968 at Haggiag's Dear Studio in Rome, with the hope that Jane Fonda—who was about to appear alongside Marquand's brother, Serge, in Vadim's *Barbarella* (1968)[8]—would take the title role (311). The lead eventually went to a relative newcomer—Ewa Aulin, Miss Teen International of 1966—but with Brando involved Marquand was able to effect a major casting coup, signing a roster of international talent, initially Richard Burton, and (later) Charles Aznavour, James Coburn, John Huston, Walter Matthau, and Ringo Starr. Haggiag, for his part, made sure that the film had money, securing a minimum guarantee of three million dollars in financing and—with Southern now substantially out of the picture—he brought in Buck Henry, fresh from his success with *The Graduate* (Mike Nichols, 1967), to rewrite the screenplay.

In an interview with biographer Lee Hill, Southern reflected on the development, and outcome, of the production package:

> The first plan for *Candy* was for David Picker, who was the head of United Artists at the time, to produce and Frank Perry to direct. Perry had just come off *David and Lisa* [1963] so he was big. We were going to get Hayley Mills to play Candy. She was perfect [. . .]. Then, my good friend Christian Marquand, the French actor who was trying to break into directing [. . .] begged me to let him have the option for two weeks for nothing, so he could put a deal together. So I did, and sure enough, Marquand immediately put Brando in the cast because Brando was his best friend. [. . .] So on the basis of getting Brando, he was able to add Richard Burton and having gotten those two, he was able to get everyone else. Then he disappointed me by casting a Swedish girl [Ewa Aulin] for the lead role, which was uniquely American and Midwestern. He thought this would make Candy's appeal more universal. That's when I withdrew from the film. The film version of *Candy* is proof positive of everything rotten you ever heard about major studio production. They are absolutely *compelled* to botch everything original to the extent that it is no longer even vaguely recognizable. (*Terry Southern: Ultrahip* 384–85, emphasis in original)

For Southern, Henry's screenplay for *Candy* lacked "credibility," failed to match the book in its "originality" and perfect (Beat-inspired) satirization of pornography (see Clayton). As noted above, Southern was especially unimpressed with a radio and print campaign, which asked the question, "Is Candy faithful?" to which the reply was "Only to the book!"[9] The advertising copy was no more than a (bad) pun, but Southern apparently took it at face value, writing to Hoffenberg (at the end of 1968) to inquire:

> Would like to know your feelings about a certain Mister Frog version of our *Can[dy]*. In my view, it was a Dumbell and Tom Fool from the opening frame. [. . .] The real point is that, good or bad, it bears precious little resem[blance] to the true *Can[dy]*—a view which would seem substantiated by the reviews in both *Time* and *Newsweek* mag[azines] this

week, the former going so far as to say the picture "is based on the novel in the same way a flea might be based on an elephant." Such not withstanding the distrib[utor] continues to use the ad: "Is Candy Faithful? Only To The Book!" I think it is important that we make serious representation to them to drop that slogan; not only is it embarrassing, but it could dramatically curtail sales of the new edition [. . .] if "word of mouth" [were to] become mere "bad mouth"; in other words, it seems fairly important that the book be identified as little as possible with the movie. (Southern, *Candy Men* 319)

Hoffenberg responded early in January 1969, writing: "I heartily agree [. . .] that something ought to be done about that '. . . faithful only to the book' nonsense" (320).

Candy premiered in New York and Los Angeles in December 1968, and later went into general release in the United States and abroad (early 1969 in London, but not until 1970 in some key European and Asian markets). Reviews typically concurred with Southern's assessment of the film. For instance, in the *New Yorker*, Pauline Kael wrote:

You can't get adjusted to *Candy*, even though it has some good bits, because, in defiance of all your expectations, it keeps getting worse than seems possible. [. . .] The material—Candide as a teen-age American girl who believes what men tell her and is pleased that they *need* her—no longer holds many surprises, so it was necessary for the movie to be very cleverly directed. It's an incompetent mess. (69–70)

Monthly Film Bulletin was even less forgiving in its evaluation, describing *Candy* as a: "frenzied, formless and almost entirely witless adaptation of the enchanting Southern-Hoffenberg pornographic parable" (80). In these reviews, *Candy* gets tagged a *BADaptation*, a deficient cinematic translation (or *mis*-translation) of Southern's literary style and sociopolitical message. Southern's work—like the film style of Stan Brakhage, which anticipated representations of the countercultural (psychedelic) experience—had developed through the 1950s and was *visionary* of the decade to come. By contrast, Marquand's film—which strove to create its own brand of epic satire *after* the revolution ("no longer holds many surprises"), emphasized Southern's picaresque style to deliver a rich tapestry of baroque tableaux ("has some good bits"), only to be condemned for its lack of cohesion ("an incompetent mess"). The film's failure was variously attributed to its slack direction, indulgent star cameos, and troubled production history,[10] but above all it was ascribed to its great tampering with the sexual excesses of the *Candy* novel—labeled "unfilmable" by *Life* magazine—and its perceived inability to translate the book's hip, porno parody into a production-code certified, mainstream film (see Dassanowsky-Harris 97).

These assessments—which valorize the source and denigrate the adaptation—focus on structure (form and content) at the expense of recognizing the *dialogue* established between text and (new) context. As Casetti describes it: "adaptation [as well as misadaptation] is primarily a phenomenon of *recontextualization of the text*, or, even better, of *reformulation of its communicative situation*" (83, emphasis in original). *Candy*'s critics—Southern included—fail to recognize that the film was not so much a corruption of a fifties' Beat or sixties' Countercultural artifact as it was a film that *repurposed* (at the end of the sixties[11]) the sexual themes at the center of novel to debunk not only current sexual politics—especially, the use of sex to create a countercultural identity—but also current myths of celebrity authorship, religious dogma, aggressive militarism, scientific positivism, and countercultural mysticism. Like other films of the period—most notably *Easy Rider* (Dennis Hopper, 1969), which it in some ways anticipates[12]—*Candy* negotiated the surrounding social and cultural changes, not by attempting a film that was "adequate" to the ideals of the counterculture, but by incorporating (however incoherently) disparate cinematic practices—mainstream, art house, exploitation—into its own positively "unoriginal" and fractured film production (see James, *Allegories* 12–18).

Good Grief! *Candy* a Movie

> There lived in the Mid-West a young lady blessed by nature with the most agreeable manners. You could read her character in her face. She combined pleasant disposition with unaffected innocence; and that, I suppose, was why she was called Candy . . .

This passage above paraphrases the opening lines of *Candide*,[13] reformulating them to indicate that (like the *Candy* novel) Marquand's film version is a self-conscious styling of the episodic form and content of Voltaire's picaresque. There have been many popularizations and updatings of *Candide*—for example, *Candide ou l'optimisme au XXe siècle* (Norbert Carbonnaux, 1960) and *Mondo Candido* (Gualtiero Iacopetti and Franco Prosperi, 1975)—and the influence of its satirical picaresque can be seen in film productions such as Lindsay Anderson's second Mick Travis adventure, *O Lucky Man!* (1973). Like these film versions, Southern-Hoffenberg's *Candy* might be described as a "free" adaptation,[14] in this case, a work that by changing the gender of the main protagonist repurposes *Candide* for the 1960s in America to provide a parody of straight pornography, popular psychology (father-daughter incest), and the portrayal of "romantic need-love" (Silva 784–85).

As a free adaptation, the Southern-Hoffenberg story does not derive directly from Voltaire—that is, there is no repetition of plot, character, or dialogue—but (in Casetti's terms) *Candy* is a "faithful" adaptation insofar as it "re-programs the 'same' reception" as its original (85): that is, it reflects "a disbelief in the efficacy of *Optimism*" (Silva 784). When Southern writes to Hoffenberg, complaining that Marquand's (bad) film bears little resemblance to the "true" *Candy*, he seems to refer to the "good" that the novel achieves in forcing readers to question the manners and morals of the day. By contrast, Marquand's *Candy*—a "faithful" adaptation that *does* adopt the title and much of the content of the book—is deemed a BADaptation for the fact it reprograms the *social function* of the work, reorienting it for a new youth audience, eschewing its critique of optimism, and "candying" the production in and through its commercial orientation and abundant use of pop cultural references and post-"summer of love" clichés. The film's "failure" to translate the hip sensibility of the Southern-Hoffenberg text, together with the film's framing sequences and episodic structure—*faithfully* replicated below, complete with *Candide*-type chapter titles[15]—conspired to anger and frustrate critics, occluding the achievements of a singular film event.

Chapter I. *How Candy left Daddy to meet McPhisto, the great poet, and how Candy did it in the limousine*. Marquand's film of *Candy* begins with an impressive, psychedelic prologue comprised of otherworldly special effects supervised by Douglas Trumbull, and accompanied by an opening theme—the acid-drenched "Child of the Universe"—co-written by jazz composer Dave Grusin and Roger McGuinn of The Byrds. Amid the cosmic reach of *Dog Star Man* (Stan Brakhage, 1962–64) and *2001: A Space Odyssey* (Stanley Kubrick, 1968), amid swirling gaseous worlds-in-formation and glistening "topographic oceans,"[16] a girl (Ewa Aulin) is revealed, sitting cross-legged, meditating on a beach (or perhaps the desert of the film's finale). A series of lap dissolves—through a kaleidoscopic rabbit-hole of leafy flora—leads to the same girl, seated in a classroom, gazing vacantly. Lost in oceanic consciousness of her thoughts, Candy is presented as the eternal innocent, a (pretty vacant) childlike marker of ego loss and cosmic spiritualism, one that resounds with the New Age sentiment of the poem, "Desiderata," circulating among the hippie community and popularized in the music charts of the time.[17] A call of "Miss Christian . . . Miss Christian" from her teacher intrudes upon the cosmic daydream: "Yes, Daddy . . . I mean, Mr. Christian," she replies.

"Daddy" Christian (John Astin) is an overt symbol of conservative American values and the postwar generation gap, an overprotective father panicked by his own incestuous thoughts towards his daughter. Mr. Christian's high school civics class not only provides an opportunity to demonstrate the patriarch's authoritarianism, but enumerate aspects of a (besieged) traditionalist American mindset, one assailed by the youth counterculture and—as the story unfolds—targeted by the film. Reaching his finger to the tip of an (obviously phallic) pointer, Mr. Christian assigns a class essay, "on the subject of the citizen's responsibility to his Government, his church, his school, his parents, his community, and his local police force." Detaining Candy after class, Daddy—as nervously played by John Astin, the kooky patriarch of *The Addams Family* television series (1964–66)—reveals himself to be the shaky cornerstone of the traditional family and (by extension) the entire American sociopolitical system. It comes as no surprise that the temple will literally come crashing down around his ears in the film's penultimate sequence. As Candy dashes from the classroom corridor, Daddy calls after her: "What's the hurry? What's all the excitement about?" Candy calls back: "McPhisto."

McPhisto—poet, adventurer, superstar, *and* bore—enters Rolling Fields Center High School auditorium, adoring students lining every row, Candy crouched in the aisle. Spotlit, McPhisto (Richard Burton) begins a tortured recital from his anthology of (faux) Romantic verse, *Forests of Flesh*:

> Life, which burned and bled in the triumph of my dream, dim days
> Where I stood steaming brightly
> In the sleep-spun, sight-stunned glamour of that eagle-crested dream
> Thrust through the draughty, tongue-tied pores
> Of those whose tender envelope of word-washed flesh
> Flinging that nameless, bitter tear

Stripped dry to the ice green, wind-whipped strawberry
    passion
Of my fractured spleen's old lymph draining,
    liquid . . . *rrlll-lust.*

With perpetually windblown hair and flowing scarf, McPhisto—the self dramatizing demagogue—addresses his (literally) swooning fans. He pompously preaches the celebration of "the virtue, the beauty, the wonder, the ultimate, ineffable desire of the ecstasy of the human spirit," and spying the mini-skirted Candy seated in the crowd, pointedly speaks of a childlike "freedom and virtue, of giving oneself without restraint, uninhibitedly, unashamedly."

If John Astin's parody of the concerned (but confused) father resonates with his role in the domestic sitcom, *The Addams Family*, then Richard Burton's rendition of McPhisto is a self-parodying star performance, one that mocks both the cult of celebrity (notably Burton's tempestuous and much publicized relationship with Elizabeth Taylor) and the pretensions of the intellectual elite. McPhisto's posturing as an underappreciated and misunderstood poet—his work "banned and burned in 27 major countries and 13 newly emergent nations"—is undermined by his own self-promotion—a direct (if hesitant) money-grubbing sales pitch for his anthology, available "for three dollars, in cash or money order" from an unassuming New Jersey postal address. Burton's boorish performance resonates with a contemporaneous fascination with, and interrogation of, the nature of celebrity stardom, most evident in the star portraits and screen tests of Andy Warhol, which culminate in *The Chelsea Girls* (Warhol, 1966), a "ruinous remake" of the tawdry *The V.I.P.s* (Anthony Asquith, 1963), an avowed favorite of Warhol's (starring none other than the Burton and Taylor franchise).

McPhisto slips Candy a note, asking her to meet him in the back of his black Mercedes stretch limousine. Here McPhisto grandly introduces himself—"I . . . AM McPHISTO"—to which the ingénue blithely replies: "Hello, I'm Candy." "A beautiful name," McPhisto tells her, "it has the spirit, and sound, of the Old Testament." He instructs his driver Zero (Sugar Ray Robinson) to take them to Candy's house, and proceeds to spin Candy an exaggerated fiction—one she immediately recognizes from the previous Tuesday's "TV Movie of the Week"—of how he rescued his friend Zero from a hostile—though, poetry-loving—warrior tribe in the Congo. En route to Candy's home at 8357½ Schweitzer Terrace (a fitting address for a heroine apparently dedicated to the "reverence for life"), Candy tells of how—moved by McPhisto's words—she believes she has a capacity to give freely of herself to whatever, or whomever, *needs* her. Gulping down liberal amounts of whisky, a drunken (sexually inept) McPhisto forces himself upon Candy, telling her of *his need*: "my huge, my giant need . . . need . . . NEED . . ."

At this point, Burton's reported "two great pleasures" in life—sex and alcohol, the latter of which reportedly contributed to his untimely death (Munn xi)—intersect with those of the sham Welsh poet. McPhisto's words reverberate, his advances documented from below, as the jammed tap of the whisky decanter floods the floor of the glass-bottomed limousine. The profanity of his actions—mashing his mouth up against Candy's sweet face, her skimpy panties immodestly exposed in the struggle—stands in contrast to the larger-than-life framing, which captures the players like figures in some baroque ceiling painting (Dassanowsky-Harris 100) and exposes the sham of a "return to Eden" utopia of free sex.

Chapter II. *How McPhisto incited the gardener Emmanuel, and how Candy did it on the billiard table*. As the limousine arrives at Candy's suburban home, a disheveled McPhisto, on all fours, slurps whiskey from the floor of the vessel. Next, a handheld camera follows Zero as he helps the whisky-sodden McPhisto through Candy's house and into the basement recreation room. Candy calls the reluctant Mexican gardener Emmanuel (Ringo Starr) into the house to help with the ironing of wet trousers and dress. "Oh no, thees no good," says a worried Emmanuel. In terms of a youth culture market, Marquand could have hoped to secure no more "stellar" performer than a member of the Beatles—Ringo Starr appearing in a feature-length film for the first time (outside of a Beatles' vehicle). Starr's exaggerated performance (and labored Mexican accent) belie the fact hat he would make the most successful transition (of the four Beatles) to acting, notably appearing as Youngman Grand, opposite Peter Sellers' Sir Guy Grand, in the adaptation of Southern's *The Magic Christian* (Joseph McGrath, 1969).

In the basement, McPhisto, still babbling about the "miracle of giving" recites poetry to a life-size marionette, an idealized version of Candy. At the same time, he urges Emmanuel to forget—as the gardener protests—that he is a "good boy," and (in a string of clichés) instructs him to give of himself, "to remember his hot Latin blood. To remember the Alamo. To remember . . . La Revolution!" Tearing away Candy's clothes, Emmanuel takes her on the billiard table while McPhisto, like

Fellini's womanizing intellectual from *Casanova* (1976),[18] mechanically fucks the marionette. Emmanuel shouts, "Viva Zapata!" McPhisto mutters Latin verse. Daddy arrives . . .

Daddy Christian, accompanied by four senior members of the school's social science committee, stands gobsmacked witness to one of the film's most explicit sequences, one in which Candy and Emmanuel's rough coupling (her naked buttocks and thighs exposed) is intercut with McPhisto's impassioned sex act which features close-up shots of the doll's carefully molded breasts, fluttering eyelids, and even an incongruous shot of a thrusting dildo. It is a sequence that not only leads (in an obvious parallel to *Candide*'s story) to Candy's expulsion from her father's house, but one that approximates the oft-cited and outrageous description of Candy's first seduction from Southern and Hoffenberg's novel:

> It was not as though [Daddy] couldn't believe his eyes, for it was a scene that had formed a part of many many of his most lively and hideous dreams—dreams which began with Candy being *ravished*, first by Mephesto [McPhisto in the film], then by foreigners, then by Negroes, then gorillas, then bulldogs, then donkeys, horses, mules, kangaroos, elephants, rhinos, and finally, in the grand finale, by all of them at once, grouped around different parts of her, though it was (in the finale) *she* who was the aggressor, she who was voraciously ravishing *them*, frantically forcing the bunched and spurting organs into every orifice—vagina, anus, mouth, ears, nose, etc. He had even dreamed once that she asked him if it were true that there was a small uncovered opening in the *pupil of the eye*, because if it were, she had said, she would have room there (during the finale) for a minuscule organ, like that of a praying mantis to enter her as well! (*Candy* 45–46, emphasis in original)

Chapter III. *How Candy was sent to school in New York, and how Candy did it in the airplane.* Consulting his liberally minded twin brother, Jack Christian (John Astin, again), and Jack's wife, the lascivious Livia (Elsa Martinelli), Daddy decides to send Candy to school in New York. At night, en route to the airport, the Christians' pristine white Cadillac is pursued by three leather-laced, bandit women on motorcycles. This highly stylized sequence also recalls Fellini (indeed, *Candy* was shot by Fellini regular, Giuseppe Maccari), but this time it is the Colosseum sequence from *Roma* (1972), or Fellini's "Toby Dammit" episode for the portmanteau film, *Histoires extraordinaires* (1968). Livia makes light of the situation, commenting that one of the women looks like an advertisement for one of Jack's magazines. *"Whips and Chains?"* he inquires. "No, the other one," she says, *"Lover Ladies."* On the tarmac, the women reveal themselves to be Emmanuel's sisters: Lolita (Florida Bolkan), Conchita (Matilu Tolo), and Marquita (Nicholetta Machiavelli). "Hey Gringo," they ask, "you in some big hurry?" They want "the little cheecken" who has dishonoured their brother: "Emmanuel *was* a good boy . . . Emmanuel was a virgin . . . Emmanuel was studying to be a priest." Jack tries to placate, offering up his wristwatch as compensation, only to be rebuked with a paraphrase—"we don't want your stinkin' watches"[19]—and a slap that sends him reeling to the ground. Even though Emmanuel appears to have been spiritually transformed by his brief encounter with the virginal Candy—"Miss Christian, stay with me," he pleads—his sisters cannot see beyond the institutionalized dogma of the church. Emmanuel is ruined, and the intended revenge—like a scene from Alejandro Jodorowsky's *El topo* (1970)—is no less than castration for Daddy: "you ruin him. We ruin you."

Gunshots from a military aircraft facilitate the Christians' escape, but Daddy sustains serious head injuries before all are taken aboard. "We've got a horizontal," says Brigadier General Smight. As played by Walter Matthau, Smight is a square-jawed symbol of U.S. militarism, a warmonger no less paranoid than *Dr. Strangelove*'s General Jack D. Ripper (Sterling Hayden). Although a unique creation of Buck Henry's, the character of Smight extends Southern's (*Dr. Strangelove*) premise that the dirtiest word for cold war capitalist America is "Communism." When Uncle Jack endeavors to secure assistance for the injured Daddy by mentioning that he has influential friends in Washington, Smight replies that having "pals in Pinkoville" won't buy any favors. A distressed Candy offers: "I'll do anything [. . .] ANYTHING" to save Daddy. Smight takes Candy forward to the cockpit, ordering the pilots aft for Daddy's much needed blood transfusion (figure 12.1).

Alone with Candy, Smight tells her "some of us haven't had much time for the nice soft easy life [. . .]. Some of us haven't had much *dolce* in our *vitas*." The ever-enduring Candy is ordered to strip down "for the sake of all that is sacred in the free world." Candy—in an iconic pose—sits up on the instrument panel, naked but for the knee-high white boots and halo-like white fur hat, arms outstretched, the star-studded night sky behind ("you are child of the universe . . ."). Pushing READY and

Figure 12.1. Ewa Aulin is a child of the universe in *Candy* (1968). Courtesy Selmur/Dear/Corona / The Kobal Collection.

JUMP signal buttons as he forces himself upon Candy, Smight inadvertently commands his twenty-four paratroopers to drop. As in Woody Allen's *Everything You Wanted to Know About Sex, But Were Afraid to Ask* (1972), Smight's orgasm is a rapid montage of plummeting chutes. Smight hurries from the cockpit, so eager to join his "boys" that he slips out of his parachute. In a mock reprise of *Dr. Strangelove*'s Major "King" Kong (Slim Pickens), who rides a phallic shaped A-bomb while orgasmically whooping and waving his Stetson, Smight rockets through the air, himself a hard shiny phallus.

Chapter IV. *How Daddy was operated upon by Dr. Krankeit, and how Candy did it on the examination table*. Posters in New York advertise a "subcranial medulla oblongotomy" performed by Dr. A. B. Krankeit (James Coburn) with "T. M. Christian as the patient." In a domed auditorium, adorned with celestial cherubs, an enthusiastic society audience applauds as Krankeit enters the ring, like a matador. Hands raised in the ready for surgical gloves, a circling camera (together with Grusin's fanfare), document the dizzying adoration of Krankeit. The boasting surgeon enumerates a number of possible procedures for Daddy's condition, and predictably elects the most radical, his first incision sending a spray of blood across his mask and forehead. Enthralled, the audience edges forward in their rows as Krankeit, soon covered from head to toe in gore—this could be Robert Altman's M*A*S*H* (1972)—ludicrously announces: "my left index finger is now fully three inches inside the patient's head. A hiccup would put a dent in the patient's speech centre that would leave him not only incapable of pronouncing the letters L, R, D, Y *and* F, but make him absolutely incapable of *digit-dialing*." But no chance of this, says a triumphant Krankeit, loudly popping a blood-stained finger from Daddy's injured head. The renegade persona of Krankeit—as filtered through Coburn's characterization of Derek Flint (*Our Man Flint*, Daniel Mann 1966; *In Like Flint*, Gordon Douglas 1967)—presents the physician as a "new false deity," substituting the alleged (sexual) shams and opportunism of the medical profession for the myth of clinical and scientific objectivity (Dassanowsky-Harris 107–8).

After the operation, Candy searches the hospital for Krankeit to learn of Daddy's progress. She finds them both in a crowded recovery room, at what Uncle Jack describes as the "best post-operative bash" he has ever attended. Uncle Jack now attempts to seduce Candy on Daddy's recovery bed, pushing Daddy to the floor in the process. He is interrupted by Krankeit's aggressive "personal assistant," Nurse Bullock (played by "Lady Rolling Stone" Anita Pallenberg[20]) who perceives Candy as sexual competition, and the hospital's self-righteous director, Dr. Dunlap (John Huston), who assails Candy, calling her "a tramp, a tart, a trollop . . . A TEENAGER." Candy faints from sheer exhaustion and is taken away by Krankeit to his rooms. At his examination table, behind a scrim—in a setting that recalls the milieu of *The Story of O* (Just Jaeckin, 1975)—Krankeit tells Candy: "slip out of your things. I'm going to examine you . . ." Nurse Bullock interrupts the scene, partly exposing her left breast, branded with a love heart and Krankeit's initials. The enraged and possessive Bullock chases Candy from the examination room to the hallway where the terrified girl is set upon by both Krankeit's mother (a cleaning woman) and a straight-jacketed, mental patient (played by screenwriter, Buck Henry).

Chapter V. *How Candy found herself on the streets of New York, and how Candy did it in the lavatory and on the piano*. Fleeing the hospital, Candy finds herself alone on the streets of New York. This leads to two further sexual encounters: first Candy enters a mob-controlled bar where she is beset by an underground filmmaker—Jonathan J. John, or J3 (Enrico Maria Salerno)—in a flooded men's room; next Candy is taken to a Gothic mansion by a hunchback-musician and human fly (Charles Aznavour) who promises her "rub-a-dub-dub" on the top of a grand piano. Pursued during these encounters by the police, Candy is finally arrested. The two cops (reminiscent of the television series *Car 54, Where Are You?* [1961–63]) plan to give Candy the "frisking of her life," but distracted by their own lewd thoughts, they lose control of the squad car, crash into a gay fashion performance (filmed with the cooperation of Judith Malina and others from New York's Living Theater group[21]), and Candy makes her escape. In these segments—the first of which is both a reprise of the whiskey-soaked limousine and David Hemmings's orgiastic tumblings with Verushka in *Blow Up* (Michelangelo Antonioni, 1966)—the film extends its interrogation of the credibility and value of artist production, and the shamanistic cult of the author-creator.

Chapter VI. *How Candy met the Guru Grindl, and how Candy did it on the road in the semi-trailer.* On the loose again, Candy accepts a ride from a big rig, only to find that its trailer is—incongruously—the temple-like sanctum of Guru Grindl (Marlon Brando). Cracking joints to comically break his meditative pose—this is Brando as Indian as riotously played by Peter Sellers (the characters of Hrundi V. Bakshi from *The Party*, [Blake Edwards, 1968] and Ahmed el Kabir from *The Millionairess* [Anthony Asquith, 1960])—Grindl tells Candy that her name is sacred, its five letters comprising the Holy pentagram. Together, he tells an incredulous Candy, they will "assume the trail of true selfishness . . . er, *selflessness*": they will "move up past the valley of material concerns, past the rocky cliffs of negative sensation, climbing, struggling, until they have attained the void . . . Beyond time, beyond space, beyond self—the void, pure energy and light" ("you are a child of the universe . . .").

"Lie down," Guru Grindl commands Candy. In search of the immutable self, Grindl takes Candy through a "breathing exercise" to immediately locate it (no surprise) in Candy's crotch. Brando's performance is now Grindl as Maharishi as "Sexy Sadie," the name (and song) John Lennon gave Maharishi Mahesh Yogi following his alleged attempt to rape Mia Farrow during the Beatles ashram retreat to Rishikesh early in 1968. The figure of Grindl not only parodies the Eastern religious experience (psychedelic transcendence) and well-meaning spirit of 1960s counterculture (acid-induced ego dissolution), but effectively denies it being any type of viable alternative to the Western institutions (and the hypocrisies of the secular world) so effectively deflated to this point in the film. Indeed. the segment is a further reprise of Candy's earlier encounters with the levitating yogi, a grotesque reincarnation the poet, the filmmaker, and the trickster (human fly). As they make their way up through the mountains, Grindl opens the retractable roof of his false temple to reveal a starry-lit night sky ("you are a child of the universe . . ."), one that is in turn revealed to be no more than another illusion, a painted canopy suspended atop the trailer. Later, the covering collapses under the weight of a fresh snowfall, showering Candy and Grindl below (just as she and the Hunchback had been showered with goose down in the previous encounter). As Candy and Grindl move through seven (sexual) stages on the trail to the void, the guru's sexual prowess is no match for Candy's unending capacity to give of herself, and the exhausted guru tells her that a "Teacher with a sacred bird" will take her on the final part of the journey. Candy and the guru travel not only towards the void but also across the United States, from New York to Las Vegas and finally into the desert where Candy—now dressed in the same white, toga-like bed sheet seen at the beginning of the film—finds the Teacher.

Chapter VII. *How Candy found enlightenment, and how Candy did it with Daddy.* "Are you the one who will take me to the void?" Candy asks the shrouded holy man. The Teacher and Candy make it to California where they enter a cave-like temple, illuminated by a thousand flickering candles. Among idols and icons, among the Buddha and Ganesha, amid an earthquake-like cataclysm, Candy and the Teacher embrace, the ecstasy of their union written on Candy's face. Opening her eyes, only now does Candy recognize the HIM: "My God. It's DADDY!" A quite deliberate variation of the deservedly outrageous words and situation that close Southern and Hoffenberg's novel—"GOOD GRIEF—IT'S DADDY!"—this (next to final) segment answers Daddy's initial prudish hysteria at the very idea of sex, closing out the film's critique of patriarchy and its institutions, and hewing close to the novel's finale in which Candy is sandwiched between Daddy ("her precious and open honeypot against the holy man's secret parts") and a giant statue of the Buddha (its nose, lubricated by the rain, "slipping into Candy's marvellous derriere") (*Candy* 222–23).

Candy's voice reverberates, providing a literal and metaphysical (sound) bridge to an external setting. Candy now transcends time and space, to cross a (Edenic) field where a happening—perhaps a hippy love-in—is in progress. Here, amid music and flapping banners, she passes by all those to whom she has given so freely of herself: McPhisto, charming a snake draped around his neck; Emmanuel with his three possessive sisters; Brigadier General Smight, on horseback with a lance; Dr. Krankeit and nurse Bullock administering youth serum; J3 filming Marquand and his crew (reflexively) filming J3; the Hunchback, assailed and dismembered by his entourage; and Guru Grindl, (falsely) levitating.

Approaching the limit of its 120-minute runtime, it should come as little surprise that in this closing segment *Candy* adopts a type of reflexivity—"[the] pandemic trope in sixties filmmaking, from structural film through the underground to the narrative art film" (James, *Allegories* 283)—to return to itself, and close out its plethora of re-enactments and references to feature films and television programs of its generation. Finally, in a reprise of the film's opening, her journey (her movement towards Eden) complete, Candy is returned to her (own) self and to the cosmos: YOU ARE A CHILD OF THE UNIVERSE . . .

Chapter VIII. *Conclusion*. Southern said that *Candy*—a film of a book that had been developed and written, more than a decade before, in the context of the aesthetic and political radicalism of (expatriate) Beat culture—should find its success via an "underground route." But by the time Marquand's *Candy* was released in late 1968 (and even later outside the United States), Warhol had already brought the amphetamine-fueled antics of the underground "above ground" with *The Chelsea Girls*, Roger Corman had appropriated the alternative vision of filmmakers such as Brakhage for the representation of the psychedelic experience in mainstream films like *The Trip* (1967), and the instant commercial success of songs like Scott McKenzie's "San Francisco (Be Sure to Wear Flowers in Your Hair)" (1967) quickly transcended the lyrics' original purpose and hippie ideal. The hippie movement had only recently been given a name (at the Trips Festival in January 1966), but as Barry Miles points out, within two years "every college town in America and most in Europe had a store where you could buy posters and rolling papers and the local underground newspapers" (*Hippie* 258). In *The White Album*, Joan Didion wrote that for many people (especially in Los Angeles) "the Sixties ended abruptly on August 9, 1969, ended at the exact moment when word of the [Manson family] murders on Cielo Drive travelled like brushfire through the community" (47). *Candy*'s near proximity to this event (along with its delayed 1970 release in some principal markets) meant that the film appeared on the cusp of cultural and generational change, that is, between the communal utopia of free sex and the commercial logic of sexploitation. A conservative work adapted from a once controversial fiction, *Candy* was repurposed—for an emergent youth audience (one with little direct experience of hippie counterculture)—and yet it adopted a radical mode of 1960s film practice—namely, "anarchic fantasy"—to gesture towards "the possibilities of the human spirit in its socially uncorrupted state" (Kelman 491; see James, "Movies Are a Revolution" 281). Marquand said that *Candy* was "absurd, grotesque and [worked] on many levels: literal, metaphoric, apocalyptic, allegoric" and ultimately—like its namesake, *Candide, or Optimism*—was essentially "optimistic in flavor" (qtd. in Shenkar 55). Freed from the shackles of fidelity and turned on to a dialogic universe Marquand's *Candy* is—can only be—a GLADaptation, one faithful only unto itself.

Notes

1. See for example Cartmell and Whelehan, Geraghty, Hutcheon, Leitch, and in particular, Stam.

2. Terry Southern and Mason Hoffenberg, *Candy* (New York: Grove Press, 1994 [1958]).

3. Voltaire, *Candide, or Optimism*, trans. John Butt (Harmondsworth: Penguin, 1983 [1947]).

4. This is the epigraph for the U.S. version of Southern and Hoffenberg's *Candy*. It translates as: "She did not know how innocent she was of the crime for which she reproached herself."

5. *Flash and Filigree* and *The Magic Christian* (Harmondsworth: Penguin, 1965), first published 1958 and 1959, respectively.

6. The inside cover of the Grove Press edition of *Candy* carries the biographical note that was invented by Southern for Maxwell Kenton: "Maxwell Kenton is the pen name of an American nuclear physicist, formerly prominent in atomic research and development who, in February 1957, resigned his post because 'I found the work becoming more and more untenable,' and has since devoted himself fully to creative writing."

7. Sellers was not signed, but went on to take the lead role in the film version of *The Magic Christian* (Joseph McGrath, 1969).

8. *Barbarella* was co-scripted by Southern.

9. For a full-page, full-color example of the ad, see *Movie News* 6.3 (March 1970): 30.

10. Novice Ewa Aulin is said to have experienced some sort of breakdown, leading to rumors that she was being drugged to keep her going through the shoot (Southern, Candy Men 313).

11. As above, the film's U.S. premiere was in December 1968, but was not released in many parts of the world—Italy, France, Japan—until 1970.

12. Candy reverses Wyatt and Billy's picaresque journey from *Easy Rider*, moving east to west, and attains the self-realization that eludes the two bik-

ers. Most significantly Candy anticipates the groundbreaking *Easy Rider* musical score from a year later.

13. *Candide* begins: "There lived in Westphalia, at the seat of Baron Thunder-ten-tronckh, a young lad blessed by nature with the most agreeable manners. You could read his character in his face. He combined sound judgments with unaffected simplicity; and that, I suppose, was why he was called Candide" (Voltaire, *Candide* 19).

14. On "free" and "faithful" adaptations, see Grant.

15. Each of the thirty chapter titles in Voltaire's *Candide* is a short (often absurd) synopsis of events, such as "How Candide was brought up in a beautiful country house, and how he was driven away," or "How Candide escaped from the Bulgars, and what happened to him afterwards," and so on.

16. Roger Dean's album artwork first appeared in the same year as *Candy*, with the "Yes" bubble logo appearing on Yes's *Close to the Edge* (1972) and *Tales from Topographic Oceans* (1973).

17. "Desiderata"—recorded with a gospel-like chorus—became a chart hit in the early 1970s has the lines: You are a child of the universe, / no less than the trees and the stars; / you have a right to be here. / And whether or not it is clear to you, / no doubt the universe is unfolding as it should.

18. Fellini's *Casanova* would feature Marquand's wife Tina Aumont.

19. The (much) paraphrased line is Gold Hat's "We don't need no stinkin' badges" from *The Treasure of the Sierra Madre* (1948), directed by John Huston who appears in Candy as Dr. Dunlap.

20. Pallenberg was the girlfriend of Brian Jones and long-term companion of Keith Richards. She appeared in *Barbarella*, played opposite Mick Jagger in *Performance* (Donald Cammell and Nicolas Roeg, 1970), and was recently in *Mister Lonely* (Harmony Korine, 2007) and *Go Go Tales* and *Napoli, Napoli, Napoli* (Abel Ferrara, 2007 and 2009).

21. Judith Malina famously appeared in Jack Smith's *Flaming Creatures* (1963), a film that Smith "theorized" in his aesthetic manifesto, "The Perfect Filmic Appositeness of Maria Montez." Smith's muse, Universal Studio's "Queen of Technicolor," Maria Montez, was Tina Aumont's mother.

Works Cited

Algren, Nelson. "The Donkeyman by Twilight." *The Nation* (18 May 1964): 509–12. Print.

———. "Un-American Idea: Sex Can Be Funny." *Life* (8 May 1964): 8. Print.

Bockris, Victor. "Terry Southern." *Interview* (20 February 1990): 126–29. Print.

Campbell, James. *Exiled in Paris: Richard Wright, James Baldwin, Samuel Beckett, and Others on the Left Bank*. New York: Scribner, 1995. Print.

Cartmell, Deborah, and Imelda Whelehan, eds. *Screen Adaptation: Impure Cinema*. London: Palgrave Macmillan, 2010. Print.

Casetti, Francesco. "Adaptation and Mis-adaptations: Film, Literature, and Social Discourses." *A Companion to Literature and Film*. Ed. Robert Stam and Alessandra Raengo. Malden, MA: Blackwell, 2004. 82–91. Print.

Clayton, Jay. "Dad Strangelove: An Interview with Nile Southern." *Nude 14* (2008). Web. 28 May 2010. <http://www.nudemagazine.co.uk/14Nile%20Southern.htm>

"Comment être vraiment femme à 20 ANS?" *Ciné-revue* 50 (1966): 10–11. Print.

Dassanowsky-Harris, Robert. "The Southern Journey: *Candy* and *The Magic Christian* as Cinematic Picaresques." *Studies in Popular Culture* 15.1 (1992): 95–111. Print.

Didion, Joan. *The White Album*. Harmondsworth: Penguin, 1979. Print.

Divine, Christian. "Southern Fried Satire: *Dr. Strangelove* to *Easy Rider*." *Creative Screenwriting* 8.4 (2001) 35–38. Print.

"Everybody's Sweet Little Swede." *The Look* (14 May 1968): 50–57. Print.

Geraghty, Christine. *Now A Major Motion Picture: Film Adaptations of Literature and Drama*. Lanham, MD: Rowan and Littlefield, 2008. Print.

Grant, Catherine. "Recognising *Billy Budd* in *Beau Travail*: Epistemology and Hermeneutics of an Auteurist 'Free' Adaptation." *Screen* 43.1 (2002): 57–73. Print.

Hill, Lee. "Terry Southern: Ultrahip." *Backstory 3: Interviews with Screenwriters of the 1960s*. Ed. Pat McGilligan. Berkeley: U of California P, 1997. 372–99. Print.

Hunter, I. Q. "Exploitation as Adaptation." *Scope*: 10th Anniversary Special Issue e-Book, *Cultural Borrowings: Appropriation, Reworking, Transformation*. Ed. Iain Robert Smith, Nov. 2009. Web. 28 May 2010. <http://www.scope.nottingham.ac.uk/cultborr_cover.php>

Hutcheon, Linda. *A Theory of Adaptation*. New York: Routledge, 2006. Print.

James, David. E. *Allegories of Cinema: American Film in the Sixties*. Princeton: Princeton UP, 1989. Print.

———. "'The Movies Are a Revolution': Film and the Counterculture." *Imagine Nation: The American Counterculture of the 1960s and 70s*. Ed. Peter Braunstein and Michael William Doyle. New York: Routledge, 2002, 275–303. Print.

Kael, Pauline. "Big Misses." *New Yorker* 44.46 (4 January 1969): 69–71. Print.

Kelman, Ken. "Anticipation of the Light." *The Nation* (11 May 1964): 490–94. Print.

Leitch, Thomas. "Twelve Fallacies in Contemporary Adaptation Theory." *Criticism* 45.2 (Spring 2003): 149–71. Print.

———. *Film Adaptation and Its Discontents: From* Gone with the Wind *to* The Passion of the Christ. Baltimore: Johns Hopkins UP, 2007. Print.

MacDonald, Ian. *Revolution in the Head: The Beatles' Records and the Sixties*. 2nd rev. ed. London: Vintage, 2005. Print.

McLaughlin, John J. "Satirical Comical Pornographical *Candy*." *Kansas Quarterly* I.3 (Summer, 1969): 98–103. Print.

Miles, Barry. *Hippie*. New York: Sterling, 2004. Print.
Munn, Michael. *Richard Burton: Prince of Players*. London: JR Books, 2008. Print.
Murf. Rev. of *Candy*. *Variety* (18 Dec. 1968): 26 & 28. Print.
Murphy, Brian. Rev. of *Candy*. *Films and Filming* (March 1969): 38–39 & 48–49. Print.
Murray, D. M. "Candy Christian as a Pop-Art Daisy Miller." *Journal of Popular Culture* 5.2 (1971): 340–48. Print.
Review of *Candy*. *Monthly Film Bulletin* 36.423 (April 1969): 80. Print.
Server, Lee. "Introduction: An Interview with Terry Southern by Lee Server." Southern and Friedman, 1–14. Print.
Shenker, Daniel. "Good Grief: It's *Candy* on Film!" *New York Times Magazine* (11 February 1968): 50–55. Print.
Silva, Edward T. "From *Candide* to *Candy*: Love's Labor Lost.' *Journal of Popular Culture* 8.4 (Spring 1975): 783–91. Print.
Southern, Nile. *The Candy Men: The Rollicking Life and Times of the Notorious Novel Candy*. New York: Arcade, 2002. Print.
Southern, Nile, and Josh Alan Friedman, eds. *Now Dig This: The Unspeakable Writings of Terry Southern, 1950–1995*. New York: Grove Press, 2001. Print.
Southern, Terry. "Flashing on Gid." *Grand Street* 10.1 (1991): 227–34. Print.
Southern, Terry, and Mason Hoffenberg. *Candy*. New York: Grove Press, 1994 [1958]. Print.
Stam, Robert. "The Theory and Practice of Adaptation." *Literature and Film: A Guide to the Theory and Practice of Film Adaptation*. Ed. Robert Stam and Alessandra Raengo. Oxford: Blackwell, 2005. Print.
Voltaire. *Candide, or Optimism*. Trans. John Butt. Harmonsworth: Penguin, 1947. Print.
Walling, William. "*Candy* in Context." *New York Literary Forum* 1 (1978): 229–40. Print.

Contributors

Tom Conley is Lowell Professor in the Departments of Romance Languages and Visual & Environmental Studies at Harvard University. Among his books are *Film Hieroglyphs* (2006), *Cartographic Cinema* (2007) and *An Errant Eye: Poetry and Topography in Early Modern France* (2011), all published by University of Minnesota Press. With T. Jefferson Kline he is co-editor of *The Wiley-Blackwell Companion to Jean-Luc Godard* (2014).

Adrian Danks is Director of Higher Degrees Research in the School of Media and Communication, Royal Melbourne Institute of Technology (University). He is also co-curator of the Melbourne Cinémathèque and co-editor of *Senses of Cinema*. He has published widely in a range of journals and books including: *Senses of Cinema, Metro, Screening the Past, Studies in Documentary Film, Studies in Australasian Cinema, Australian Book Review, Screen Education, Quarterly Review of Film and Video, 1001 Movies You Must See Before You Die* (Cassell Illustrated, 2004), *Traditions in World Cinema* (Edinburgh University Press, 2006), *Melbourne in the 60s* (Circa, 2005), *24 Frames: Australia and New Zealand* (Wallflower Press, 2007), *Cultural Seeds: Essays on the Work of Nick Cave* (Ashgate Publishing, 2009), *World Film Locations: Melbourne* (Intellect, 2012), and *Twin Peeks: Australian and New Zealand Feature Films* (Damned Publishing, 1999). He is currently writing several books including a monograph devoted to the history and practice of home moviemaking in Australia, a book examining "international" feature film production in Australia during the period 1945–75 (*Australian International Pictures*, with Con Verevis), and an edited companion to the work of Robert Altman (Wiley/Blackwell).

Tessa Dwyer teaches in the School of Culture and Communication at the University of Melbourne. She has published widely in international anthologies and journals including *A Deleuzian Century?* (Duke, 1999), *Words, Images and Performances in Translation* (Continuum, 2012), *Linguistica Antverpiensia*, *South Atlantic Quarterly*, *The Translator* and *Velvet Light Trap*. She is on the Advisory Committee of Melbourne art publication *un Magazine* and has co-edited a special issue of online journal *Refractory* on the subject of split screens.

Kate Egan is lecturer in film and television studies at Aberystwyth University, Wales. She is author of *Trash or Treasure? Censorship and the Changing Meanings of the Video Nasties* (Manchester University Press, 2007) and *The Evil Dead* (Wallflower Press, 2011) and co-editor (with Sarah Thomas) of *Cult Film Stardom: Offbeat Attractions and Processes of "Cultification"* (Palgrave Macmillan, 2012).

I.Q. Hunter is Reader in Film Studies at De Montfort University, Leicester. He is the author of *British Trash Cinema* (British Film Institute, 2013), editor of *British Science Fiction Cinema* (Routledge, 1999), and co-editor of numerous books including *Science Fiction Across Media: Adaptation/Novelisation* (Glyphi, 2013), *Controversial Images: Media Representations on the Edge* (Palgrave Macmillan, 2012) and *British Comedy Cinema* (Routledge, 2012). His next books are *Cult Film as a Guide to Life* and *Psychomania*.

Adrian Martin is Associate Professor in Film and Television Studies at Monash University, Melbourne, and Distinguished Visiting Professor at Goethe University, Frankfurt. He is author of numerous articles and book chapters, and co-editor of *LOLA* magazine. His books include: *Phantasms* (McPhee Gribble, 1994), *Once Upon a Time in America* (British Film Institute, 1998), *The Mad Max Movies* (ScreenSound Australia, 2003), *Last Day Every Day* (Punctum Books, 2012) and (in Spanish) *Sublimes obsesiones* (Altamira, 2004) and *¿Qué es el cine moderno?* (Uqbar Editores, 2008). He is also co-editor (with Jonathan Rosenbaum) of *Movie Mutations: The Changing Face of World Cinephilia* (British Film Institute, 2003).

R. Barton Palmer is Calhoun Lemon Professor of Literature and Director of Film Studies at Clemson University. He is the author or editor of nearly forty books devoted to various literary and cinematic subjects, including (with Robert Bray) *Hollywood's Tennessee: the Williams Films and Postwar America* (University of Texas Press, 2009), (with Steven

Sanders) *The Philosophy of Steven Soderbergh* (The University Press of Kentucky, 2009), *To Kill a Mockingbird: The Relationship between the Text and the Film* (Methuen, 2008), and *Nineteenth and Twentieth Century American Fiction on Screen* (Cambridge University Press, 2007). His edited collections include *Film Stars of the 50s* (Rutgers University Press, 2010) and (with David Boyd) *Hitchcock at the Source: The Auteur as Adapter* (SUNY Press, 2011). His next anthologies include: (with Steven Sanders and Aeon Skoble) *The Philosophy of Michael Mann* and two volumes, co-edited with Robert Bray, *Modern British Drama On Screen* and *Modern American Drama On Screen*.

Claire Perkins is Lecturer in Film and Television Studies at Monash University, Melbourne. She is author of *American Smart Cinema* (Edinburgh University Press, 2012) and co-editor of *Film Trilogies: New Critical Approaches* (Palgrave Macmillan, 2012). Her writing has also appeared in the journals *Velvet Light Trap*, *Cinemascope* and *Studies in Documentary Film*, and in the anthologies *Shining in Shadows: Movie Stars of the 2000s* (Rutgers University Press, 2012) and *Second Takes: Critical Approaches to the Film Sequel* (SUNY Press, 2010).

Murray Pomerance is Professor in the Department of Sociology at Ryerson University. He is author of *Alfred Hitchcock's America* (Polity Press, 2013), *The Eyes Have It: Cinema and the Reality Effect* (Rutgers University Press, 2013), *Tomorrow* (Oberon Press, 2012), *Edith Valmaine* (Oberon Press, 2011), *Michelangelo Red Antonioni Blue: Eight Reflections on Cinema* (University of California Press, 2010), *The Horse Who Drank the Sky: Film Experience Beyond Narrative and Theory* (Rutgers University Press, 2008), *Johnny Depp Starts Here* (Rutgers University Press, 2005), *An Eye for Hitchcock* (Rutgers University Press, 2004), *Savage Time* (Oberon Press, 2005), and *Magia D'Amore* (1999). He has edited or co-edited numerous volumes, including *The Last Laugh: Strange Humors of Cinema* (2013), *Hollywood's Chosen People: The Jewish Experience in American Film* (Wayne State University Press, 2012), *A Family Affair: Cinema Calls Home* (Wallflower Press, 2008), *City That Never Sleeps: New York and the Filmic Imagination* (Rutgers University Press, 2007), *Cinema and Modernity* (Rutgers University Press, 2006), *From Hobbits to Hollywood: Essays on Peter Jackson's "Lord of the Rings"* (Rodopi, 2006), *American Cinema of the 1950s: Themes and Variations* (Rutgers University Press, 2005), *Where the Boys Are: Cinemas of Masculinity and Youth* (Wayne State University Press, 2005), *BAD: Infamy, Darkness,*

Evil, and Slime on Screen (SUNY Press, 2004), and *Enfant Terrible! Jerry Lewis in American Film* (New York University Press, 2002). His *Marnie* will appear in 2014. He is editor of the Horizons of Cinema series at the State University of New York Press and the Techniques of the Moving Image series at Rutgers University Press, and, (with Lester D. Friedman and Adrienne L. McLean, respectively), co-editor of both the Screen Decades and Star Decades series at Rutgers.

Jeffrey Sconce is Associate Professor in the Department of Radio/Television/Film at Northwestern University. His publications include *Sleaze Artists: Cinema at the Margins of Taste, Style, and Politics* (Duke University Press, 2007) and *Haunted Media: Electronic Presence from Telegraphy to Television* (Duke University Press, 2000). His essay "'Trashing' the Academy: Taste, Excess, and an Emerging Politics of Cinematic Style" (first published in a 1995 issue of *Screen*) is an ongoing point of reference for discussions of paracinema and questions of taste and cultural value in film studies.

Jamie Sexton is Senior Lecturer in Film and Television Studies at Northumbria University, UK. He is the co-author of *Cult Cinema* (Wiley-Blackwell, 2012), co-editor of *No Known Cure: The Comedy of Chris Morris* (British Film Institute, 2013), and co-edits the book series *Cultographies* (Wallflower/Columbia University Press).

Constantine Verevis is Associate Professor in Film and Television Studies at Monash University, Melbourne. He is author of *Film Remakes* (Edinburgh UP, 2006), co-author of *Australian Film Theory and Criticism, Vol. I: Critical Positions* (Intellect, 2012), and co-editor of *Second Takes: Critical Approaches to the Film Sequel* (SUNY Press, 2010), *After Taste: Cultural Value and the Moving Image* (Routledge, 2011), *Film Trilogies: New Critical Approaches* (Palgrave-Macmillan, 2012), and *Film Remakes, Adaptations and Fan Productions: Remake/Remodel* (Palgrave Macmillan, 2012).

Index

Note: Page numbers followed by n indicate endnotes; page numbers followed by f indicate figures.

ABC television, 221
Abossolo M'bo, Emile, 173
Ackroyd, Peter, 105–6
Adams, Michael, 200, 211
adaptation studies. *See* BADadaptation
Addams Family, The (television series), 226, 227
Adler, Luther, 114
Agamben, Giorgio, 105
AIDS epidemic, 96, 98
Á l'aventure / On with the Adventure (2009), 171–72, 177
Alexander, John, 153
Alexander, Nathan, 115–17
Alfie (1966), 15, 209, 211
Algren, Nelson, 220
Alien (1979), 119
A-list features, 8, 9
Alive (2002), 111
Allen, Karen, 95
Allen, Woody, 25, 197, 199, 231
Almodóvar, Pedro, 173
Altman, Rick, 53, 58, 60n14
Altman, Robert, 232
American International Pictures, 47–48
L' amore (1948), 175
Anchor Bay Entertainment, 181, 184

Anderson, Lindsay, 225
And God Created Woman (1965), 220
Andrews, Julie, 76
L' ange noir (1994), 173–74
Les anges exterminateurs / The Exterminating Angels (2006), 168, 171
Angry Silence, The (1960), 199
Aniston, Jennifer, 25
Antonioni, Michelangelo, 15, 28, 76–77, 200–201, 203, 233
Apocalypse Now (1979), 34
Archer, Eugene, 73
Argento, Dario, 45
Armageddon (1998), 25
Army of Darkness (1992), 184
Artaud, Antonin, 4
Artists and Models (1937), 151
Asia Extreme, 46
Asquith, Anthony, 227, 233
Astin, John, 226, 227, 229
Atlantic Library, 217–18
Auden, W. H., 207
audience/spectators
    bad cinema and, 8
    explosive apathy (Sconce) and, 9–10, 26, 27–28, 38–39, 40n3
Aulin, Ewa, 221, 222, 225–26, 231f, 236n10

Aumont, Tina, 220, 237n21
Austin, Bruce, 139
Australia (2009), 173
auteurism, 7–8, 11
   auteur stars, 14–15
   Brisseau as auteur, 167–68
   classical auteur theory, 13
   cult films and, 135–36
   nature of auteur, 149–50
Auteurs and Authorship (Grant), 13
Aznavour, Charles, 221, 233

back-projection. See rear-projection
BADadaptation
   Candy (1968) and, 15–16, 215–36
   of *The Magus* (Fowles), 197–200
   origins of term, 212n1
   questions for assessing, 216
Badley, Linda, 182
"bad" objects, 8, 10, 11, 16, 53,
   58–59, 216, 220
Bale, Christian, 126
Bamber, David, 114, 117–18
Bannen, Ian, 114
Barbarella (1968), 221, 236n8, 237n20
Bardem, Javier, 35
Bardot, Brigitte, 220
Barr, Roseanne, 34, 35
Barthes, Roland, 40n1, 82n4
Bates, Alan, 203
Battle Beyond the Sun (1963), 48
Battle of Algiers, The (1966), 111
Bay, Michael, 25
Bazin, André, 135
Beast of the City, The (1932), 69
Beat, 224
Beatles, The, 219, 228, 233
Bekmambetov, Timur, 31
Bellour, Raymond, 162
Ben & Arthur (2002), 202
Benjamin, Walter, 12, 57, 61n16,
   61n19, 130, 131
Benny, Jack, 149, 151–63
Benshoff, Harry, 205, 212

Benton, Robert, 113
Bergen, Candice, 198, 202, 202f,
   210, 211
Bergman, Ingmar, 40n3, 49
Bergman, Ingrid, 73, 137f
Berkoff, Steven, 114
Berthelot, André, 107, 126n1
Bertolucci, Bernardo, 45
Betz, Mark, 48, 51
Birds, The (1963), 74, 203
Birth of a Nation, The (1915), 90
black humor, 174
Black Tulip, The (Dumas), 109
Blake, Robert, 153
Blakeston, Oswell, 133–34
Blow-Up (1966), 28, 203, 233
B movies
   A-list features versus, 8
   as paracinema, 5
body genres (Williams), 9, 32
Bogart, Humphrey, 66, 70, 136–37,
   137f
Bogdanovich, Peter, 48, 73–74
Bolkan, Florida, 230
Bong, Joonho, 2
Bonnie and Clyde (1967), 203
Boom! (1968), 201, 202
Bordwell, David, 24–25, 28–29, 40n2,
   69, 171
Born to Be Bad (1950), 7, 7f, 88
Borzage, Frank, 68
Bourdieu, Pierre, 4–5, 6
Bourguignon, Serge, 209
Bourne, Chris, 171–72
Boys in the Band, The (1970), 94, 95
Brabin, Charles, 69
Bradley, Truman, 158
Bradshaw, Peter, 1–3
Brakhage, Stan, 223, 225, 235
Branagh, Kenneth, 115
Brando, Marlon, 220–22, 233
Braveheart (1995), 108
Bray, Christopher, 198, 209
Brazilian film, 47

Breillat, Catherine, 172
Brennan, William, 88, 102
Breton, André, 33
Briggs, Joe Bob, 190–91
Brisseau, Jean-Claude, 14, 167–78
Brolin, Josh, 35
Brooks, Richard, 96
Brophy, Philip, 47, 48, 178
Brown Bunny, The (2004), 200
De bruit et de fureur / Sound and Fury (1988), 169–70, 176
bullet time, 32, 40n4
Bullitt (1968), 92–93
Burchill, Louise, 60n15
Burks, Robert, 78
Burton, Richard, 221, 222, 226–28
Burton, Tim, 201
Byrds, The, 225

Cabinet of Dr. Caligari, The (1920), 132
Cacoyannis, Michael, 203
Caesar and Cleopatra (Shaw), 113–14
Cahiers du cinéma, 135
Caine, Michael, 15, 197–99, 202, 207, 209–11
Callenbach, Ernest, 135
Cameron, Ian, 65
Cameron, James, 36–37
Cammell, Donald, 204, 237n20
Campbell, Bruce, 14–15, 181, 182, 184–94
Campbell, Colin, 143n1
Campbell, James, 217
camp material, 9, 10, 133
Candide, or Optimism (Voltaire), 15–16, 216, 218, 219, 224, 236n3, 237n13, 237n15
Candide ou l'optimisme au XXe siècle (1960), 224–25
Candy (novel), 15–16, 216–24, 229, 234–35, 236n2, 236n6
Candy (1968), 15–16, 216, 223–36, 231f

Candy Men (Southern), 218–23
Cannes Film Festival, 1–2, 90
Cannon, Danny, 25
Car 54, Where Are You? (television series), 233
CARA (Classification and Ratings Administration), 90, 100
Carax, Leos, 1–4
Carbonnaux, Norbert, 224–25
Carcassonne, Philippe, 66
Carnal Knowledge (1971), 89, 103n5
Cartmell, Deborah, 236n1
Casablanca (1942), 25, 120, 136–39, 137f
Casanova (1976), 228–29, 237n18
Casetti, Francesco, 216, 224, 225
Castellari, Enzo, 44
Cather, Kirsten, 49
Céline (1992), 175, 177
Certeau, Michel de, 155
Chaffey, Don, 212–13n4
Chamber, The (1996), 111
Changeling (2009), 112–13
Chaplin, Charlie, 132
Charles, John, 48
Chelsea Girls, The (1966), 227, 235
"chick flicks," 34
Choses secrètes / Secret Things (2002), 168, 169, 175–76
Christmas in July (1940), 14, 152, 156, 159, 161
Chute, David, 44
Ciao Manhattan (1972), 220
Cimino, Michael, 197
Cincinnati Kid, The (1965), 220
Cineaste, 141
Cinema 2 (Deleuze), 3–4
Cinema of Invention, The (Ferreira), 178
Cinema Scope, 172
Cinémathèque française, 151
Ciné-revue, 220
Clagett, Thomas D., 100, 103n4

Classification and Ratings
   Administration (CARA), 90,
   100
Clayton, Jay, 222
Cleese, John, 114
Cléo de 5 à 7 / Cleo from 5 to 7
   (1962), 51–52
Clockwork Orange, A, 103n5
Clooney, George, 21–23, 23f
Close to the Edge (1972), 237n16
Close Up, 132, 133
Cobra Woman (1944), 5f
Coburn, James, 221, 231–32
Cocteau, Jean, 134
Coen, Ethan, 25, 35, 111
Coen, Joel, 25, 35, 111
Colchart, Thomas (pseudonym for
   Francis Ford Coppola), 48
Collins, Robbie, 1
comic pornography, 215–37
Commando (1985), 120
Confessions of a Cultist (Sarris), 136
Conley, Tom, 13–14, 149–63
Connery, Sean, 76
Conrad, Joseph, 34–35
consumerism, 8
Cooper, Gary, 151
Cooper, Merian C., 69
Coppola, Francis Ford, 34, 48
Corman, Roger, 47–48, 200, 235
Corrigan, Timothy, 14, 46
Costner, Kevin, 200
Counterculture, 224, 235–36
Count of Monte Cristo, The (Dumas),
   109–10
Cousins, Mark, 8
Craig, Daniel, 112
Cremator, The / Spalovač mrtvol
   (1969), 45
Crippen, Hawley Harvey, 109
La croisée des chemins (1975), 174
Cromwell, John, 66
Crowley, Martin, 94, 95

Crowther, Bosley, 49–52
Cruise, Tom, 112, 115
Cruising (novel), 92–93, 95–96,
   103n4
Cruising (1980), 11, 85–103
   community standards and, 86–90,
      100–101
   divided artistic judgments, 88–90,
      99–100
   identity politics and, 11, 91–98,
      100
   moral badness and, 85–89
   pornography and artistic freedom,
      100–103
   as sequel to action thrillers, 92–95
   subterranean aspects of gay
      subculture, 94–98
Cult Film Reader, The (Mathijs and
   Mendik), 60n5, 129
cult films, 129–43
   auteurism and, 135–36
   as badfilms, 199
   Candy (1968), 15–16, 216, 223–36,
      231f
   Casablanca (1942), 25, 120,
      136–39, 137f
   characteristics, 129, 133–34, 138,
      139–40
   critical analysis of, 6
   The Evil Dead (1981), 14–15,
      181–95, 183f
   The Magus (1968), 15, 16,
      197–213, 202f
   negative connotations, 130–34,
      139–43
   as paracinema, 5
   post-cult culture, 12–13, 139–41
   reception-based approach in, 8
   The Rocky Horror Picture Show
      (1975), 139
   shifts in perceptions, 131, 134–39,
      142–43
   subtitles and, 45–49

Cult Movies (Peary), 139
Cultural Studies and Cultural Values (Frow), 6–7
Curran, Brian, 46, 56–57, 60n8
Curtiz, Michael, 25, 120, 125, 136–38

Dadaism, 33
Dancer in the Dark (2000), 2
Daney, Serge, 167
Danish film, 51
Danks, Adrian, 10–11, 13, 65–84
Dankworth, John, 211
Dante, Joe, 56–57
D'Antoni, Philip, 92–96, 103n4
Darabont, Frank, 111
Dark Knight, The (2008), 35, 126
Dassanowsky-Harris, Robert, 224, 228, 232
David and Lisa (1963), 222
Davis, Bette, 173
Davis, Kathleen, 55–57, 56, 57, 60n17
Dawn, Norman, 68–69
Day, Barry, 136–38
Day, Doris, 81
Dead Man Walking (1995), 111
Dead Reckoning (1947), 66, 69–73
Dean, Roger, 237n16
De Baecque, Antoine, 168
Deep Throat, 103n5
Delabastita, Dirk, 53
Deleuze, Gilles, 3–4, 6, 16–17
Dell, 220
de Man, Paul, 57, 61n16
DeMille Cecil B., 72, 82n7
Demme, Jonathan, 120
Denis, Claire, 51, 52, 53, 175
Deren, Maya, 134
Derrida, Jacques, 10, 45, 54–58, 60n15, 61n16
Deutsch, Andre, 218
De Witt, Cornelius, 109

De Witt, Johan, 109
Dickens, Charles, 107
Didion, Joan, 235
Die Hard 2 (1990), 39
Disney, Walt, 132
Distant Trumpet, A (1964), 151
Dixon, Wheeler Winston, 79
Doane, Mary Anne, 53, 60n14
Dog Star Man (1962–64), 225
La dolce vita (1960), 203
Doniol-Valcroze, Jacques, 178
Donnie Darko (2001), 141
Doors, The, 35
Douglas, Gordon, 232
Dr. Crippen (1962), 109
Dr. Crippen an Bord (1942), 109
Dr. Strangelove, or How I Learned to Stop Worrying and Love the Bomb (1964), 219, 230, 231
Dr. Strangelove, The Loved One (1965), 220
Drew, Ellen, 160
Dreyer, Carl, 175
Drifter, The (1913), 82n5
dubbing, 10, 46, 48–53
Duck Soup (1933), 157, 159
Duel (1971), 103n4
Duff, Charles, 106
Dumas, Alexandre, 109–10
Dumont, Margaret, 157, 159
Duvall, Robert, 34–35
Duvivier, Julien, 82n6
DVD commentaries. See *Evil Dead, The* (1981) DVD commentaries
Dwyer, Tessa, 10, 43–64
Dyer, Richard, 94, 98
Dylan, Bob, 219

Each Man in His Time (Walsh), 151
Eastwood, Clint, 111, 112–13
Easy Rider (1969), 224, 236–37n12
Ebiri, Bilge, 1
Eco, Umberto, 139

Edwards, Blake, 233
Egan, Kate, 14–15, 181–96
Eisenstein, S. M., 4
Eliot, T. S., 198
Elite Entertainment, 181, 184, 190–91
Elsaesser, Thomas, 7–8, 13
Emmanuelle (1974), 45
Emmanuelle IV (1984), 220
Empson, William, 207
Engels, Erich, 109
English, John, 111
Ernst, Max, 33, 35
Esper, Dwain, 200
"event" films, 2
Everything You Wanted to Know About Sex, But Were Afraid to Ask (1972), 231
Evil Dead, The (1981) DVD commentaries, 14–15, 181–95, 183f
   amateur aspirations, 192–93
   audience reactions, 190
   distinctive personalities, 190–92
   historical context, 188–90
   sequels, 184, 191–93
Evil Dead Companion, The (Warren), 184
Evil Dead II (1987), 184, 191–92
Executioner's Song, The (1982), 111
Existentialism, 203, 208, 210
Exorcist, The (1973), 99
exploitation films, 47, 200–201, 204, 216
   critical analysis of, 6
   in paracinema, 9
   in post-cult culture, 12–13
explosive apathy (Sconce), 21–40
   aggressive stylistic lexicon of, 22–25, 28–32, 36–39
   Apocalypse Now (1979), 34–35
   comic approach, 9–10, 23, 27–28, 33–34, 35, 40n3

   extreme detachment and violence in, 27–32, 35–37
   impact aesthetic (King) and, 10, 28–32, 36–37
   The Matrix (1999), 9, 32, 40n5
   No Country for Old Men (2007), 35
   origins and evolution, 32–37
   in popular culture, 37–39
   Robocop (1987), 9, 36
   spectacle versus classic narration, 24–27
   Syriana (2005), 9, 21–23, 23f
   Terminator series, 36–37
   Wild in the Streets (1968), 33–34
Eyes Wide Shut (1999), 168

Famous Monsters of Filmland (Dante), 56–57
Fan, The (1949), 72
Fan Cultures (Hills), 130
Faraldo, Claude, 174
Farber, Manny, 13, 201
Far from Heaven (2002), 67
Farrelly Brothers, 174
Farrow, Mia, 233
Fassbinder, Rainer Werner, 60n11, 169
Fawkes, Guy, 108
Fear and Loathing in Las Vegas (1998), 199
Fellini, Federico, 203, 209, 228–30, 237n18
Felsher, Michael, 184
Female Animal (1970), 48–49
Fernau, Rudolf, 109
Ferrara, Abel, 237n20
Ferreira, Jairo, 178
Ferrell, Will, 23
Ferrer, José, 166
Feyder, Jacques, 134
Fidler, Tristan, 190–91
Fielding, Henry, 110

Fielding, Raymond, 71, 82n4
Fifty Worst Movies of All Time, The (Medved et al.), 200–201
Figgis, Mike, 99, 185
film brut, 201
Film Comment Top Films of 2012, 1
film noir, 66, 159, 166, 173–74
film objects, 9
Film Quarterly, 135
Films and Filming, 136–38
films maudits, 201
Fincher, David, 15, 208
Finney, Albert, 209
fireball fleeing, 38–39
Fisher, Terence, 212–13n4
Five Screenplays by Preston Sturges (Henderson), 163n4
Flaming Creatures (1963), 237n21
Flash and Filigree (Southern), 218, 236n5
flashback, 159, 198, 204–5, 207
flash-cuts, 204
Fleischer, Richard, 111
Fleming, Victor, 156
"flubtitles," 10, 45, 51, 56, 60n4
Flubtitles website, 60n4
Flynn, Errol, 125
Foley, James, 111
Fonda, Jane, 221
Fontaine, Joan, 7f, 70–71
Ford, Harrison, 112
Foreign Correspondent (1940), 75, 80, 82n11
Forster, E. M., 203
Foster, Jodie, 123
Foster, Marc, 111
Foucault, Michel, 86, 102, 105, 106–8, 110–12
Four Quartets (Eliot), 198
fourth wall, 26
Fowles, John, 15, 197–213
Fox, Megan, 27f
Foxe, J., 108

Fox Studios, 68
Frankfurt School, 130
French Connection, The (1971), 92–93, 99
French film, 15, 44, 51–52, 53, 131–32, 167–78, 203, 211, 220
French New Wave, 15, 203, 211
Freud, Sigmund, 35–36, 155
Friday the 13th series, 35
Fried, Debra, 66
Friedkin, William, 11, 13, 88–103
Friend, Philip, 109
Frow, John, 4, 6–7
Fujiwara, Chris, 60n6
Fuller, Samuel, 168
Full Metal Jacket (1987), 60n13

Gaghan, Stephen, 9, 21–23
Gallo, Vincent, 200
Game, The (1997), 15, 208
gaming consoles, 38
Gance, Abel, 4
Ganz, Bruno, 114
Gardner, Reginald, 157
Garfinkel, Harold, 122, 123
Garland, Judy, 112
Garnett, Tay, 111
Garrel, Philippe, 82n3
Gay Activists Alliance, 91
General Foods, 159
Geraghty, Christine, 236n1
German film, 44, 51, 130–31
Gert, Valeska, 134
Gibson, Mel, 108
Gilbert, Lewis, 15, 203, 209
Gilliam, Terry, 199
Girodias, Maurice "Gid," 217–21
Giuliani, Pierre, 151
Godard, Jean-Luc, 156, 169, 174, 203, 211
Go Go Tales (2007), 237n20
Gojira / Godzilla (1954), 45
Gondry, Michel, 2

Good German, The (2006), 67
Gorgon, The (1964), 212–13n4
Gottlieb, Henrik, 51, 53
Graduate, The (1967), 203, 221
Grandrieux, Philippe, 175
Grand Street, 217
Grant, Barry Keith, 13, 14, 140
Grant, Cary, 73, 74f
Grant, Catherine, 182, 185, 186, 191, 193–94, 237n14
Gray, Jonathan, 182, 185
Great Depression, 160
Greek Tycoon, The (1978), 209
Green, Guy, 15, 197, 199, 204, 205, 207–8
Green Mile, The (1999), 111
Greutert, Kevin, 25
Griffith, D. W., 25, 90
Gross, Jerry, 48–49
Grusin, Dave, 225, 231
Guinness, Alec, 114
Guins, Raiford, 195
Gunning, Tom, 111
Guns of Navarone, The (1961), 209

Hackman, Gene, 112
Haggard, H. Rider, 210
Haggiag, Robert, 221
Halloween series, 35
Hammer, 212–13n4
Haneke, Michael, 45
Hannibal (2001), 123–24
Hanson, Miriam, 50
Happening, The (2008), 197
Hark, Tsui, 171
Harlin, Renny, 39
Harper, Graeme, 140
Harrington, Curtis, 48
Hathaway, Henry, 111
Hawkins, Joan, 9, 48
Hawks, Howard, 13
Hayden, Sterling, 230
Haynes, Todd, 67, 173
Heart of Darkness (Conrad), 34–35

Heaven's Gate (1980), 197
Hedren, Tippi, 76
Hemmings, David, 203, 233
Henderson, Brian, 161, 163n4
Henry, Buck, 221–22, 230, 232
Hérédia, Lisa, 175
Herz, Juraj, 45
Hickman, Bill, 93
Hill, Lee, 222
Hiller, Arthur, 97
Hillis, Aaron, 1
Hills, Matt, 130, 140
Histoires extraordinaires (1968), 230
Hitchcock, Alfred, 11, 13, 65–68, 72–81, 82n2, 82n11, 82nn8–9, 93, 120, 172, 203
Hitchens, Christopher, 106
Hitler, Adolf, 12, 114–19, 126
Hoberman, J., 139
Hoffenberg, Mason, 15–16, 216–24, 229, 234–35, 236n2, 236n4
Hoffman, Dustin, 28
Hollywood vs. Hard Core (Lewis), 100–101
Holy Motors (2012), 1–4, 3f, 16–17
Honda, Ishiro, 45
Hong Kong cinema, 42–45, 56, 171
Hooper, Tobe, 193
Hope, Bob, 151
Hopkins, Anthony, 114, 120, 121f, 123–24
Hopper, Dennis, 112, 200, 224
Horn Blows at Midnight, The (1945), 13–14, 149, 151–63, 154n
Hour of the Wolf, The (1968), 40n3
Howard, Trevor, 120
Huillet, Danièlle, 82n3
Hundred Headless Woman, The (La femme 100 têtes) (Ernst), 33
Hunter, I. Q., 10, 15, 16, 197–214, 212n3, 212–13n4, 216
Huston, John, 120, 221, 232, 237n19
Hutcheon, Linda, 236n1
hypnosis, 166, 177

Iacopetti, Gualtiero, 224–25
identity politics, 11, 91–98, 100
Imanjaya, Ekky, 46, 47, 60n7
IMAX, 31
impact aesthetic (King), 10, 28–32, 36–37
Incredibly Strange Films (Vale and Juno), 139–40
Independent Frame Process, 79
Indonesian New Order exploitation films, 47
industrialized system of aesthetic production, 6, 8
Inglourious Basterds (2009), 44, 114–15, 118
In Like Flint (1967), 232
Internet Movie Data Base (IMDB), 181, 184, 192, 199
Interpretation of Dreams, The (Freud), 155
intertextuality
  in film adaptations of novels, 206, 209, 213n5, 215
  in post-cult culture, 12–13, 139–40
irony, 12–13, 50, 136, 138, 140, 173, 174, 212, 220
I Spit on Your Grave (1978), 190
Italian film, 44, 45, 221
I Want to Live! (1958), 111

Jackson, Peter, 45, 112
Jacobi, Derek, 114
Jacobs, Steven, 82n8
Jaeckin, Just, 45, 232
Jagernauth, 2
Jagger, Mick, 237n20
Jaka Sembung / The Warrior (1981), 47
James, David E., 224, 235, 236
James Bond series, 120–21
James I, 108
Jancovich, Mark, 134, 140
Jarrott, Charles, 220
Jaws (1975), 28, 103n4

Jeffrey, Richard, 65
Jenkins v. Georgia, 103n2
Jentsch, Ernst, 35–36
Jewison, Norman, 220
Jodorowsky, Alejandro, 212, 230
Joffé, Roland, 199
Johnston, Joanna, 117–18
Jones, Brian, 237n20
Jones, Christopher, 33–34
Joslin, Allyn, 153
Jourdan, Louis, 70–71
Judge Dredd (1995), 25
jump cuts, 188–89
Juno, Andrea, 139–40
Jurgensen, Randy, 96

Kael, Pauline, 8, 13, 223
Karina, Anna, 15, 198, 203, 209
Karzhukov, Mikhail, 48
Kashpirovksy, Anatoly, 45–46
Keighley, William, 125
Kelly, Grace, 74f
Kelman, Ken, 236
Kennedy, Jayne Jain, 46
Kenton, Maxwell (pseudonym for Terry Southern), 218–19, 236n6
Khrushchev, Nikita, 151
Kibbee, Guy, 153, 157
Kill Bill: Vol. 1 (2003), 44, 59n2
Kill Bill: Vol. 2 (2004), 44
King, Geoff, 28–32, 38
King and Four Queens, The (1956), 162n1
King Kong (1933), 69
Kirkland, Bruce, 193
Kitamura, Ryûhei, 111
Klinger, Barbara, 182, 185, 189, 195
Klushantsev, Pavel, 48
Koch, Howard, 136
Kohn, Eric, 1
Korine, Harmony, 237n20
Kozyr, Aleksandr, 48
Kracauer, Siegfried, 12, 130–31, 132
Krohn, Bill, 100

Kubrick, Stanley, 40n3, 60n13, 219, 225
Kuntzel, Thierry, 162

LaBeouf, Shia, 27f
Lady in the Water, The (2006), 197
Lady Vanishes, The (1938), 82n9
Landis, James, 47
Land of the Dead (2005), 112
Lang, Fritz, 4, 155–56
Larrabee, Eric, 135
Last Movie, The (1971), 200, 202
Last Year at Marienbad, The (1961), 200–201
Laughton, Charles, 72, 120
Laura (1944), 177–78
Lavant, Denis, 2, 3f
L'avventura (1960), 15, 203, 210–11
Lawrence of Arabia (1962), 209
Lean, David, 209
Ledger, Heath, 35, 126
Legrand, Gérard, 178
Le Guern, Philippe, 142
Leguizamo, John, 112
Leitch, Thomas, 213n5, 215, 236n1
Lengel, Frances (pseudonym for Alexander Trocchi), 217–18
Lennon, John, 233
Lentz, Harris M., 48
Leroi, Francis, 220
Lester, Michael L., 120
Letans, Iris, 220
Letter, The (1940), 173
Letter from an Unknown Woman (1948), 70–71
Lev, Peter, 60n11
Lévi-Strauss, Claude, 155
Lewis, Jon, 100–101, 103n5
Lewis, Joseph H., 168, 172
Lewis, Philip E., 60n15
Life of Pancho Villa, The (1912), 151
Liliom (1930), 68
Liotta, Ray, 123, 124

Living Theater group (New York), 233
Lloyd, Christopher, 112
Lloyd, Frank, 120
Lodge, Guy, 1
Lollipop (Southern), 219
Looking for Mr. Goodbar (1977), 96
Lord of the Rings: Return of the King (2003), 112
Lord of the Rings: The Two Towers (2002), 43, 44f, 45, 59
Lord of the Rings series, 185, 201
Lorre, Peter, 120
Losey, Joseph, 201
Lubitsch, Ernst, 157
Lucas, George, 28, 119
Lucas, Tim, 199, 201, 203, 212
Luhrmann, Baz, 173
Lust for Life (1956), 209
Lynch, David, 2
Lyne, Adrian, 99
Lynn, Robert, 109

Macbeth (Shakespeare), 169
Maccari, Giuseppe, 229
Machiavelli, Nicholetta, 230
Macpherson, Kenneth, 132–33
Maddin, Guy, 82n3
Magic Christian, The (novel), 218–19, 228, 236n5
Magic Christian, The (1969), 228, 236n7
Magic Voyage of Sinbad, The (1962), 47
Magus, The (novel), 15, 197, 199, 201, 205–12
Magus, The (1968), 15, 16, 197–213, 202f
Maharishi Mahesh Yogi, 233
Making Love (1982), 97
Malick, Terrence, 2, 175
Malina, Judith, 233, 237n21
Maltese Falcon, The (1941), 120

Maltin, Leonard, 197
Man, Paul de, 55
Mandarin film, 44
Mandeville, B., 107
Manhunter (1986), 123
Maniac (1934), 200
Mann, Daniel, 232
Mann, Michael, 123
Manos: The Hands of Fate (1966), 200
Manson family, 235
Man Who Knew Too Much, The (1956), 80, 81
Man Who Made Movies: Raoul Walsh (1973), 162n1
Man Who Wasn't There, The (2001), 111
Marnie (1964), 11, 65, 68, 73–78, 80, 81
Marquand, Christian, 15–16, 216, 220, 221–25, 235–36
Marquand, Serge, 221
Martin, Adrian, 14, 99–101, 165–79
Martinelli, Elsa, 229
Marx Brothers, 159
Marxism, 8
Masato, Harada, 60n13
M*A*S*H (1972), 232
Masson, Alain, 170, 175
Mastroianni, Marcello, 203
Mathijs, Ernest, 8, 129, 140
Matrix, The (1999), 9, 32, 40n5
Matthau, Walter, 117, 221, 230
Maurice, Alice, 53, 60n14
Mazurki, Mike, 159
McCarey, Leo, 157
McCarthy, Frank, 151
McElhaney, Joe, 80
McGilligan, Patrick, 149, 162n1
McGowen, Randall, 106
McGrath, Joseph, 228, 236n7
McGuinn, Roger, 225
McKay, Adam, 23

McKenzie, Scott, 235
McLaglen, Victor, 109
McQuarrie, Christopher, 115–17
McTeague, James, 108
Medhurst, Andy, 97–98
Medved, Harry, 200–201
Medved, Michael, 200–201
Meisner, Günter, 114
Méliès, Georges, 23–24, 153
melodrama, 173–74, 176
Mendes, Eva, 3f
Mendik, Xavier, 8, 129, 140
Le mépris (1963), 203
Merlin, 217
Miike, Takeshi, 45
Miles, Barry, 235
Milestone, Lewis, 120
Miller v. California, 86–87
Millionairess, The (1960), 233
Mills, Hayley, 222
Minnelli, Vincente, 173, 209
Mister Lonely (2007), 237n20
Mitchum, Robert, 72
Mix, Tom, 109
Mogg, Ken, 76
Mondo Candido (1975), 224–25
Mondo Macabro, 46–47
Monroe, Marilyn, 151
Monster Chiller Horror Theater, 40n3
Monster's Ball (2001), 111
Montaigne, Michel de, 162–63n3
Montez, Maria, 4, 5f, 237n21
Monthly Film Bulletin, 223
Moore, Julianne, 123
moral badness, 85–89. See also *Candy* (1968); *Cruising* (1980)
Moran, Dolores, 153
Moran, Percy, 109
Mottram, James, 1
Movie Man (Thomson), 76
MPAA (Motion Picture Association of America), 186–87
Mraovich, Sam, 202

MTV Movie Awards (2009), 23
Mueller-Stahl, Armin, 114
Mulvey, Laura, 67–68, 77, 82n2
Munn, Michael, 228
Murnau, F. W., 4
Musy, Jean, 168
Mutiny on the Bounty (1935), 120
Mutiny on the Bounty (1962), 120

Napoli, Napoli, Napoli (2009), 237n20
NBC, 9–10
Négret, François, 170f
neo-formalism, 24–25
New Age, 175, 226
Newman, Paul, 75, 76
Newmeyer, Fred C., 154–55
Newsweek, 219
New Wave, 15
Nichols, Mike, 89, 203, 221
Niebo Zowiet (1959), 48
Night at the Opera, A (1945), 159
Night of the Hunter, The (1955), 72
Nighy, Bill, 115
Noce blanche / White Wedding (1989), 170, 170f
No Country for Old Men (2007), 35
Noé, Gaspar, 175
Nolan, Christopher, 35, 126
Nornes, Abe Mark, 42–43, 48, 50, 51, 52, 53, 60n9, 60n13
North by Northwest (1959), 74, 120, 126
Nossack, Hans Erich, 118
Notorious (1946), 73, 80
La notte (1962), 77
Nowell-Smith, Geoffrey, 44

Objective, Burma (1946), 156
Oliveira, Oswaldo de, 47
Olsen, Christopher, 81
O Lucky Man! (1973), 225
Olympia Press, 217–18, 219
O'Malley, David, 192

One Million Years BC (1966), 212–13n4
Ophuls, Max, 70–71
Other Guys, The (2010), 23
Other Side of Midnight, The (1977), 220
Our Gang series (1922–44), 153
Our Man Flint (1966), 232
Owen, Clive, 112
Ozon, François, 174

Pacino, Al, 95, 98f
Païni, Dominique, 66, 67
Pallenberg, Anita, 232, 237n20
Las Palmas Film Festival (Spain), 169
Palmer, John, 220
Palmer, R. Barton, 8–9, 11, 13, 85–104
Pang, Laikwan, 59n2, 61n18
Pangborn, Franklin, 157, 159, 160, 161
paracinema (Sconce), 4–6, 8, 9, 45, 140, 186–87, 190, 193–94. *See also* B movies; cult films
Paracinema magazine, 45, 47
Paradis, Vanessa, 170, 170f
Parker, Deborah, 191
Parker, Mark, 191
Party, The (1968), 233
Pasolini, Pier Paolo, 45, 100, 175
Peary, Danny, 139
Penn, Arthur, 203
Pépé le Moko (1937), 82n6
Perez, Faustino (pseudonym for Mason Hoffenberg), 218–19
Performance (1970), 203, 204, 237n20
Perkins, Claire, 1–18
Permissive (1970), 204
Perry, Frank, 220, 222
Peters, Bernadette, 28
Phantom Speaks, The (1945), 111
Pialat, Maurice, 168
Picasso, Pablo, 209

Picasso Summer, The (1969), 209
Pickens, Slim, 231
Picker, David, 222
Pierrot le fou (1965), 211
Plainsman, The (1936), 72, 82n7
Planeta Bur (1962), 48
Plan Nine from Outer Space (1959), 202
Playboy magazine, 219
Pleasence, Donald, 109
Polan, Dana, 7, 85, 87–88
Pola X (1999), 1
Pomerance, Murray, 11–12, 105–27
Pontecorvo, Gillo, 111
Porton, Richard, 172
post-cult culture, 12–13, 139–41
Postman, The (1997), 200
Postman Always Rings Twice, The (1946), 111
Postman Always Rings Twice, The (1981), 111
Potamkin, Harry Allan, 12, 130, 131–33
Powell, Dick, 159–60
Powell, Michael, 155–56
Powers, John, 1, 44
Pratley, Gerard, 134–35
Preminger, Otto, 66, 72, 166, 177–78
Presley, Delma E., 208
Prévert, Jacques, 177
A Prisão / *Bare Behind Bars* (1980), 47
process cinematography, 70–71, 75, 79–80, 82n1. *See also* rear-projection
Prosperi, Franco, 224–25
Psycho (1960), 78, 120, 172
psychoanalysis of cinema, 166
Psychotronic Encyclopedia of Film, The (Wheldon), 139–40
Psychotronic Video magazine, 45, 47
Ptushko, Aleksandr, 47
Pullen, Richard, 185
Pulp Fiction (1994), 67

punctum (Barthes), 67–68, 82n4
Putnam, 219
Putra, Sisworo Gautama, 47

Quel maledetto treno blindato / *The Inglourious Bastards* (1978), 44
Quéré, Julie, 168
Querelle (1982), 60n11
Quick and the Dead, The (1995), 112
Quinn, Anthony, 198, 202, 203, 209, 210

Rafelson, Bob, 111
Raiders of the Lost Ark (1981), 28, 112
Raimi, Sam, 14–15, 112, 181–95
Rains, Claude, 125
Rank Organisation, 79
Raoul Walsh (Giuliani), 151
Rappaport, Mark, 82n3
rappers, 38
Rathbone, Basil, 125
Ray, James, 108
Ray, Nicholas, 7, 88
Ray, Robert B., 138
Reagan, Ronald, 90
realism, 11, 68, 205, 210
  antirealism versus, 172, 177–78
  explosive apathy (Sconce) versus, 21–23
rear-projection, 10–11, 65–82
  benefits of, 81
  critique of, 66–67, 68–69, 71–72, 78–79
  Dead Reckoning (John Cromwell), 66, 69–73
  emergence of, 68–69, 82n6
  in Hitchcock films, 11, 65–68, 72–81
  nature of, 66–67
  "reappearance" of, 67
Rebecca (1940), 80
Rechy, John, 93
Redgrave, Corin, 198

Renaissance Pictures, 181, 184, 187
Resnais, Alain, 200–201, 204
Revel, Coralie, 168
Revolt of Marnie Stover, The (1956), 162n1
Rich, Ruby, 46
Rich and Strange (1937), 82n9
Richards, Keith, 237n20
Richardson, Tony, 220
Richter, Hans, 134
Rickitt, Richard, 75
River of No Return (1954), 66
Robbins, Tim, 111
Robin Hood (1938), 125
Robinson, Sugar Ray, 227
Robocop (1987), 9, 36
Rock, The (1996), 25
Rocky Horror Picture Show, The (1975), 139
Roeg, Nicholas, 204, 212, 237n20
Rogers, Tom, 23
Rohmer, Eric, 168
Roma (1972), 229–30
Romero, George A., 112
Romney, Jonathan, 2
Room, The (2003), 200, 202
Room with a View (Forster), 203
Roseanne, 34, 35
Rosenbaum, Jonathan, 2, 139
Rossellini, Roberto, 175
Roth v. United States, 88–89
Rotterdam Film Festival, 172
Routt, William D., 173
Russell, Jane, 151
Russell, Ken, 212
Russian films, 44–48
Russo, Vito, 91, 94

Saboteur (1942), 80
Sade, Marquis de, 102, 211
Sadko (1952), 47
Safety Last (1923), 154–55
Salerno, Enrico Maria, 232–33
Salò (1975), 100
Salt, Barry, 82n6
Samberg, Andy, 23
Samuels, Stuart, 139
"San Francisco (Be Sure to Wear Flowers in Your Hair)" (1967), 235
Sarris, Andrew, 13, 73, 74, 78, 99, 136
Les savates de bon dieu / Workers for the Good Lord (2000), 167, 172–73, 176
Saw 3-D (2010), 25
Scarlet Letter, The (1995), 199
Scarlet Street (1945), 155–56
Schaefer, Eric, 48, 60n10
Schiller, Lawrence, 111
Schindler's List (1993), 116
Schoedsack, Ernest B., 69
Schrader, Paul, 175
Schwarzenegger, Arnold, 36–37, 112, 120
science fiction, 36–37
Sconce, Jeffrey, 4–6, 8–10, 21–41, 46, 60n3, 140–42, 186–87, 187, 190, 193–94, 200
Scorsese, Martin, 67, 208
Scott, Lizabeth, 66, 70
Scott, Ridley, 119, 123–24
Scott, Tony, 99
SCTV
  "Farm Film Report," 9–10, 27–28, 40n3
Seagal, Steven, 112
Seaver, Richard, 217
Sebald, W. G., 118, 119
Sebastian, John (pseudonym for Curtis Harrington), 48
Sedaka, Neil, 28
Seidelman, Susan, 34
Seldes, Gilbert, 135
Sellers, Peter, 221, 228, 233, 236n7
Selmur Productions, 221
Server, Lee, 217
Seven Lively Arts, The (Seldes), 135

Seven Types of Ambiguity (Empson), 207
Seven-Ups, The (1973), 93
Sexton, Jamie, 12–13, 129–45
Sgt. Pepper's Lonely Hearts Club Band (1967), 219
Shadow of a Doubt (1943), 80
Shakespeare, William, 53, 169
Sharman, Jim, 139
Shaw, George Bernard, 113–14
She (novel), 210
She (1964), 210, 212–13n4
Shear, Barry, 33–34
She-Devil (1989), 34, 35
Shenkar, Daniel, 236
Shields, Brooke, 28
Shin, Chi-Yun, 46, 60n7
Shirley Valentine (1989), 203
shockwave surfing, 38–39
Shohat, Ella, 52
Shonteff, Lindsey, 204
Showgirls (1997), 212, 212n3
Showgirls, Teen Wolves and Astro Zombies (Adams), 200
Shutter Island (2010), 67, 208
Shyamalan, M. Night, 197, 208
Siegel, Mark, 139
Sight and Sound, 2, 8, 199
Silence of the Lambs, The (1991), 120, 121f, 123
Silva, Antonio Marcio de, 47
Silva, Edward T., 225
Silver Lion Award, 47
Simon, Alex, 95, 96
Singer, Bryan, 114, 118
Sirk, Douglas, 173
Sixth Sense, The (1999), 208
Smith, Alexis, 153, 154f, 157, 159
Smith, Jack, 4–6, 5f, 237n21
Smith, Justin, 134, 140, 141
Social Text (Wilson), 99
sociology of symbolic forms (Bourdieu), 4–5
Soderbergh, Steven, 67

Sontag, Susan, 13
sound synchronization, 44, 53, 71, 99
Southern, Terry, 15–16, 216–24, 228, 236n2, 236n4, 236n8
Spadoni, Robert, 53, 60n14
Spanish films, 48–49
Spellbound (1945), 80–81
Spielberg, Steven, 28, 96, 103n4, 112, 116
Spoto, Donald, 65, 68, 75–76, 76
Spottiswoode, Raymond, 81, 82n2
Stairway to Heaven (1945), 155–56
Stallone, Sylvester, 112
Stam, Robert, 52, 213n5, 236n1
Stamp, Terence, 115
Stanfield, Peter, 141
Starr, Ringo, 221, 228
Star Wars (1977), 28, 31, 119, 125
Stauffenberg, Claus Von, 115–18
Still of the Night (1982), 113
Stone, Oliver, 99
Stone, Sharon, 112
Story of O, The (1975), 232
La strada (Fellini), 209
Straub, Jean-Marie, 82n3
Strauss, Frédéric, 173
Streep, Meryl, 28
studio system, 8, 67–70, 138, 151, 153–54
Sturges, Preston, 14, 152, 159, 163nn4–5
sublime conception of cinema (Deleuze), 3–4, 16–17
subtitles, 10, 43–61
   with bootleg DVDs, 43–45, 46–47, 52, 59
   Crowther on potential of, 49–52
   Derrida and failure of translation, 45, 54–58
   dubbing versus, 10, 46, 48–53
   film versus literary translation, 45, 48–49, 52–53
   as "flubtitles," 10, 45, 51, 56, 60n4
   intercultural cult of, 45–49

subtitles (continued)
  lack of quality control, 53, 58–59
  politics of translation, 46, 50–51
  with spaghetti Westerns, 44
  with Tarantino films, 44
  Zontar "bad classics," 45, 47, 56–57, 60n3
Surrealism, 4, 33, 34, 133, 166
Syriana (2005), 9, 21–23, 23f

Tales from Topographic Oceans (1973), 237n16
Tapert, Robert, 14–15, 181, 185–86, 188, 189, 191, 193–94
Tarantino, Quentin, 44, 59n2, 67, 114–15, 201
Tartan, 46
Taylor, Elizabeth, 227
Taylor, Greg, 133, 134
Taylor, Sam, 154–55
Telotte, J. P., 140
10 Rillington Place (1971), 111
Teorema (1968), 175
Terminator, The (1984), 36–37
Terminator 2: Judgment Day (1991), 37
Texas Chainsaw Massacre, The (1974), 193
Thackeray, William Makepeace, 106–7
Thérèse Requin (1928), 134
Thomas, Derek (pseudonym for Peter Bogdanovich), 48
Thompson, J. Lee, 209
Thompson, Kristin, 40n1, 69, 177
Thomson, David, 66, 67, 76, 77, 79, 81, 82n2, 82n10
Thousand and One Nights, A, 176
3-D, 31
Tierney, Gene, 177
Timecode (2000), 185
To Be or Not to Be (1942), 157–58
To Catch a Thief (1954), 74f, 81, 82n11

Tokyo! (2008), 2
Toland, Gregg, 80
Tolo, Matilu, 230
Topaz (1969), 75
El topo (1970), 212, 230
Torn Curtain (1966), 75–76
Touch (1996), 175
Transformers: Revenge of the Fallen (2009), 25, 26–27, 27f
translation errors, 10, 43–61
Traveller's Companion, 218–19
Treasure of the Sierra Madre, The (1948), 237n19
Tree of Life, The (2011), 2
Trier, Lars von, 2
Tringham, David, 205
Trip, The (1967), 235
Trip to the Moon, A (Méliès), 153
Trocchi, Alexander, 217–18
Troeltsch, Ernst, 143n1
True Crime (1999), 111
True Grit (1969), 111
Truman Show, The (1998), 210
Trumbull, Douglas, 225
Turpin, Dick, 108–9
Twin Peaks: Fire Walk with Me (1992), 2
2001: A Space Odyssey (1968), 40n3, 225

Ulmer, Edgar G., 168, 172
Umland, Rebecca, 192–93
Umland, Sam, 192–93
Under Pressure (1935), 162n1
Unforgiven (1995), 112
United Artists, 220–21, 222
U.S. Supreme Court
  Miller v. California, 86–87
  Roth v. United States, 88–89
Universal Studios, 4
Until She Screams (Hoffenberg), 218–19
Upchurch, Alan, 47

Vadim, Roger, 220, 221
Vale, Vivian, 139–40
Valkyrie (2008), 114–19
Van Damme, Jean-Claude, 112
Varda, Agnès, 51–52
Vartan, Sylvia, 174
Vasey, Ruth, 79
Vendredi Soir / Friday Night (2002), 51, 53
Venice Film Festival, 47
Venuti, Lawrence, 45, 50, 54, 55, 59, 60n12, 61nn17–18
Verevis, Constantine, 1–18, 10, 15–16, 212n1, 215–39
Verhoeven, Paul, 9, 36
Vertigo (1958), 68, 74, 80
Verushka, 233
V for Vendetta (2005), 108–9
video games, 38
La vie comme ça / Life the Way It Is / Life's Like That (1978), 168
villains and villainy, 11–12, 105–26
  capital punishment as public entertainment, 105–13
  degradation ceremonies, 122–26
  examples of villains, 12, 35, 112, 114–19, 120, 121f, 123–26
  historical villains in film, 12, 108–9, 114–19, 126
  pure screen villains, 11–12, 119–26
Vincendeau, Ginette, 2
V.I.P.s, The (1963), 227
Voltaire, 15–16, 216, 218, 224, 236n3, 237n13, 237n15
Voyage to the Planet of Prehistoric Women (1968), 48
Voyage to the Prehistoric Planet (1965), 48

Wachowski, Andy, 9, 32
Wachowski, Larry (now Lana), 9, 32
Wagner, Richard, 117
Wahlberg, Mark, 23
Walker, Gerald, 92–93, 95–96, 103n4
Wallace, William, 108
Walsh, Raoul, 13–14, 149, 151–63
Wanted (2008), 31
Warburton, Eileen, 199, 205
Warhol, Andy, 227, 235
Warner Brothers, 40n4, 69
Warren, Bill, 182, 184, 187
Warren, Hal, 200
Waters, John, 201
Watney, Simon, 97
Watt, Michael, 53, 60n13
Way Hollywood Tells It, The (Bordwell), 24–25
Weber, Max, 125
Weiner, Adam, 23
Weiner, Debra, 149
Weintraub, Jerry, 96, 101
Weir, Peter, 210
Weisman, David, 220
Weldon, Michael, 47–48
Wells, Vernon, 120
Wheldon, Michael, 139–40
Whelehan, Imelda, 236n1
Whirlpool (1949), 166, 177
White Album, The (Didion), 235
Who Framed Roger Rabbit (1988), 112
Wiene, Robert, 132
Wild in the Streets (1968), 33–34
Wild Strawberries (1957), 49
Willemen, Paul, 4
Williams, Billy, 202, 212
Williams, Linda, 9, 32
Willis, Bruce, 39, 112
Wilson, Alexander, 91–92, 96, 99, 101
Wilson, Colin, 201
Wise, Robert, 111
Wiseau, Tommy, 200, 202
Witnail & I (1987), 141
Wizard of Oz, The (1939), 112, 156
Wollen, Peter, 13

Woman in the Window, The (1944), 155–56
Women in Love (1969), 212
Wood, Edward D., Jr., 200, 202
Wood, Robin, 73–74, 76, 92, 95, 96, 99
Wood, Sam, 159
Wuttke, Martin, 114
Wyler, William, 173

Yates, Peter, 92–94
Young and Innocent (1937), 82n9

Zabriskie Point (1970), 28, 200–201
Zarchi, Meir, 190
Zemeckis, Robert, 112
Zontar: The Magazine from Venus, 45, 47, 56–57, 60n3
Zorba the Greek (1964), 203, 209, 211

www.ingramcontent.com/pod-product-compliance
Lightning Source LLC
Chambersburg PA
CBHW070757230426
43665CB00017B/2393